The Ballad of Tommy LiPuma

Also by Ben Sidran

Black Talk: How the Music of Black America Created a Radical Alternative to the Values of Western Literary Tradition

Talking Jazz: An Oral History

A Life in the Music: The True Story of Everything I Ever knew

There Was a Fire: Jews, Music and the American Dream

The Ballad of

Tommy LiPuma

Ben Sidran

NARDIS BOOKS
Madison, Wisconsin

NARDIS BOOKS
PO Box 2023
Madison, Wisconsin 53701
nardisbooks.com

Nardis Books is an imprint of Unlimited Media Ltd.

The author has curated a playlist of songs referenced in the text:
https://bit.ly/LiPumaBookPlaylist

Book design: Isabelle Wong, Sara DeHaan
Cover photos: Hollis King
Photo credits: pp. 51–56, courtesy of the LiPuma Family Archive; pp. 167–171,
courtesy of the Rock & Roll Hall of Fame; pp. 203–210, courtesy of the
LiPuma Family Archive unless noted otherwise

Printed in the United States of America

Publisher's Cataloging-in-Publication Data

Names: Sidran, Ben, author.
Title: The Ballad of Tommy LiPuma / Ben Sidran.
Description: Includes index. | Madison, WI: Nardis Books, 2020.
Identifiers: LCCN: 2019911191
ISBN: 978-0-578-55660-4 (cloth) | ISBN: 978-0-578-62566-9 (ebook)
Subjects: LCSH LiPuma, Tommy. | Sound recording executives and
producers—United States—Biography. | Sound recording industry—United States.
| BISAC BIOGRAPHY & AUTOBIOGRAPHY / Entertainment & Performing Arts |
BIOGRAPHY & AUTOBIOGRAPHY / Music
Classification: LCC ML429.L565 2020 | DDC 781.49092—dc23

For Gilda Sharon

I hope I didn't bring you down.

—Lord Buckley

Contents

Prelude:

Dinner with Tommy

To his friends, there was nobody like him. To the millions who purchased the records he produced, his signature sound was something magical. And to those who are hearing about him for the first time, you are in for an American journey unlike any other.

Tommy LiPuma was a self-invented polymath straight from the streets, a rough-and-tumble Cleveland guy who lived through the wildest days of the record industry and went on to spectacular success, selling over seventy-five million albums and helping to establish musical genres that sold millions more.

Tommy had an ear for music, and listening to music with him was like shining a light into the darkness. He not only knew how to make great records, he also knew why. He heard inside the music for the human component. A recording wasn't merely an artifact, it was a snapshot of the soul of a person and a song at a magic moment. Slightly curated, of course—that was production.

This is not the definitive history of Tommy. These are the stories he told me over a period of years. Decades, actually. We met in 1972 when I signed to his record label, Blue Thumb, and for the next forty-five years we spent hours, even days, together, in and out of recording studios, restaurants, nightclubs, you name it.

Tommy and Ben in a recording studio in Manhattan, November 19, 1991.

His greatest pleasure was talking about the music and the people and the business he loved, but he was also an avid follower of art, literature, politics, and films and would happily discuss whatever subject was on the table. Mostly, *hanging* was his forte. He loved being with creative people, enjoying a good bottle of wine, exchanging war stories, and laughing, always laughing. Tommy raised hanging out to a high art.

One of his favorite films was *My Dinner with André,* in which a couple of guys spend a couple of hours sitting around a dinner table talking about life. But few who sat around dinner tables with Tommy—and there were many, some legendary, from Miles Davis and George Benson to Diana Krall and Barbra Streisand—knew the details of his personal story, how he got into the business of music or why he was so empathetic with the artists he produced. That's what this book attempts to explain.

—Ben Sidran, May 2020

intro:

A Moment in Time

In the spring of 1977, the George Benson album *Breezin'* had been nominated for four Grammy Awards including Album of the Year and Record of the Year, the top prizes that the Recording Academy has to offer. It was an unprecedented recognition for a jazz album, one that normally goes to top rock or pop acts.

Tommy had gone through hell and high water to make that record, but like everyone else, he was surprised when, first, it started to get significant crossover airplay, and then again when it started to sell, and then it kept selling, and by the end of the year it was an outright phenomenon. One doesn't expect that to happen when you make a jazz record. With jazz, you basically trust that the musicians and the songs you've chosen are compatible, that the feeling in the room is conducive to something fresh and alive happening, and that you manage to capture it without too much trouble. Sounds simple, but that's the trick: "Try not to try too hard," as James Taylor once said. Tommy knew he had something special here, but nobody could have predicted the gigantic success of that record.

He and George went to the Grammy Awards ceremony together, expecting nothing more than to have a good time and see some old friends. They were up against records like Paul Simon's "Fifty Ways to Leave Your Lover," so they had little hope of winning.

They wound up sitting right next to a group called Dr. Buzzard's Original Savannah Band, a zany group of kids all dressed up in vintage gear and having a ball. "One of the guys," remembers Tommy, "was wearing a khaki army officer's uniform, one of the chicks was decked out in 1940s jitterbug regalia, and every time something came up that they could dance to, they did it, spilling out into the aisle and carrying on. It was pretty hard to take the whole thing too seriously."

As the night went on, their expectations seemed to be confirmed: Every one of the awards that he and George were nominated for went to somebody else. At the very end of the evening, Barbra Streisand came out and announced, "The last award of the evening; the Record of the Year." She read the list of nominees, opened the envelope, looked at the camera, and said, "And the winner is . . . 'This Masquerade,' George Benson and Tommy LiPuma.'" The crowd erupted in applause, the band started playing the song, and Tommy and George looked at each other in disbelief.

Tommy says he has no memory of what happened next: getting out of his seat, going up on the stage. Maybe down deep, he knew in that moment that his life had changed, but that's definitely not what he was thinking. Actually, he was thinking nothing at all. It was just a blur. He does recall that on the way home, the limo driver offered him a free ride, and also that he didn't stop smiling for three days.

Shortly thereafter Tommy ran into Barbra Streisand at the Palm restaurant in Los Angeles, and on the way out she stopped at his table to congratulate him again. She was chatty and complimentary, and then, just before she left, she gave him a penetrating look and said, "You played me that song first, didn't you?" She was suggesting that he had offered her "This Masquerade" before cutting it with George Benson. In fact he had not, but somehow, he says, he couldn't help himself. He said, "Yeah, Barbra, I did." She smiled and said "I thought so" and turned and left.

Track One:

A Dirt Path

Tommy's story begins in a small Sicilian village on a windswept mountainside fifty miles southwest of Palermo. The village is named Alimena, and at the turn of the twentieth century it was home to a couple of thousand people and a few hundred goats, chickens, donkeys, and various other animals that could be used for food, transportation, or both. Think of the village of Corleone in *The Godfather* but smaller, dustier. We're talking about a way of life that was closer to the fifteenth century than to the world of today.

From a distance, Alimena looked like a pile of limestone rocks perched high on a hill. Water was scarce, plumbing virtually nonexistent, and everybody drew their water from a communal well in the center of town. On Saturdays, the day when people took their bath, there were long lines at the well, and hauling buckets of water back to the house was a full-time job. When Tommy's father, Salvatore, was a boy, it was his job.

The LiPuma family lived in Alimena as far back as anyone could remember. The extended family numbered in the dozens, a close-knit group that gathered every weekend to play guitars and mandolins and sing songs that went back to the beginning. Nobody knew where or when that was, but it didn't matter; music was part of their history, it was in the blood.

The LiPumas rarely, if ever, left the village. There was really no place to go and few ways to get there. The nearest village was Villarosa, ten miles away, and it took a whole day to get there on foot, or four hours by horse or bicycle, *if* the paths were clear. And once you were there, where were you? Often you couldn't even understand some of the locals because, like Alimena, each town had its own dialect.

Sal LiPuma, the second of Giuseppe and Giuseppina LiPuma's three sons, worked like a man from the time he was a small boy. At age six he woke up at sunrise, hitched up the family donkey, and spent the day leading the animal up and down the mountain paths, hauling buckets of limestone rock from the family mine down to the town. The mine, a hardscrabble open-pit affair, was the family business, and everybody contributed.

The paths Sal and the donkey walked had been walked for hundreds, if not thousands, of years. Generations of boys just like him had beaten that permanent groove into the Alimena hillside. Sometimes Sal would find an artifact from the Byzantine period on the side of the road. He never picked it up.

In the winter, when it was too cold to work the mine, Sal still woke early and took the donkey to the top of the mountain to collect snow and bring it down to a cave near the mine. There he and his brothers compressed it into blocks of ice that they stored until the following summer, when they sold it as "air conditioning" down in the village. Day after day, year after year, he walked that path, the hard clanking bell on the donkey the sound marking time. Years later, Sal told his son Tommy, "By the time I was six years old, I was already tired of living."

One Saturday, in July 1905, when Sal was twelve years old and working the mountain with the mule, his father, Giuseppe, went into town to pass some time at a bar. On weekends the place would fill up with men sitting around eating lupini beans, drinking small glasses of grappa, and gossiping.

This Saturday, Giuseppe, who had a reputation for having a short temper, picked a fight with one of his competitors in the limestone business, a man named Sapienza. Nobody remembers exactly how it started or what it was about, but everybody agreed that the outcome was a scandal: Giuseppe slapped Sapienza across the face. In public. In this part of the world, that was cause for retribution. The bar went silent. But Sapienza just sat there, calmly sipping his grappa.

However, two days later, as Giuseppe was riding his donkey into town with his youngest son, Tony, on the blanket in front of him, they spotted somebody up ahead hiding behind a bush. "Look, Pa," said the boy, "there's Mr. Sapienza," but Giuseppe just shrugged him off. When the donkey and its riders passed the bush, Sapienza jumped out and, in a flash, stabbed Tommy's grandfather in the back with a long carving knife, virtually disemboweling him on the spot. Giuseppe LiPuma died that night at home, and Sapienza disappeared from Alimena the next day.

Word soon came that Sapienza had fled to America. It wasn't justice that he was afraid of; it was revenge. In Sicily, a grudge like this could last years, even generations, and everyone knew "If you kill the father, you had better kill the sons too," because they would be coming for you.

Giuseppe's death left Giuseppina, thirty-two years old, with five children and no income. There was the limestone mine, of course, but unfortunately Giuseppe's partner in the business, his brother-in-law, took advantage of the situation and stopped giving Giuseppina her share of the money. Soon she and her children were reduced to scavenging for food and clothing on the streets.

Other family members brought clothes and food to Giuseppina and the children when they could. One uncle was the barber in the village, and he tried to teach Tommy's uncle Joe the trade. But nothing came of it, and for months, the family barely survived. Finally, after two years of scraping and scrapping and doing odd jobs, Joe managed to put together enough money to buy a boat ticket to America. He was going to find Sapienza and kill him.

Joe arrived at Ellis Island in 1907 and after asking around discovered that Sapienza was on the run, headed out west, possibly to California. The man, they said, was always looking over his shoulder, knowing somebody was coming after him. Joe had no money and spoke no English, so he sought out his mother's brother—a man named John Tedesco. Tedesco had arrived in America a few years earlier and had settled in Cleveland. Joe went to Cleveland, put down some roots, took a job as a clothing presser, and started saving money again. After four years, he had saved enough money to bring over his brother Sal from Sicily. The plan was for the two of them to search for Sapienza together.

Sal spent three days on a mule traveling the fifty miles from Alimena to Palermo, another week going from Palermo to Napoli on the Italian mainland by a combination of animals and boats, and three more weeks sailing the thousands of miles to New York City. And that is how Tommy's father, Salvatore LiPuma, arrived in America on March 14, 1911, aboard the *Sant' Anna,* a freighter that would be torpedoed and sunk by a German submarine off the north coast of Africa just a few years later at the start of World War I. He was eighteen years old. And the boys never did find Sapienza.

In the old country there had been no work and no future, but in America the future had arrived and was parading down Main Street; there was work for everyone. In Cleveland, they were building the new City Hall, and even though Sal didn't speak English he devised a plan to get himself a job: He met a guy in the "Little Italy" section of town who was already on the job, and one morning Sal woke up before the sun rose and went to sleep across this guy's front door. When he left for work, he literally had to step over Sal, who woke up and followed him to the construction site and got himself hired.

His job was carrying bricks in a basket hanging from a wooden pole he carried on his shoulder. It was hard labor, but he saw, without exactly understanding, that groups of men standing around with nothing to do one day were gone the next, and he figured out that if you didn't look busy, you were fired. So anytime he had nothing to do, he simply moved bricks from one part of the work site to another and then back again, just to appear busy. But it only worked for so long—eventually he, too, was fired. Then he went to work on the crew putting up the Terminal Tower, the largest building in Cleveland and the model for the *Daily Planet* building in the legend of Superman (a myth created by two young guys from Cleveland).

Sal and Joe were working one job after another and sending money back home to Sicily, and over time, they managed to bring the rest of the family to America. In 1913, they brought their brother Tony, and then in 1914, they brought over their mother and their two sisters, Domenica and Marietta.

The LiPumas were part of a flood of immigrants from hardscrabble towns and villages all across Italy making their way to the new world. Like the Guerra family—Salvatore and Teresa Guerra, along with their children, Frank and Rose—who arrived in America at Ellis Island a decade before Joe and Sal. First they settled in Hackensack, New Jersey, where little Rose became a poster child for the new America, speaking perfect English by the time she was five and excelling in school. In another time or place she might well have gone on to college. But when her father lost his job, she, too, was forced to quit school and pick up odd jobs, often working in sweatshops. Eventually the Guerras also moved to Cleveland.

Both the LiPumas and the Guerras were members of the Alimenese Club in Cleveland, a social organization of expatriates from Alimena that met once a month to have a meal, play cards, and keep memories of the old country alive. The women wore long dresses in the Sicilian fashion, and when the meal was finished, they cleared the tables while the men took their chairs and drinks into the backyard and sang songs, songs that have since faded into obscurity, in part because they were sung in an old dialect that no one understands today, but people who were there say these songs sounded more like laments.

At one of these gatherings, sixteen-year-old Rose Guerra met twenty-two-year-old Salvatore LiPuma, and they began courting. Their grandmothers had been friends in the old country and made the introduction. Sal, who by this time was going by the name of Sam, was still working construction, but he managed to come home every night, wash his face and hands, change into nicer clothes, and go by Rose's house. There they sat together in the family parlor, along with Rose's parents, and passed time in the traditional way.

The big question on everyone's mind was citizenship. To become an American citizen one typically had to wait for years and then study for the big test. But there was an alternative: If a man enlisted in the army and was honorably discharged, he was automatically granted citizenship, and so, too, were his wife and children. Sam wanted to marry Rose, and he wanted to become an American citizen, so he and his brother Tony both enlisted just as the First World War was winding down. They were sent to a boot camp in Georgia in the spring of 1918.

After a few weeks of basic training, Sam jumped on a train and went back to Cleveland, where he and Rose were married on June 1, 1918. It's not clear whether his English was so bad that he didn't understand the consequences of his actions or that he simply didn't care, but when he returned to boot camp a married man he was busted for going AWOL and thrown into the brig. There he became the jailhouse barber and spent the rest of the war in comparative comfort. In fact, he never worked a day of construction again in his life and remained a barber to the end.

When the war officially ended on November 11, 1918, Sam and Tony returned home to Cleveland and opened a barbershop down on Fourteenth Street. Sam and Rose had their first child, Joe, on October 10, 1919. It was a long, hard delivery, and immediately after Joe's birth, the doctor had to set the baby aside and work to save Rose's life; eventually she went on to give birth to four more children (one who died very young), Tommy being the youngest.

By the mid-1920s, Sam had moved the family to a bigger house on East 111th Street, just south of Woodland Avenue. This area of Cleveland was known as Bloody Corners because it was ground zero for the Sicilian families fighting for control of the bootlegging business. Not long after he moved there, Sam, too, got into the racket.

It wasn't a big leap. Back in the old country, every family made their own wine—it was just a normal part of most meals, a social lubricant as well as a connection to the deep communal past, more of a sacrament than a path to intoxication. So by making his own alcohol, Sam was merely upholding a family tradition. In addition, as a barber, he ordered hair tonic in quantity, and hair tonic, too, contained alcohol. By edging into bootlegging, Sam was just expanding his operation. Soon he had set up his own still and was producing his own brand of drinkable alcohol. Even after Prohibition ended in 1933, bootlegging remained a popular way for people to make a little extra money. Sam stayed in it until early 1940.

Being an aspiring capitalist, he also discovered there was money to be made selling raw sugar: You couldn't get busted for selling it, and everybody needed it to make whiskey. So he started dealing in bulk sugar as well, and that's when he received a visit from the Lonardo family.

The Lonardos were the dominant crime family in Cleveland. "Big Joe" Lonardo supplied corn sugar and granted "franchises" to bootleggers all over town. The Lonardos worked with their *paisanos* the Porrellos to control the market, but the Porrellos got tired of the arrangement and went into business for themselves; each family formed an army and hit the mats. Bodies began turning up regularly—that's how the neighborhood became known as Bloody Corners. This was the start of the "Sugar Wars" in Cleveland, and Sam LiPuma had accidently stepped right in the middle of them.

After he received his visit from the Lonardos, Sam decided to move the family up to East 153rd Street and Kinsman. There he and his brother built a three-family home; Sam's family lived on the first floor, Tony's on the second, and their mother, Giuseppina, and their aunts on the third. It was a little piece of the old world, a mixed neighborhood of Italians and Jews, more respectable than Bloody Corners but with plenty of numbers runners, bootleggers, and wiseguys within a radius of a few blocks.

Joe, the eldest of the LiPuma children, had the hardest time adjusting; raised in a three-family house where everyone spoke Sicilian, he barely spoke English. His parents found him a tutor, but the tutor spoke Italian, not the Sicilian dialect that Joe knew, so the lessons were virtually useless. Joe did poorly at school; his hero was Lucky Luciano, the mobster. By the time he got to high school, Joe would show up dressed like a gangster, in a full-length overcoat, gray felt fedora, and triple-A shoes with white stitching around the soles.

He dropped out of high school and became what his father bitterly referred to as a "drugstore cowboy," because he mostly just loafed around Levitt's soda fountain, a little joint across the street from their house. When his father finally lost patience with him and pulled him off the streets, Joe took a job at a linen cleaning company, where he worked until the day he had to handle damp, bloody sheets from a mortuary. After that, it wasn't hard for Sam to persuade him to become a barber.

For the next year, Sam dropped Joe off at the entrance to the barber college, but even as the car pulled away from the curb, Joe would be heading for the pool hall. Joe made it through barber college and went to work with his father, first at the barbershop and then in the bootlegging business.

At seventeen, Joe was delivering whiskey and picking up cash for Sam's operation. He drove a 1935 Ford coupe with a rumble seat and a V-8 engine that would do 100 mph, the perfect moonshiner's car, outfitted with truck springs on the rear so it wouldn't ride too low when it was loaded with five-gallon cans of alcohol. (On the way home, after the booze was delivered, Joe would put cement blocks in the back so the car wouldn't "ride high"; riding too high or too low was a dead giveaway to the cops.)

Once he was hijacked by the same guys he had just sold the whiskey to—threading his way home through the back roads at night, they forced him off the road, held him up at gunpoint, and told him, "Don't do nothing stupid"—and once he drove right into a federal roadblock. But luckily that night, Joe had his grandmother Giuseppina along for cover: just a boy and his grandmother out for an evening's drive. When the cops looked in the window all they saw was an old woman knitting, and they waved Joe through.

This was the family life into which Tommy LiPuma was born on July 5, 1936; his brother Joe was seventeen, his next brother, Henry, was fifteen, and his sisters, Josephine and Terese, were twelve and nine. Years later, Henry told Tommy that he had been an accident and that his father had wanted his mother to have an abortion, but his mother refused. So Tommy was not only an accident but a product of his mother's love, independence, and determination.

And even though Joe was the oldest of the five LiPuma children, he was really in the middle, in between the old Sicilian ways and the new American reality, between the protection of his grandmother's generation and the unknown future of the wide-open roads.

It's the story of many first-generation families in America. What remains so remarkable is that in just one short generation, the LiPuma family would travel from the donkey paths of a Sicilian mountainside to Hollywood's red carpet.

Track Two:

Growing Up Cleveland

Tommy's family was close in a way that only immigrant families can be. His brothers Joe and Henry slept in the same bed until they were twelve and ten, even though they were completely different as people—"like Cain and Abel," Tommy says.

Through his whole life, Joe remained more Sicilian than American. Every Saturday on his way to work, he would stop by the Lamarca brothers' barbershop to check in with all the neighborhood wiseguys; he admired their pockets full of cash and their slicked-back hair. In the end, it turned out the Lamarca shop was under surveillance by the feds and several of the regulars went to jail, but Joe was never questioned.

Henry, on the other hand, was a real middle-American kid who went on to become a high school teacher and the owner of a small insurance agency. From the beginning, all he wanted was to blend in, to be normal. He went to Shaker Heights High, where, Tommy says, he "fell in with a crowd of guys with names like Dave Morgan and Jim Milligan." Henry was a preppy dresser and a country club golfer; Joe worked in the barbershop, Henry sang in a barbershop quartet.

These two forces, the new world and the old, the love of the old traditions and the allure of the American dream, shaped not only Tommy's family but also the music Tommy would one day come to love and produce.

When he was growing up, the music in Tommy's house was mostly the pop music of the day. The one exception would be on Sunday mornings when the *Italian Hour* came on the radio, hosted by a guy named Louie DiPaolo and brought to you by Gust Gallucci's Italian specialty store downtown. For that one hour of the week, nobody but Sam could touch the radio. Otherwise, it was in the hands of Tommy's two teenage sisters.

The music they listened to was what teenagers everywhere were listening to: Frankie Laine, Jo Stafford, the Mills Brothers, Johnny Mercer's "Ac-Cen-Tchu-Ate the Positive," Les Brown's "Sentimental Journey," Harry James's "It's Been a Long Long Time." In the 1940s, kids sat in front of the radio for hours, swooning over songs, going around the dial searching for programs like *Your Hit Parade*. It was the start of teenage America.

From the time he was able to talk, Tommy was singing. The first song he learned was "Paper Doll" by the Mills Brothers. He would sing it nonstop, and when he went for a ride with his father, Sam would say to Tommy, "Sing me that Doll song." Their '41 Oldsmobile had no radio, and Tommy was the entertainment.

He always had a good ear for music. He remembers once his mother tried to make him take a nap by singing him a lullaby. "My mother, bless her heart, could not carry a tune," he says, "and when she got a few bars into the song, apparently I told her, 'That's okay, Mommy, stop singing and I'll go to sleep.'"

And then there was Eddy. Eddy lived across the street from the house where Tommy grew up, in a small frame house with an old wooden swing on the front porch. Eddy was in his thirties but he was born with cerebral palsy and had the mind of a five-year-old. He spent his days dressed in overalls and an old cap, swinging on the porch swing, just watching life pass by. Sometimes Tommy, who was five years old himself, would go over and sit next to Eddy on the swing and talk with him. He could hardly understand what Eddy was saying, but the man was so gentle and nice that they would sit together and swing for hours. Eddy's heavy work boots had literally worn big grooves in the porch. Years later Tommy took a friend to see Eddy's porch; the grooves were still there. Tommy shook his head and said, "You can see his whole life in that floor."

So at a very tender age, Tommy had already demonstrated a fine ear for music, a love of swinging, and a deep compassion for people—all the tools he would need for a future as a record producer. The only thing lacking was the motivation. That would come in a few years.

In the spring of 1941, somebody tipped off the feds that Sam LiPuma was operating a still. When they came to the house with an arrest warrant for him, Tommy's brother Joe stepped up and claimed the operation was his. He knew if his father went to jail, there would be no one to take care of the family; it would be like Sicily all over again. Joe was sentenced to a year in jail. It was enough to get Sam out of the bootlegging business, but the feds continued to come by his shop every so often just to check up on him. They would say, "We want to check that delivery of hair tonic you just got." Sam would say, "Go ahead, take a drink."

Eventually Sam paid off the right guy and Joe received a new trial, at which he was acquitted. He was out of jail by the fall of 1941, and within weeks of his release, he received his draft notice. When he and the other inductees marched from the federal building to the train station, his father Sam marched right next to him, all the way down Euclid Avenue, wearing a clean white shirt and a stiff straw hat, proud to be an American.

Joe didn't come home until the Japanese surrendered four years later, after he had made landings with the 27th Infantry Division on Makin Atoll, Eniwetok, Saipan, and Okinawa. After forty-eight months in the Pacific it was a miracle he came back at all. He had earned several ribbons including the Bronze Star. Meanwhile, Henry, who had enlisted in 1941, was stationed in an office, never left the United States, and spent the war pushing papers; in Joe's eyes, it was further proof that Henry was a weakling.

The neighborhood where Sam moved next was primarily Jewish. There were still a lot of wiseguys hanging out, including both Don King, the fight promoter who went to jail for murder, and Shondor Birns, who was eventually blown up by the mob. Tommy ended up with mostly Jewish friends, including his best friend, Errol Kwait. Tommy called him Ede (pronounced "E.D."), and between the ages of six and ten, he and Tommy were inseparable, in and out of each other's houses at all hours of the day and playing in the streets until after dark. Their favorite game was pretending that they were big-league baseball players, throwing grounders to each other and announcing the imaginary game for hours.

Years later it would occur to Tommy that one of the reasons he was so comfortable in the record business was that it was primarily a Jewish business and he was always comfortable around Jews. So when Ede went to a Jewish Federation camp, Tommy went too—he even had his own yarmulke and could say the *bruchas* (the blessings over bread and wine).

Tommy says he didn't really understand what being Jewish meant until the day his father took him to visit a cousin, Frank, who manufactured pasta for a living. Sam parked the car in front of Frank's place and told Tommy to wait for him there. Tommy was sitting behind the wheel, pretending to be driving, when he noticed three kids throwing stones at a building. The building was a Jewish synagogue.

Tommy rolled down the window and asked why they were throwing stones, and they said, "'Cause that's where the Jews pray." "And they used the expression *ammazza cristiani*," he remembers. "I knew enough Italian to understand that meant 'Christ killers.'" It was his first introduction to anti-Semitism.

"I was very fortunate that my parents were not particularly prejudiced," Tommy says. "Well, to a point, meaning I'm not sure how they would have felt if I came home with a black wife. Actually, come to think of it, I do know exactly how they would have reacted to that. Because once we had a big family picnic in the park, about thirty or forty people, and it started to rain heavily and everyone ran for the shelter. It turns out there was a group of African Americans who also ran for cover, and my relatives were not too happy about sharing the shelter with them. On the African American side, they were having a great time, playing music and laughing, while everyone on our side had a *farbisseneh* face on.

"I was digging the action across the room and I recognized a friend of mine who was part of their group. We caught each other's eye and ran toward each other and hugged. We talked for a while, then hugged again, and I went back to the Italian side of the shelter. All of my relatives looked at me like I had just caught the plague."

There was also a time that Tommy's father had his African American porter from the barbershop come over on a Sunday to paint window screens. When it was time for dinner, Sam brought him a plate of pasta. After they had all finished eating and Tommy's mother was washing dishes, Sam came in with the porter's empty plate and said in Italian, "This is the plate the porter ate from." Tommy's mother asked him in Italian with a straight face, "What do you want me to do, throw it out?"

"Looking back," says Tommy, "I think if I wasn't an atheist, I probably would have taken up Judaism. To me, it's the most civilized form of religion I can think of, at least the reformed Jews are. I can remember the first service I went to with Ede. Everyone in the congregation was able to get up and say something, unlike the Catholic faith that I was brought up in, where everything was hush-hush and very serious and there was a lot of talk about hell and mortal sin."

And he saw that superstition and the old ways could create a lot of misery. He had a friend named Donny, from a rough-and-tumble Italian family with five kids. Donny's father was old world too, a mechanic who used to sit down to eat dinner with black grease on his hands. From time to time, he would reach across the table and slap Donny if he didn't like his son's behavior. "He was," says Tommy, "an absolute animal." One day Tommy went over to their apartment to see his friend, and Donny's little sister, a girl about four years old, was alone in the living room. Tommy asked her, "Is Donny here?" and she said, "He's in the other room." When Tommy went into the bedroom he found Donny and his two brothers bound and gagged.

In many ways it was a dark time. World War II cast its shadow over much of Tommy's childhood. There were air raid alerts at night, when you were required to turn off all your lights and the Civil Patrol people wearing white helmets would walk the neighborhoods, making sure you obeyed orders. One night his father was standing at the window smoking a cigarette when the Civil Patrol knocked on the door and told him, "No cigarettes. No lighters. Nothing." Darkness, darkness.

The war worked its way into his consciousness in ways big and small; when he went to see a Saturday matinee, he would bring a piece of junk metal and throw it onto the pile for the "war drive," and then he got in for free. As a kid, he was a car fanatic, and they even stopped making cars from 1942 to 1946; instead, the automobile factories were producing army vehicles.

With both his brothers in the military, Tommy became the center of his family's attention, and he was, in his own words, "spoiled and pampered," not just by his mother but also by his two sisters. Josephine (the younger of the two, whom he called Babe) took on the role of surrogate mother; it was Babe who called him home for dinner when it was getting dark outside and he and Ede were playing ball.

His older sister, Terese, was a normal teenager with lots of boyfriends. He was only nine when Terese met her future husband, Jimmy, who showed up one day in a convertible with a rumble seat. Jimmy loved music and knew that Tommy did too. One day, as they were driving downtown to pick up Terese, the song "I Miss You So" by the Cats and the Fiddle came on the radio. Tommy just flipped out over the song. He couldn't stop talking about it. So Jimmy drove straight to a record store and bought him the record. It was the first record Tommy ever owned. "I remember this," says Tommy, "as one of the happiest days of my life."

And then his life changed 180 degrees.

It happened one afternoon when he and his pals were playing baseball in an empty lot. In his neighborhood, they played hardball, not softball, and he was at shortstop when a big kid a few years older and a whole lot stronger came up to bat. On the first pitch this kid hit a line drive directly into Tommy's left hip. The ball was hit so hard that it literally knocked Tommy out. When he came to, he was lying on the ground with everybody standing around him asking if he was okay. He shook it off and went back to the game.

But a month later he started complaining to his mother that when he sat down he would have a hard time standing up. He limped around for a bit, but the next thing you know, he would be out running around, so his mother paid no attention. Gradually, though, over time, the pains came closer together, until one day, he found himself in an altered state of consciousness, apparently floating in a corner of the ceiling, looking down on himself laid out on the couch. He remembers feeling "absolutely great," the coolest of cools, a number eleven on the scale of one to ten. He had the sensation that there were voices in his presence and they sounded troubled but he couldn't figure out what was wrong. He was in a coma.

And then, suddenly, he woke up, back in his body, with his brother Henry trying to shove a thermometer in his mouth. Tommy was running a temperature of 104 and was delirious. He passed out again and when he woke up the next morning, he was lying in a pool of sweat; the fever had broken temporarily, but that's when he really started going downhill.

He was in and out of fevers for days. Nothing could touch it. Not even his Grandmother's old Sicilian concoction made from bone marrow broth. None of the medicines or therapies worked, and finally they took Tommy to a hospital, where he was diagnosed with a life-threatening staph infection.

A few months before he was struck by the baseball, he had gone into the hospital for a tonsillectomy, where, quite possibly, he had contracted the initial infection that then lay dormant, circulating in the background, until the ball hit him, and then it (the infection) settled in his hip and eventually went raging through his system.

In time, they put a name to his disease: "osteomyelitis," an infection of the bone. Today it would be treated with surgery and intravenous antibiotics for six weeks. Back then, it took them months just to make the diagnosis and two years more to get it under control.

Until they were able to make the diagnosis, the doctors tried everything. At one point, they thought there was something wrong with the leg itself, so they put him in traction, suspended above the bed in a frame made of steel pipes and canvas. Tommy was forced to lie there with his back and arms on the pipes and an eight-pound weight pulling on his bad leg. It was sheer torture, and it probably did more harm than good. He suffered "that particular version of the Spanish Inquisition" for two months.

Ultimately, penicillin saved his life. It was a new drug, discovered at the end of the Second World War, and for days, they gave him injections in his hip every three hours. When the veins in his hip collapsed, they used the veins in his leg. He never did get any feeling back in his leg where the nerves were destroyed by all those injections.

When they sent him home, his mother set up a bed for him in the sunroom just off the kitchen so she could keep an eye on him. He spent the next two years in that bed. The first year, he was not allowed to leave the house, a kind of a prisoner, and he came to know what it felt like, at ten years old, to be handicapped among other children, "a freak."

From his bed, he could hear all his friends playing outside, but he couldn't join them. At one point his parents brought his bed out to the front porch and every so often one of his friends would come over. One day, while he was on the porch yelling to his friends, "Come on over," he heard one of them say, "I don't want to go over there. He's a cripple." And then another kid said, "No, let's go over. He's got great toys." And they all came over to play with his toys. "I can remember," Tommy says, "that even though I had heard them say it, and it hurt me deeply, I was so desperate for friendship that I just pretended that I hadn't." He believes that this moment—one of the most vivid of his childhood—propelled him to become what he later described as "the nicest guy in the room." If so, in the ironic way of personal history, it too contributed to his eventual success as a producer.

The days passed into nights and the nights passed into days and nothing was changing. It was relentless, terrible pain; whenever they had to move him, even to change the sheets on the bed, it was excruciating. His only comfort was the little tabletop radio his mother had bought for him. He listened to the adventures of the "The Green Hornet," "The Shadow," "The Lux Radio Theatre," "Fibber McGee and Molly," "Duffy's Tavern, where the elite meet." This little radio had his undivided attention.

And then one night, just by chance, lying in bed, he turned the dial and hit WJMO, the local R&B station. That night, he heard Ruth Brown singing "Mama He Treats Your Daughter Mean," and a whole new world opened up to him. "It was like she was reaching out to me through that little speaker," he says. "Just the sound of her voice and the bass and drums; I don't know exactly what it was about that music, but I felt like it was my best friend. That music saved my life."

From that moment on, he spent his nights searching for more of the music that moved him so powerfully, having no idea where this emotion was coming from, until much later, when he heard Mahalia Jackson sing Duke Ellington's "Come Sunday." Then he realized it all came out of the black church. It was the same soulfulness. He grew to love songs that spoke of overcoming tragedy through a greater caring, songs that "hurt so nice." "I've come to realize," says Tommy, "that ballads and the blues is where I live."

He became addicted to WJMO. He heard Charles Brown singing "Driftin' Blues" and "Merry Christmas Baby"; Lionel Hampton's "Hey! Ba-Ba-Re-Bop"; Louis Jordan singing "Ain't Nobody Here but Us Chickens" and "Let the Good Times Roll"—Louis Jordan ruled the airways back then; Nat Cole with "Route 66," and Cab Calloway's "The Honey Dripper." Up to that point he had only known the music his sisters were listening to. But when he heard this music, it was like falling down the rabbit hole in *Alice in Wonderland*. Every day, when he woke up, he couldn't wait to turn on the radio and take the next trip.

By the time he found King Records—Red Prysock, Earl Bostic, Tiny Bradshaw, Bill Doggett—he was a convert to black music. He had found heaven. And nobody else around him knew anything about it. It was his secret; it was the first time he truly understood there was a positive side to being an outsider.

Because when he listened to this music he just *knew* there was a better place and it was possible to get there. "Hearing all this great music," says Tommy, "took me out of my troubles and gave me a future."

At one point, the city of Cleveland sent a tutor over to Tommy's house. "She looked like the witch on the bicycle in *The Wizard of Oz*," Tommy remembers. "And she had a horrible cough—she couldn't stop coughing."

He hated these lessons, and after a couple of weeks, Tommy appealed to his friend Ede to help him hide the books she had brought. He figured if the books were gone, maybe she would stop coming over to the house. When the teacher returned the next day, Tommy told her, "I don't know where the books are." The woman became so outraged that Tommy became frightened and confessed, "Oh, I just remembered where they are."

But two months later the visits finally ended with a call from the city saying they were sending over a new tutor. The old one had died of tuberculosis. So then Tommy had to go through a series of tests to determine whether he had contracted tuberculosis. No wonder he didn't open another book for twenty years.

Finally, the infection in his hip simply exploded. The doctors didn't know what to do or what they were looking for, but they knew they had to do something. And that's when things got really dark. Eventually, Tommy suffered through three major operations.

When he awoke from the first surgery, he was in a plaster cast from the top of his toes to just under his armpits. He had the use of his right leg and his arms and that was it. He was kept flat on his back for for almost eight months. Every two or three months, they would put on a new cast: to remove the old one, they used a round electric saw that vibrated instead of rotating to lessen the possibility of cutting the patient. It wasn't foolproof.

When the doctors realized he was going to have to stay in the hospital for a long time, they recommended he go to the Rainbow Hospital for Children, a long-term care facility that was supposed to provide a more normal environment. Rainbow had a school, or at least they had classtime, and they had doctors on staff in case there was an emergency. Tommy remembers, "They told me, 'Oh, it's in the country and you're going to have campfires and marshmallows,' and I thought, 'Oh, this is gonna be great.'"

But when he got there, the first thing they did was take away every personal object he had, even his little radio and his comic books, and put him in an isolation chamber for two weeks. In those times, polio was rampant, and they had to "air everything out." After two days, they returned his radio—"I got my best friend back," says Tommy—but he was still living in a glass enclosure wearing nothing but a smock. When his parents came to visit him, they had to wear masks, wash their hands, and stand on the other side of the glass.

"It's difficult to verbalize how completely lost I felt," Tommy says. "I realized I had gone from the frying pan into the fire. I had thought this was going to be a fun place but instead it began with weeks of pure hell. I was completely alone." Years later, Tommy would develop an unusual style of producing records, choosing to remain on the same side of the glass as the musicians out in the studio, as opposed to working from the control room as most producers did; perhaps there was some distant memory involved, of never wanting to be separated from what he loved by a sheet of glass.

At the end of this period of isolation, they put Tommy on a cart and wheeled him down a long hallway and into a large room. Beds lined both sides of the room and kids were moving around everywhere on carts like his, propelling themselves by pushing on the wheels. It was a special ward for kids with any number of medical problems that they couldn't solve, including polio.

The kids who were able to propel themselves on the carts could go to breakfast, lunch, and dinner in the cafeteria on these vehicles. The kids with polio didn't go anywhere. "It really gave me the sense," says Tommy, "that no matter how bad off I was, I wasn't *that* bad off. There were even a couple of kids there that didn't seem to have anything wrong with them, but it turned out they had rheumatic fever, so they probably didn't live very long, certainly not as long as some of the rest of us. It teaches you that looks can be deceiving. It definitely leveled the playing field as far as me succumbing to self-pity."

At Rainbow he became friends with a young girl who had polio. "I can still see her face," he says, "like it was yesterday; she was so sweet. She was in an iron lung—there must have been at least ten kids in iron lungs, kids who could barely move one finger—and she was lying with her head out and a mirror above her so you could see her face. I woke up one morning and she was gone. I asked the staff where she was and all they said was she was moved to another room." He learned later that she had died in the middle of the night.

And while the nurses were generally very professional, some of the young nurses' aides, students from a private woman's school right next door, were over their heads. One morning, an aide who was probably only eighteen years old and trying to act grown up brought Tommy a watery soft-boiled egg for breakfast. "I looked at this thing shimmering there in the cup and I told her I couldn't eat it. She said, 'You *are* going to eat this.' I said, 'No, I'm not.' And then she started shoving spoonfuls of this disgusting egg down my throat. Moments like that I just felt totally lost."

But kids have a way of surviving the most adverse conditions. "One good thing about Rainbow Children's Hospital," Tommy says, "was that you were with kids your own age and everybody was in the same boat, more or less, so you could feel comfortable with each other and you were still able to act like a kid. We invented games, like we used to make slingshots out of Erector Set kits and rubber bands and we would have slingshot wars. It was normal kid stuff, even though we were all physically messed up and rolling around on these carts."

"Sometimes I would lie there and wonder what happened to me. I had a lot of time to think about it. It was like yesterday I was outside running around, a very athletic, normal, happy kid, not a thought in my head. And then suddenly the bottom fell out. It was like I was blindsided. A good part of the rest of my life has been spent trying to figure out how to deal with this curve ball that was thrown at me"—or rather, the line drive that knocked him out cold.

"I was raised Catholic," Tommy recalls, "but I wouldn't say we were religious. I remember asking my father during those horrible years, 'Do you believe in God?' He said, 'I don't believe.' He hardly ever went to church. But when he did go to church, he never knelt. Everybody else would kneel. My father would not."

When he was finally discharged from the hospital, Tommy's left leg was two inches shorter than his right, he was two years behind his friends in school—twelve years old and still in the fifth grade— and music was his only friend. When he was taken out of school two years before, he had been a normal kid; now he was the geek in the room, with a pronounced limp and, as fate would have it, an equally pronounced interest in the opposite sex.

"I reached my sexual potential pretty early on," says Tommy, "and the first time I got a crush on a girl was an experience I do not like to remember. Basically, I experienced a lot of rejection in school. It built up to the point where, on the one hand, I would over-compensate, be a people pleaser to get acceptance, and on the other hand, I would retract, withdraw inside myself. I wouldn't want to go anywhere because when you met someone, you noticed that the first thing they did was look down, like they were checking out the dam-aged goods. I was constantly aware of being different."

That summer, Tommy went to a camp for handicapped kids called Camp Cheerful. There he found respite from being the most physi-cally handicapped kid in the room; at Camp Cheerful, he almost felt normal, just another kid living in the Chippewa bunkhouse. Then when summer was over, he returned to the brutal reality of public school.

"Years later," says Tommy, "Miles Davis said to me that the first time he wasn't conscious of his blackness was when he went to Paris. It was the first time that he wasn't constantly aware of the color of his skin. And that's basically how it was for me: Going to the school for crippled children or to Camp Cheerful, you never thought about what was wrong with you. You were just a kid with other kids and you were all more or less in the same boat. When I was there, I never thought that somebody was looking at my leg.

"I can't explain how it feels to be the freak in the room, but I've come to believe that it was some kind of test. A test you either pass or fail. You can either use all that pain you walk around with in some creative way, like a good many of the artists I've worked with do, or you can let it destroy you. I wasn't going to let that happen to me. That doesn't mean that I walked away unscathed. To the contrary, you still have the pain and the scars and all the emotional baggage to deal with. You've just taken a detour from total destruction.

"Over the years, some of the artists I've worked with, they're freaks, walking around with mental scars rather than physical ones, but the scars are still there and have the same effect on their actions." Perhaps one of the reasons Tommy was so successful as a producer is that he understood the unspoken terror of hiding something deep inside.

When Tommy returned to school, everything he did was an attempt to prove he was as good as everyone else. He even joined the wrestling team in his last year of junior high and held his own, winning a match or two; clearly, he was developing a serious competitive edge. The body may have been weak, but the spirit was getting stronger and stronger.

His father, too, cut him no slack. From the minute he was able to walk again, his father put him to work shining shoes at the barbershop: "I can remember his customers saying, 'Sam, whadaya doing with the kid?' And he would say, 'No, that's-a okay. He's-a doing fine. Don't worry. He's doing all right.' He didn't want me to feel like I was something special or out of the ordinary in any way."

Sam promoted Tommy's independence in his old-school way. If Tommy wanted to go home from the barbershop early, he would have to take the bus. But Sam had a scheme to save a few cents; he would borrow a pass from the barber who worked for him and walk Tommy to the bus stop. Then he would get on the bus with Tommy. The first time this happened, Sam told him, "Look, when I get on, I'm-a gonna sit next to you and hold out-a my hand like this and you gonna hand me the pass." They got on the bus and sat next to each other and Tommy slipped Sam the pass and Sam got off at the next stop, walked back to the shop, and returned the pass to the second barber. All to save a nickel.

"I grew up with what they called a 'depression mentality,'" says Tommy. "The Great Depression was a part of my own experience because it affected all of these working-class people around me to the extent that they believed it could come back again at any time. This is how my father lived. He was traumatized and he watched every penny, literally."

Sundays were slow on the street but Sam would still take Tommy with him when he went down to clean the shop. He would pull the shoeshine chair out to the sidewalk, and while he was cleaning, Tommy was shining shoes. Shoeshines were fifteen cents apiece and there was always some guy who gave Tommy a dollar and wanted change. His father would check the guy out to see if he could afford it, and then he'd say, "All I have are half dollars." So the guy would have to give Tommy a half a buck. Or if his father thought this was going too far, he'd give the guy four quarters—never less than four quarters—so Tommy knew he was always going to get at least a dime tip.

"He was teaching me a work ethic," says Tommy. "It wasn't just about the value of the dollar; it was about the value of hard work. When I would complain about the business to him, he would say, 'You don't know what work is like. This is nothing. This is a luxury; my hands are clean.' And he would stay at the shop as long as people were coming in, until eight o'clock at night if that's what it took, and he started at eight in the morning. If they were coming in the door, he'd stay."

When all of Tommy's friends were going to go to camp for Easter vacation and Tommy wanted to go too, Sam said, "Okay, you-a go down there and shine shoes and whatever you make, I'll put in the difference." Camp cost forty dollars. So while everybody else was outside playing, getting ready for vacation, Tommy was shining shoes. He ended up making thirteen dollars for the week: six days, fifteen cents a shine; he shined over eighty pairs of shoes. His father put in the other twenty-seven dollars and Tommy went to camp.

"He never just handed over any money," says Tommy. "At the time I resented it so much. Later on, I realized that my father, in his own primitive way, was trying to teach me that nobody was going to give you something for nothing. And don't feel sorry for yourself because nobody's going to feel sorry for you. Your life is in your own hands. He did it without saying it."

The next year, at thirteen, Tommy worked as a vendor at the Cleveland Indians ballgames. He was too young to sell beer, so he sold peanuts, where the profit margin was smaller and he had to hustle harder to make any money at all. The job was a real window into the sordid underbelly of Cleveland commerce.

"I worked with this guy named Pete," says Tommy. "He was just a complete whack job. He was headed for the pen or somewhere worse. One day Pete took me under the bridge where tramps hung out. It was dank under there and there were a couple of guys huddled together. He said, 'Man, check this out,' and I suddenly realized that one of these guys was giving head to the other. Back then, your parents wouldn't think anything of putting you on a bus and saying, 'See ya later.' That's how you learned the facts of life. No wonder by the time we reached eighteen, we were gone."

There were a lot of wounded first-generation kids in America that were saved by the music, who heard something in the music that was about freedom or equality or just possibility. Tommy was one of them. It was the sound of escape and it was the sound of recovery all at once.

When he would go to weddings, Tommy would always stand in front of the band; he never got any farther than the musicians. And when he would go to a restaurant, there were often small projectors called MovieTones, little stand-alone viewing stations playing films of live music. For a few pennies, you could see short clips of Louie Prima, Benny Goodman, and Artie Shaw.

At first Tommy thought he might want to play drums. But when he got to Warrensville Heights Junior High, Mr. Newman, who taught music, said to him, "Hey, you love music. Why don't you get into the band?" and Tommy said, "Well, the only thing I can play is a little piano." (He had been taking lessons before he got hit by the baseball.) Mr. Newman took him into the band room and said, "Pick an instrument." And the first thing he picked up was a clarinet. Not long after, he found the saxophone. And that was it.

"I found my voice," he says. "The minute I picked up the sax-ophone, I found my comfort spot. From then on, the only thing I thought about was music. Within a year I was playing pretty decent. I was even starting to get gigs."

It was the year of Rosemary Clooney's big hit "Come On-a My House," and Tommy remembers hearing it at the little corner drug-store where they had pinball machines and a jukebox. He was sup-posed to be in tenth grade but was still an eighth grader. And there was a girl—his first real crush—who worked at the drugstore. He was mad for her and for Rosie Clooney's song. Between visiting her at the drugstore and playing saxophone, he had very little time for school.

Plus he was insecure about education in general. "When I first went back to public school," he remembers, "they gave me an IQ test. And tests of any sort just made my brain shut down. The min-ute I saw them, I froze. It was the time factor, I think; you only had so much time, and as the clock ticked, I would just panic. I hated the clock." One day, his brother Henry broke the news to him: he had scored an 85 on the IQ test. Henry said, "Well, it's average."

But then Tommy found out it wasn't average, it was below average, and it affected him deeply. From then on, he believed that he wasn't smart. It didn't occur to him or anyone else that he just wasn't good at taking tests.

School held no interest for him, with one exception: "The only time I ever felt a sense of accomplishment, a sense of self-satisfaction, was when I was playing music," he recalls. It took him out of his shell and brought him to a place where he was doing something that people were digging. He was "somebody" when he had the horn.

"I remember being in junior high and walking from class to class humming tunes in my head, thinking about the music," he says. "Other kids would be walking around trying to figure out how to solve this problem or that problem and I'd be thinking, 'What if I played this, or how could I sing that?' I dreamed about being a great saxophone player in one of the big bands like Stan Kenton or Count Basie or Woody Herman. If people talked to me, I would be like, 'Huh? What?' I would be completely off. Music was all I thought about. Music and girls."

By the time he was sixteen, he was playing gigs. Frankie Yankovic, the polka king, was like the Rolling Stones in Cleveland, so Tommy joined a polka band, playing in beer joints for hard drinkers. He worked Fridays and Saturdays, and within a few months he knew every polka tune there was. He became a working musician, and if he was late coming home, he would always leave his saxophone case behind his father's chair in the living room so that in the morning, his parents would know he got home all right.

The following year, Tommy's first year in high school, the orchestra director was not sympathetic to Tommy at all. Especially if becoming a working musician conflicted with school events. It came to a head over a concert for the school orchestra, booked on a Friday night when Tommy already had a gig. When Tommy told the orchestra director that he wasn't able to play the school concert, the director kicked him out of the orchestra. "He might as well have simply told me to leave school," says Tommy. "But that was only the first part of the punishment. Then he gave me an F in music. You need to be brain-dead to get an F in music, and I got an F in music." He was sixteen years old and in eighth grade.

And that was the year he discovered jazz. Somebody played him George Shearing's "Lullaby of Birdland," and he was hooked. Within the year he was digging Horace Silver's "Room 608," a fast, complicated, funky song he heard on the radio. And from there, Pandora's box opened. He became "a jazz junkie," he says, up on all the latest records.

With school quickly fading from view, and nothing on the horizon but a life as a musician, his father enrolled him at the local barber college, the same one his brother Joe had gone to. His father would drop him off in front of the college and Tommy would walk up the stairs, across the building, and down the stairs on the other side, just as his brother Joe had done years before, but unlike Joe, who would go to the pool hall, Tommy went straight to the Record Rendezvous. "The Vous" as the famous Cleveland disc jockey Alan Freed used to call it, was a fantastic record store. They had everything and would play whatever record you wanted to hear. Tommy would hang out there all day and then take the train home.

In those days, the guys who worked behind the counter at the Vous could spot a customer a mile away. You might have something in mind when you walked in, but you always walked out with more than you bargained for. They'd say, "Hey, did you hear the new Miles," or "Horace has a new thing," and they'd put it on the turntable and the next thing you'd know you'd buy three more albums than you planned to. These guys were masters of upselling.

One day somebody at the Vous turned Tommy on to Miles Davis's *Birth of the Cool*. There was something about this recording he just couldn't get over. The music was cool and organized, passionate and hip; it was like a glimpse into the future, and he wanted to be part of that future. It changed the way he listened to music.

Tommy finally quit school in the tenth grade. He was eighteen and working at his father's barbershop. Every morning, Tommy and Sam drove into the city together, Tommy feeling like a prisoner. When they got to the Lorain–Carnegie Bridge, which joined the east side and west side of Cleveland, Tommy would get that sinking feeling in his stomach. He knew he had to spend the rest of the day cutting hair, which he hated. The barbershop was located near the Tremont steel factory, where the mills would dump all their waste into the Cuyahoga River. The smell in the air could be awful and the area was becoming run down. At Sam's shop, they were starting to get "the lowest of the low" as far as Tommy was concerned.

Sam, who was always looking for an angle, and with a thought toward boosting business, got the idea to hire a Puerto Rican barber to attract all the Puerto Ricans who were moving into the neighborhood. For a while, there was Sam, Tommy and, in the third chair, a Puerto Rican barber who spoke little English. Within a couple of weeks, the joint was rolling with Puerto Ricans, all speaking Spanish, and Sam and Tommy were totally out of the action. Tommy was starting to go crazy. Plus he wasn't making any money to speak of.

As fate would have it, a friend of Tommy's father—they called him Joey Baloney because his name was Joe Balone—had a barbershop on Fleet Avenue, right in the middle of the steel district, and he offered Tommy a job. At the time, all Tommy wanted to do was make some money to get a car so he could get some chicks. So he left his father's shop and went to work with Joe.

The first thing he did was buy a car. It was a '35 Ford. He got it for about $400 in 1954. It opened up opportunities for him immediately. One night he was working a gig at a place called Darrow's and the club owner said, "You know, Sam Butera's in town. He thought maybe he'd come over and jam but he doesn't have a car. But if somebody could go pick him up . . . " Sam was Louis Prima's sax man and one of Tommy's heroes; Tommy immediately volunteered to be the designated driver.

Tommy drove downtown to the radio station where Butera was being interviewed and picked him up. In the car, Tommy started telling him how much he liked his playing but Sam just turned to Tommy and said, "Hey, man, you know where I can lay some pipe around here?" Tommy said, "Yeah, Sam, we're going to pipe-laying central."

His next car was a '54 Ford Fairlane. This one cost $2,400 brand new and his father loaned him the money, which he paid back, with interest, at $25 a week. It was a beautiful car, pink and black with a futuristic design. But Joe Balone's barbershop was in a neighborhood where both Republic and Bethlehem Steel were located, two huge factories that put out so much pollution over the course of the day that the entire neighborhood would be covered in thick soot by evening. Most of the customers at the shop wouldn't take their weekly bath until they had their haircut, so Tommy would literally be shaving strips of dirt off their necks. And after work, he would walk outside to find his beautiful new car covered with soot. Again, he had gone from the frying pan into the fire.

Tommy ultimately spent three years working at Joe's barbershop on Fleet Avenue. Time was passing.

When he was young, many of his friends had been Jewish, but when he left school and started cutting hair, suddenly everybody he hung out with was Sicilian. It was what he refers to as his *goomba* period. "My old Jewish friends were off going to the theater and reading books—they had found Salinger and Mailer—and I was like, 'Hey, baby, what's shakin'?'"

That's when he started playing with the Sammy Dee Orchestra. Sam Denardo had the most popular band in Cleveland, and wherever they played, there was a line of people waiting to get in. All the guys in the band were jazz fanatics. Sicilian jazz fanatics. Tommy even started singing a few "jump" tunes, like "Gimme That Wine."

The guys who hung around with the band were all from a pretty rough Sicilian crowd; a few of them actually became "made men." Tommy's old Jewish friends didn't understand what was happening to him. Even his old friend Ede remembers, "There was one guy named Squirrel Mongeluzzi and he was the head of one of the gangs in high school. I used to think if I ever ran into Squirrel, it might be all right because Tommy might be there too. Tommy might be with the Squirrel." In fact, Tommy never knew him, but the point was, he could have.

"I'm not sure how I managed to stay out of trouble," Tommy says. "One time, we were all at my friend Tony's house and a couple of guys came over. They said, 'Are you ready to go?' We said 'yeah' and when we got in the car, they said they were going to rob a drugstore. I said, 'Tony, I'm gonna take the bus home.' He said, 'No, no, you're not gonna be involved.' But I split."

Everybody in the Sicilian crowd was a sharp dresser. They wore black draped pants with the three-quarter-inch raised waist, tailored so they would fit tight around the ankles, with monogrammed white-on-white shirts with the large "Mr. B" (Billy Eckstine) rolled collar. They had ducktail haircuts, and for a while, even Tommy took to wearing a star sapphire pinky ring.

Like all the kids his age, he saw the movie *Blackboard Jungle* when it came out in 1954, but by that time he was such a bebop fanatic, and ran with such a heavy crowd, that he thought it was more or less a joke. In fact, a few months after "Rock Around the Clock" became a huge hit, the Sammy Dee band was playing a gig and Bill Haley and the Comets came to town and played a set on their stage. "They played 'Rock Around the Clock,' Tommy remembers, "and it was terrible. They were so loud, and the sound in the room was so awful, you couldn't hear a thing. So that was rock and roll music to me."

A local disc jockey in Cleveland named Chris Miller just loved the Sammy Dee band. He believed in them so much that he managed to get them an audition for the Arthur Godfrey television show. One night after a gig, everybody hopped in their cars and drove straight to New York City; they stayed in a big suite at the Park Sheraton Hotel on Seventh Avenue (the same hotel where the Sicilian gangster Albert Anastasia got whacked). It was a wild first time in the big city for Tommy, but in the end, nothing came of the audition, and the Sammy Dee band settled for being celebrities in Cleveland.

Not long thereafter, another Cleveland disc jockey named Phil McLean decided to start his own television program, a local version of *The Dick Clark Show* on Saturdays, and he asked Sammy Dee and the guys to be regulars. The band was in residence for a couple of months and became huge in the Cleveland area. Pretty soon they were working four or five nights a week. It was becoming a full-time gig for Tommy.

Sammy Dee and Tommy both played the sax. At the dances, Sammy would get on one side of the auditorium, Tommy would get on the other, and they would meet in the middle, blowing their horns. They called it "the battle of the saxes," and the act went over well, especially at large dance halls like the Twilight Gardens in Eastwood, out by Lake Erie.

It was at the Twilight Gardens that Tommy met his first real girl-friend, Ninfa. She ran with the heavy Sicilian crowd that followed the band, and she was the girl that everybody wanted to date, eighteen and gorgeous with smoldering Sicilian looks. Tommy was crazy about her, and at one point he even thought they might get married, although in retrospect, he says it was pretty obvious that they were going in different directions. "We would drive around in my pink and black Ford listening to Alan Freed on WJW," says Tommy, "and I remember once sitting in that car late at night and her saying to me, 'Tommy, you got your eyes in the stars; come back to earth.'"

At one point, they stopped seeing each other and Tommy heard through the grapevine that she had married someone else. He was heartbroken, but a few months later, she left the guy and she and Tommy got back together again. The relationship was on and off for several more years.

Ninfa "was a tough broad," says Tommy, "which I respected. Her father was definitely connected. During the prohibition he was involved in bootlegging, driving a truck. He knew the biggest people in town. They used to come by the house. In those days, there was a guy named Dominic Sospirato. They called him the bagman. He would go back and forth to Vegas with a suitcase full of money because the Cleveland mob owned the Stardust hotel."

Ninfa's father was Licatese, which meant he was from the town of Licata, in Sicily. And Licata had the largest number of guys who ended up made guys. "They used to make the guys in the basement of the Roman Gardens and I always thought that maybe Ninfa's father had a tighter connection to this scene than people thought. He worked at the newspaper, but he also worked at the racetrack at night selling tickets. It was probably a cover for all the cash he had coming through. But he was one of those guys, if he didn't want to tell you something, you couldn't get a word out of him."

Tommy was still working at the barbershop on Fleet Avenue and hating it. One day, a friend of his named Jim Lang told him, "I think there's a barbershop for sale in the Keith Building." The shop was only open by appointment and they were closed on Saturdays, perfect for a guy who was playing gigs at night and didn't want to come in early to cut hair. Tommy asked his father for another loan to purchase the shop and the money to refurbish it. "He went with me to take a look at the premises, and thank God he liked it."

Tommy kept that shop for five years; it would become his entrée into a whole new world.

The Keith Building was in Playhouse Square, a very hip area where many of the radio stations were located: WJW, where Casey Kasem worked, was across the street, WERE was not far away on Thirteenth, WGAR was on Twelfth, and WHK was on Forty-sixth. And the Palace Theater was right there too—a fantastic old venue where Lew Wasserman, who would one day run the giant MCA media empire, started as an usher. Playhouse Square was where all the action was; even Bob Feller, the famous fastball pitcher for the Cleveland Indians, had an office in the Keith Building and became one of Tommy's customers.

The record business was still young and it was attracting a lot of miscellaneous guys, guys who were looking for the main chance and often had a background of dubious repute. One of them, Ernie Farrell, always wore a sharp, shiny suit, liked to hang out at a small hoodlum club on the west side of town named Felice's, and was definitely connected. When they first met, he told Tommy he was "in construction" and described how he got in the business: He had convinced some guy that he could crew a job when he didn't even have a crew. When the guy said, "Well, I want to see what kind of equipment you have," Ernie took him to a place where another construction company stored its vehicles and said, "Well, here it is. Here's my stuff." Ernie subsequently talked his way into the record business and showed up one afternoon at Tommy's barbershop in Playhouse Square, looking for a trim before he pitched the radio jocks.

Instead of the sharkskin suit, Ernie was now wearing a full-blown ski outfit—knit sweater, special shoes, the whole thing—and when Tommy asked him what he had been up to, Ernie told him he had scored a huge job laying concrete around the Cleveland Museum of Art, and the night he finished the job, there was a huge rainstorm, the worst storm that Cleveland had ever seen, and the whole area flooded. The flood ruined the concrete, of course, and because Ernie didn't have the right insurance, he went bust. So then he became an Arthur Murray dance instructor. And within a year, the former gangster, contractor, and dance instructor had found his way into the record business as a promotion man.

A lot of Tommy's clients at the Keith Building were promotion men like Ernie; in fact, Ernie was the guy who first brought the famous deejay Casey Kasem into Tommy's shop. Then another friend of Tommy's from the old days, a guy named Johnny Musso, got a job as a promotion man at Decca Records and he, too, started coming into the shop. He brought in deejays like Phil McLean and Big Wilson, two of Cleveland's hottest radio personalities. And guys like Bob Skaff and his brother Phil, who were working their way up in the record distribution game, became customers too. Soon the shop was a record biz hangout and Tommy was thinking, "This is where I belong!" He was twenty-three and eager to expand his horizons, but every time he would bring up the possibility of a job, they would say, "Man, you don't want to get into the record business. You have a nice business right here. You're doing all right."

But Tommy was a complete record freak; he spent every loose dollar he had on jazz records. He wasn't crazy about most of the popular music of the day, but he did love the Moondog's radio program. The Moondog was Alan Freed, the man credited with naming this new music "rock and roll," and his radio program would go on at ten o'clock on WJW. Tommy had been listening to Freed since he was eighteen years old, cruising down Chagrin Boulevard with Ninfa or sitting in his car at Manner's Big Boy drive-in. Like thousands of other Cleveland kids, Tommy would hear the Moondog's theme song—a slow drag called "Blues for the Redboy," the most gutbucket thing you ever heard—followed by Freed's trademark wolf call, and he knew he was in for three hours of the hippest groove music on the planet: Ruth Brown, Charles Brown, Big Maybelle, Nat King Cole. Freed might have named the music "rock and roll," but back then he was playing nothing but straight-up, life-changing rhythm and blues.

When Tommy wasn't in the barbershop or working with the Sammy Dee band, he was sitting in at local nightclubs, trying to get his saxophone chops together. It was all about trying to find a *sound*. It wasn't just about playing in tune or playing the right notes; you were looking for a special *sound*. It wasn't like anybody ever told him, "Hey, you gotta find your own sound." He was just hearing all these cats and he realized everybody he dug had their own voice. Guys like Stan Getz and Lester Young and Paul Quinichette, they were his guys. They called Quinichette "the vice president" because Lester Young was "the president" and some guys starting calling Tommy "little veep" because he was starting to sound a bit like Quinichette.

There was a brother named Weasel Parker who worked in the music store where Tommy got reeds for his horn. Parker also played sax, and one day he said to Tommy, "Hey, man, I play at this joint at Seventy-ninth and Cedar called the Corner Tavern. You should come down and sit in." Tommy knew that a fantastic Hammond B3 organ player named Labert Ellis also worked at the club. By then Tommy had heard Jimmy Smith and was a fan of the B3 sound, so he started going down to the Corner to sit in every chance he had. He was chasing the jazz train.

The Corner Tavern was one of those local dives where you had to keep your coat on in the winter because there was no insulation in the walls and the wind came whistling through the joint. One night, along with the wind, Tommy heard a voice that would open his ears permanently. The jukebox at the Corner Tavern was loaded with hip jazz cuts, and on this night, when the band took a break, Tommy heard a flurry of notes come out of the speaker that was so wild and ferocious that he jumped up and ran to see what it was. It was Charlie Parker playing "Just Friends." He recalls, "It was the most amazing thing I had ever heard. What he did to that song was unbelievable. So of course the first thing the next morning I went down to the Vous and I bought *Charlie Parker with Strings*. And that's when I really started to put all this music together."

Tommy kept gigging with Sammy Dee and jamming at the Corner Tavern until the following year, when he was twenty-four; that's when he joined up with Nick DeCaro and his brother Frank. Frank played drums, Nick played accordion, and together with various bass players they sang in close harmony, like the Four Freshmen, who were popular in jazz circles at the time. (Tommy specialized in the falsetto parts.)

They became a "territory band," working all through the Midwest. They went as far east as the Catskills in New York, where they were once booked at an Italian resort in a town called Caro. The entertainment there opened each night with a house band; the leader of the band played two bass drums and had an act with a monkey that would dance and put his hands over his ears. That was the whole act—the monkey pretending to hate music. The drummer was named Pete Bennett, and he went on to become a big-time record promotion guy, even working with the Beatles, the Rolling Stones, and Sam Cooke a few years later. This, too, is how the record business started.

In this very room one night came several guys from the famed Nola Recording Studios in New York City. Nola was a rehearsal and recording space, and at the end of the evening one of these guys said to Tommy, "Listen. Are you guys looking for work? I've got a good friend who's got an agency. His name is Joe Glaser. Let me see if I can get you an audition." Now Joe Glaser was one of the biggest agents in the world; he handled Louis Armstrong and was clearly connected, all the way back to Al Capone. Sure enough, the guy from Nola was telling the truth; he got Tommy and the boys an audition with Glaser, and one night after the gig in Caro, they all headed to New York City to audition.

They set up at Nola, and at the appointed hour, in walks Joe Glaser himself, along with one other guy, Oscar Cohen. Oscar was Louis Armstrong's personal representative, and he didn't say a word, not to Tommy or anybody else in the band; he just sat there, impassive. The guys did their whole show, and when it was over, Oscar said, "You'll hear from somebody," and then they all got up and left. Tommy, Nick, and Frank immediately went out and bought two tuxedos (used)—one white and one red—and went home to wait for the call. When it came, it was from a guy named Joe Mussi at the Chicago office of Associated Booking, and he said, "Are you guys ready to work?" And that was that. They were on the road. But not the road they had anticipated.

The first thing Associated Booking did was put them on a tour of Army bases. Everybody met up in Chicago, a motley collection of acts including a big show band, a comedian—a woman who, Tommy remembers, "was not at all funny"— a trio of over-the-hill singers called the Bon Bons (three blondes who looked alike and could have been sisters), and Tommy's group. They got on the bus and started hitting every Army base down through Illinois, Kansas, Tennessee—as far South as Florida.

In the 1950s, the late-night air was jumping with the best music in the world, and it became one of the few things the musicians lived for. Riding on the bus, Tommy and the guys discovered the 50,000-watt clear-channel radio stations that played great jazz—one night, outside Pensacola, they realized they were listening to Ben Webster on a station coming in from Windsor, Canada.

Needless to say, life on the road was rough. They played small bases, SAC missile launch and control sites mostly, with maybe a hundred people at each one. The "artists" would perform in class-room spaces, where the audience would sit in school chairs (complete with the little table on the arm for writing) and the women would change and do their makeup in the kitchen. "When we would leave," Tommy remembers, "these chicks were such hardcore road rats that they'd fill their suitcases with whatever canned goods they could cop from the kitchen. We played gigs like that for months, eating out of suitcases, and we thought, 'Hey! We're in showbiz!'"

The routing was all over the place, one joint leading to the next in an endless parade of second-rate gigs. Once Associated Booking got them a month-long gig at the Duluth Hotel in Duluth, Minnesota, where they worked the Black Bear Lounge—of course there was a giant stuffed bear in the lobby. It was the dead of winter, and so cold that the band left the hotel only one time during the entire month. A lot of these joints would have gambling in the basement or in a back room and the music was just a cover. There was one place in Terre Haute, Indiana, an old theater that was set up like a supper club, and for the first two nights there were literally no people in the room. The woman who ran the club told the band not to worry about it, just do their set. The third night the place was jammed. It turned out the former projection booth had been converted into a gambling room for blackjack and dice. Nobody listened to the music.

Tommy, Nick, and Frank stayed on the road for almost a year. They would go from Indianapolis to Fargo and then turn around and go back to Streeter, Illinois. Then they'd check in with ABC and find out the next gig was back in Minot, beyond Fargo, and they'd simply turn around and go back, like rats in a maze.

What finally got Tommy to abandon the road wasn't the music or the routing or even the nasty joints, but his health. He had picked up a "social disease" somewhere along the line and ended up in a hospital on a catheter for five days. When he got out, he went straight back to Cleveland and started over. As a barber.

He found a job in a shop across from his old place in the Keith Building. The guy who owned it thought that because Tommy knew a lot of people in town he would be good for his business. Tommy lasted one day. At six o'clock he went to the owner and said, "I'm really sorry, but I can't do this." Every bad dream he ever had about cutting hair had come back to him that afternoon.

When he got home that night, his father said, "So, how much-a you make today?" He said, "I don't know. Twenty, twenty-five, something. But I quit." "You quit? What, are you crazy? Why do you quit?" Tommy said, "I don't know what I'm going to do, but all I know is I'm not doing this. If I have to be a beach bum, I'll be a beach bum. But I'm done cutting hair."

Tommy often thought about what would have happened to him if his friend Jim Lang hadn't told him about that barbershop in the Keith Building. He wouldn't have discovered the record business or met all of the people whose hair he cut on their way to promote the latest "hit," including the one guy who finally gave him a job: a guy named Jack Bratel. Bratel called Tommy out of the blue just two weeks after he quit cutting hair for the last time. People say "out of the blue," but this was really out of the dead of night. Tommy was sitting at home with his head in his hands when the phone rang.

Jack managed MS Distributing. MS stood for Milt Salstone, who owned the company, based in Chicago, and he had just opened a branch in Cleveland. Jack told Tommy he didn't have anything big to offer but there was a job packing records in the backroom for $50 a week. Tommy was thrilled and ran to tell his father the good news.

Sam said, "Fifty a week when you can make a hundred twenty-five cutting hair? Are you crazy?" But it turned out to be one of the greatest introductions to the record business Tommy could have had, because working in the shipping room gave him a sense of how the whole thing worked: The promotion men went out and got the records played on the radio, and then the orders would start coming in, and then the boxes got packed and records got shipped out. Follow the money.

At MS, Tommy got to know some of the legendary men of the music industry, guys like George Goldner and Harry Finfer. Goldner was one of the pioneers of payola (pay for play) who had actually discovered Frankie Lymon and the Teenagers—they had a huge hit with "Why Do Fools Fall in Love?"—and George made a lot of money, but he was a terrible gambler and wound up trading all of his rights to the notorious gangster Morris Levy to erase a bad debt, and now he was back on the streets hustling again. He and Finfer were traveling together; technically they were competitors but they were sharing expenses and were still good friends. It was Christmastime when they arrived at MS in Cleveland to plug their products and spread a little cheer.

Tommy remembers Finfer coming into the back room where he and the guys were packing boxes. Finfer was wearing a long black coat and made it a point to shake hands all around, and before he left he tipped each guy twenty bucks. When George discovered that Harry had greased the crew, he went into the back room, shook hands all around, and then, instead of tipping everybody himself, he said, "My guy Finfer took care of you guys, right?" That same afternoon, Tommy took Finfer up to WHK to meet the disc jockey Neil McIntyre, and when Harry shook Neil's hand, Tommy could see Harry had watches all the way up to his elbow. "Go ahead," he said to McIntyre, "pick a watch." You could learn a lot about the business from the back room.

And then one day, Tommy actually met Milt Salstone himself. The man was like a myth; few people had ever seen him. But that afternoon, while Tommy was packing records in the back room, a very suave guy with a dark Florida tan walked in wearing a checked coat with a burgundy handkerchief and a burgundy tie. He looked around for a minute and then walked up to Tommy and said, "How you doing?"

Tommy said "Okay." Milt said, "You got any change?" Tommy reached into his pocket and pulled out seventy-five cents. Milt took the change, threw it against the wall, and said, "You like what I did with your money?" Tommy said "No." Milt said, "Well, I don't like what you're doing with my money." And he pointed to the cardboard that littered the floor, pieces of packing material that Tommy had wasted. "I never forgot it," Tommy remembers. "This is a nickel-and-dime business. And whatever job you do in this business, whatever role you have to play, you're supposed to care enough to do it right."

Within a month, Tommy was promoted to salesman at MS, but it turned out he wasn't particularly good at selling to retailers. For one thing, he wasn't good with numbers. For example, when he went to meet Leo Mintz, the guy who owned the Record Rendezvous, Tommy remembers it was a total disaster. "I was really nervous because I knew he was a tough guy. I was kind of fumbling around and he was getting angrier by the minute, mumbling 'What the fuck, they sent out some amateur here.' Some way or other I got through it and I must have answered him back in a way that he liked because when the transaction was done, he said, 'Let's go have a drink.' Of course, Leo was an alcoholic . . ." And suddenly Tommy had scored with the man who owned his favorite record store. But it was one of his few victories as a salesman.

And then finally, a gig promoting records opened up. Unlike a salesman, who had to know numbers and units, a promotion man had the sole task of taking care of disc jockeys, making friends, buying lunch, going along to get along, and Tommy took to it like a duck to water. Bratel gave him his send-off speech. He said, "Look, every record you go out with ain't a hit. And what you have to do is make your bets based on what you think you can get played." So Tommy learned to deliver all the records, but to hold back the one he believed in until the end of his pitch, and then say, "Look, this is the one that I think has a shot." By operating in this way, program directors and disc jockeys came to trust him.

The first record he "broke" (got played on the air) was "The Boll Weevil Song" by Brook Benton. Then a few weeks later he heard something on a Jack Jones album that caught his ear. "We had Kapp Records as one of our accounts," Tommy remembers, "and I didn't like the album, but I heard this one ballad that I thought was really good. The song was called 'Lollipops and Roses,' and I mentioned it to Jack Bratel." Jack was impressed enough to pass along the information to MS in Chicago and Kapp Records in Los Angeles. He told them, "You know, our guy in Cleveland is getting this record played, and he's getting calls for it." Kapp ended up putting it out as a single and it became a hit all around the country.

Up until that point, Tommy had been strictly a jazz freak. But with this initial success, he started to realize, "Hey, I like this pop music."

Within a couple of months Tommy had become successful enough to rent a little pad of his own and move out of his parents' house. This was a major decision; in Sicilian families, nobody left home until they were married. Tommy was the first in his family to make the leap, and his father didn't talk to him for six months. He took Tommy's leaving as a personal insult. Tommy was twenty-five years old.

And then one of Tommy's old customers from the barbershop at the Keith Building, Bob Skaff, called him from LA. Several months before, Skaff had left his job in Cleveland and moved to the West Coast, where he became head of national promotion for Liberty Records. He was calling to say his local promotion guy was leaving and did Tommy want the job. Tommy jumped at the chance.

Back when he was still cutting hair, even before his time as a touring musician, he had seen a film called *Strangers When We Meet*. It starred Ernie Kovacs, Kirk Douglas, and Kim Novak, and, Tommy remembered, "The story was about an architect (Douglas) who gets his dream job to build a home for a very successful TV star (Kovacs) on a beautiful piece of land in the Pacific Palisades area of LA. Most of the film was simply beauty shots of the city as the architect was seducing the girl (Novak), and even though it was a nothing movie, when I saw the landscape of LA it was love at first sight: beautiful scenery, warm climate, and fabulous women."

From that moment on, he knew he was going to leave Cleveland some day and move to LA. "When I got the call from Bob Skaff it took me about three minutes to make up my mind," he says. "I told my father I was moving and he asked me what it paid. I told him, 'A hundred twenty-five a week.' It was the same money I was making in Cleveland. He said, 'What, are you crazy? You're going to move three thousand miles for the same money?' But I was already gone."

The day he actually left Cleveland was a freezing cold Sunday in February. He was wearing a suit and a tie, an overcoat, gloves, and a Stetson hat. "I was dressed sort of like George Raft in *Whistle Stop*," says Tommy. "I wanted to make a good impression." His father and mother drove him to Hopkins airport, and the last thing he did before he got on the plane was stop at a vending machine and buy a life insurance policy (they used to sell them at airports) and hand it to his mother. "When I saw the look on her face," he says, "I realized it was dumbest thing I'd ever done."

Giuseppe LiPuma.

Sal LiPuma in uniform.

The Corner of Kinsman Road near where Tommy lived.

Tommy and the infamous
rumble seat Ford.

Hank, Sam and Tommy
at war's end.

Tommy tugging mom's apron strings.

The Chippewa cabin at Camp Cheerful.

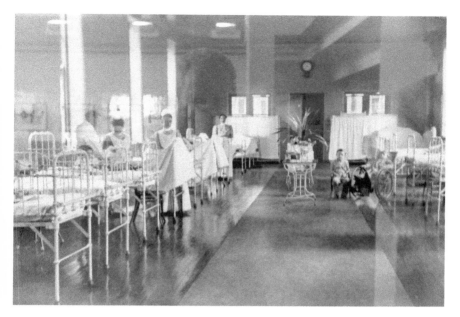

The hospital ward where Tommy recovered as a child.

Tommy just out of the hospital.

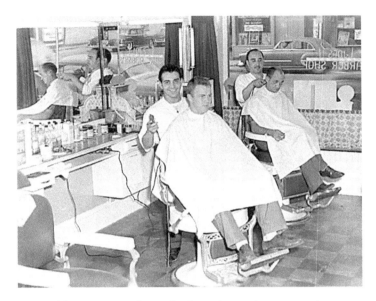

Tommy at work as a barber; the smile is not real.

The band with the DeCaros, Tommy
at far right and Nick above him.

Meet Johnny Carson

There's a moment when you first land in LA that is magical. Like that moment in *The Wizard of Oz* when the house falls from the sky and the world goes Technicolor. The first thing you notice is the light—things seem lit from within—and then the endless parade of characters. And of course there's that smell in the air, like flowers and smoke; something sweet with just a little hint of danger. The day he arrived, Tommy's life went from mundane black-and-white to a Technicolor fiction before he even hit the curb.

Bud Dain, the guy whose job he was taking, met him outside the baggage claim dressed in casual gabardine slacks and a sport shirt. In his suit and overcoat and Stetson hat, Tommy looked like he was from another planet, a refugee from a different time. Bud ignored the outfit and said, "We're going directly to a Starlets baseball game and Skaff will meet us there." They jumped in the car, pulled on to the freeway, and headed for the game; on the radio, the Shirelles were singing "Will You Still Love Me Tomorrow?"

At the ballgame, Tommy got some strange looks because of his George Raft getup—he had prepared for a serious meeting and here he was with a bunch of guys drinking beer out of paper cups. There were also a couple of girls with the party; LA was a company town and this was a company picnic. Tommy immediately got with the program. There was electricity in the air, the smell of perfume and cigarettes, and Tommy couldn't help thinking that when he was a kid, he was the guy walking up and down the aisles shouting "Peanuts!"

After the game, Bud checked him in to the Carolina Pines Motel, just north of Sunset and La Brea, where he would be staying until he got established. Tommy threw his suitcase in the corner and put his coat and hat in the closet, and when he moved out three weeks later, he took the suitcase but left the coat and hat behind. That's how long it took him to go native.

That first night, after the ballgame, Bud took him to a club on Sunset called Pandora's Box, a funky little showroom in West Hollywood. A few years later, it would become famous as the epicenter of the "curfew riots" that put the Sunset Strip on the map and inspired Steve Stills to write the hit song "For What It's Worth." The place was always well attended by record business types, and on this night, the singer Jackie DeShannon was going to sit in with the band. Tommy immediately grasped that Bud had a thing for her. They strolled in a little past ten and Tommy came face-to-face with a piece of his musical future.

Up onstage, sitting at the piano, was a very serious-looking six-foot-tall dude wearing a blue suit, a pink tie, and a big rock and roll pompadour. He was playing in a style Tommy had never quite heard before, a kind of Texas stride, but slicker, less rough than the country and western version. Most of the boogie players of the day, like Jerry Lee Lewis or Little Richard, were basically playing four chords, but this guy had a real handle on the harmonic spectrum, and he wasn't afraid to roll 'em. His name was Leon Russell, and he had just arrived in LA from Tulsa, Oklahoma. Along with Leon on the stage that night were the guitarist David Gates and the bassist Carl Radle; Tommy had been in town less than twenty-four hours and he'd already discovered three of the best studio musicians in town, musicians he would work with for years to come.

The next day was a Monday, and Bud started taking him around and introducing him to the guys who ran radio in LA. LA was a "breakout city," which meant that if you could get something played there it had a good shot all across the country, and KFWB was the radio station in town. KRLA had a bigger wattage than KFWB but they played what they called "good music," like KNPC, and then there was KGFJ, which was the R&B station. So KFWB was the deal; if you got something played on that station, if the record "had the goods," you would know it. No excuses.

Tommy thought he knew the job pretty well, but in LA he discovered just how green he really was as a promotion man. The record business was just about to take off in LA, and he was up against guys like Joe Smith, head of national promotion for Warner Bros., and Gil Bogus, the national guy for Motown, who were *serious* promotion men. They had numbers in their phone books that had never been listed, and they knew where all the bodies were buried.

Tommy learned that all these guys hung out at Aldo's, a coffee shop right downstairs from KFWB, and he spent a lot of his time there, picking up tips, listening to stories, learning the ropes. Watching these guys operate was a graduate education.

In those days, disc jockeys could vote on what records they played. There was the Top Forty, which was the playlist, things that were definitely going to get on the air, but then there was also an "extras list," the records that the disc jockeys could play if they wanted to. Tommy's job, like every promotion man, was to get his records played, if not on the regular playlist, then at least on the extras list. If you had the number one record, they *had* to play it every hour. Otherwise, getting your record on the extras list was often the best you could do, and everyone was trying to do it.

But even when your record was on the extras list, that's when your work really started. Because once you got it on the list, then you had to actually get it played. Just because it was on the extras list didn't mean it *would* get played; it meant it *could* be played.

A lot of promotion men would go back to the office at this point and say "Well, I got the record added to the list" and then go to lunch, but of course, if it didn't get played, it didn't sell through, and the whole process stopped there. The proverbial tree had fallen in an empty forest. The bottom line was the song had to get played, and to do that, you had to get tight with the disc jockeys. The job of a promotion man was really a very personal, intimate one. Disc jockeys had to trust you, they had to like you, and they had to be willing to take a chance on your behalf.

Tommy spent most of his time knocking on doors and trying to take disc jockeys out for a drink, lunch, dinner, anything; for weeks, he was pretty much on his own in a city he didn't know. He remembers looking into the mirror one morning and seeing this guy looking back at him with a quizzical expression. "Like I was thinking, 'Man, what am I doing here?' I missed my family and my friends. I had that feeling you get as a child, knowing you had felt safe in your mother's arms and that you could always go back there, but this time, that wasn't going to happen. This was the absolute moment of truth for me. I knew I couldn't go back home and I wasn't going to let myself go down." Failure was not an option.

One source of comfort for Tommy was the large number of Jews in the music business. "I realized," he says, "that hanging out with Jewish people always reminded me of home. I had grown up with Jews—I went to Jewish camp and learned Jewish prayers—and suddenly in LA, here I was, kind of back home again, in a cultural sense. I always felt very comfortable in the Jewish world."

In LA he found himself a long way from being "this heavy *goomba* in Cleveland," totally immersed in the Sicilian hoodlum thing; he was now in a world of books, movies, music, publishing, all the

Jewish industries. The record business was about to explode world-wide and Tommy was positioned to become a partner in the culture business. "When I moved to LA, my world changed completely," Tommy says. "My mind became a sponge. And one of the main reasons was a guy named Bobby Dale."

His first week in LA, they told him, "There's this guy at KFWB who you absolutely have to get next to; he's tough, but he's very important. They listen to him at the station because he's got great ears and they know he's not in anybody's pocket. The guy you gotta get tight with is Bobby Dale."

It took Tommy three weeks just to get up the courage to call him and say, "Hey, when you get off tonight can we go have a drink?" Bobby had the 9 p.m. to midnight slot, and he agreed without hesitation. When his shift ended, Tommy was there in the parking lot. They drove to PJ's on Crescent Heights and Santa Monica Boulevard, a joint where everybody in the business would go after hours. You walked in and there was a long bar on the left that ran fifty feet back to the room where there was another smaller space with an intimate club atmosphere; that's where the band was set up. Depending on the night, you might see someone famous, like Steve Allen or Mel Torme, sitting in. The place was a great hang, open until 2:30 a.m.

But that night Bobby was in no mood for entertainment; he just wanted to do some serious drinking. He and Tommy said very little to each other on the way over and Tommy was already thinking that this was one of the toughest characters he had ever met, and he had met a few. When they arrived and took a seat at the bar, Bobby told the bartender, "Two Cutty and soda, tall." The bartender brought him the two Cuttys and he knocked them both back, guzzled the first one and then downed the second one. Then he said, "Two more."

Same thing. Downed them both with no obvious effect. Unfazed, he ordered two more. At one point he asked Tommy what music he listened to, and when Tommy mentioned somebody, he said, "Aw, fuck that guy; he's bullshit."

But after they hung out a few more times, Bobby seemed to relax around Tommy, his defenses dropped and one night he invited Tommy over to his house to listen to some music. And that was the night, Tommy remembers, that his mind started expanding.

"Now I could hold my liquor," says Tommy, "but this was like being on a roller coaster. At the house, we started juicing, and he opened up with Thelonious Monk. Then he put on Chuck Berry, 'Johnny B. Goode.' I was never a Chuck Berry fan, I was a bebop fanatic, and he saw right away that I wasn't digging this. He said, 'You don't dig him, do you?' And I said, 'No, I just don't get it.' So he started walking me through the lyrics to the song, and just hearing Bobby talk about them, I suddenly realized that Chuck Berry was a serious poet. It was like a kind of epiphany: when I heard the song through Bobby's ears, the music just let me in. And when the music lets you in, then you really get into it. Pretty soon, I was a Chuck Berry fan."

Bobby taught him not only about the value of pop music but also about films and literature. "One night, out of nowhere, he asked me if I knew George Bernard Shaw. When I said no, he said, 'He's a playwright,' and he started to tell me about *My Fair Lady* and where it was taken from. Then he said, 'Shaw wrote this book called *Man and Superman*. This is a part of *Man and Superman*. It's called *Don Juan in Hell*,' and he played me a recording featuring Charles Laughton. From the opening lines—'No light, no sound, no time, nor space. Utter void'—I loved it and was hooked."

Then Bobby played Tommy a spoken-word record with Charles Boyer, Agnes Moorehead, and Sir Cedric Hardwicke. He started throwing out all these names and Tommy started paying attention:

James Thurber, Somerset Maugham, Aldous Huxley, some of the Beat writers like Jack Kerouac and William S. Burroughs. "It kind of stunned me," he says. "There were so many elements that were coming out of these conversations that I thought were just incredible, to the point where the next day, after hanging with Bobby all night, I would go out and buy the books. And I started reading. And I never stopped." It was Bobby Dale who turned on that light for Tommy.

Bobby was always throwing off great lines from some book he was reading or a film he had seen, and Tommy was picking them up like "a bird picking up bread crumbs in Central Park." Within a short time, Tommy was passionate about books—fiction, history, biographies, whatever he could get his hands on; in the midst of hustling records to radio stations, Tommy went to the school of Bobby Dale. "Meeting Bobby and becoming his lifelong friend," says Tommy, "was like going to Harvard for me, an education in art and life."

And yet, as Bobby's own biographer wrote, "He taught the politics of life while simultaneously struggling with his own." Bobby was not a happy camper.

Bobby Dale was very self-conscious about his looks. He was a big guy, about six foot one, with a definite paunch, and he stood in a perennial slouch, wore tortoiseshell glasses, and was balding. He had, as the saying goes, a perfect "face for radio." And there was a visceral sadness about him, something that seemed as deep as an ocean. But his mind and sense of humor made up for whatever he imagined his shortcomings to be, and his casual, offhand hipster delivery and flat Minnesota accent (he was originally from the Twin Cities) was the perfect combination to hold your emotional hand through the long LA night. His one-liners were often hilarious and his digressions and improvisations were in a category all their own. But first and foremost, Bobby Dale was a great music man. If he believed something was a hit, you didn't bet against him.

A few months after Tommy met Bobby, Liberty Records released a single by an obscure R&B group named the Rivingtons. The record was called "Papa Oom Mow Mow" and it was a silly song with nonsensical lyrics, but the group could really sing and the thing was incredibly infectious. It was like one big hook. Tommy thought it had a chance to be a "pick hit"—a "pick hit" was a record that a disc jockey thought was hot enough to knock the previous "pick" off the list—so he delivered the record to KFWB, made his pitch to the record librarian, and then forgot about it. That was on a Tuesday.

The following Sunday night, Tommy was relaxing at home when he got a call from Bob Skaff. Bob asked Tommy if he was listening to KFWB, and when Tommy said no, he said, "Man, you got to turn it on, Bobby Dale is playing the shit out of 'Papa Oom Mow Mow.'" Bobby was not just playing the song; he was playing it over and over again, twenty times in a row. The song would end and Bobby would say, "Now we're gonna hear . . ." and bam! He'd play it again. For over three hours, that's the only thing he played. The next day, the distributor came in for ten thousand records. As a promotion man, Tommy was finally off and running in LA.

Bobby was also the guy who introduced Tommy to the great record producer Phil Spector. Back in 1958, Bobby had turned "To Know Him Is to Love Him" into a hit for Phil's group the Teddy Bears, so Phil loved Bobby and gave him carte blanche at his recording sessions. Sometimes Tommy would go along, sit in the back, and watch Phil work his magic. Seeing how Phil Spector made hit records was an eye-opener. There was an art and a craft to it, and Phil Spector definitely had his own style. Style turned out to be the most important part of the magic.

At one point, Phil went to work for Liberty—it didn't last long, he soon left and formed his own company, Philles Records—and while Phil was at Liberty, he discovered a song by Gene Pitney called "He's a Rebel." After Phil started his own company, one of the first things he planned to do was cut this song with a group called the Crystals. Phil's old boss at Liberty, Snuff Garrett, also remembered the song, and when Phil left, maybe to get back at him, Snuff decided he would cut it too, so it was off to the races to see who would get it to radio first. The fly in the ointment was that Snuff had just signed the singer Vikki Carr, and Vikki was definitely not the "he's a rebel" type, but Snuff was determined to get a version of the song out on the street before Phil Spector could.

Today it takes several months between the time a song is recorded and the time it's sent to radio. There are marketing plans and art department decisions and budget considerations. But in those days, the days of the Wild West in the record business, you could cut a record one day, and the next day the promotion man would have pressings and be touting it at radio. The whole thing could happen in two days.

Tuesday was the day KFWB added records, so Snuff was cutting his version of "He's a Rebel" with Vikki Carr on Monday. It was literally going to be a twenty-four-hour turnaround. Tommy went to United Recorders in Hollywood to wait while Snuff and Vikki cut the song. At one point, something familiar caught his ear; he walked out of the studio and heard the same song coming from the session across the hall. He opened the door and there was Phil Spector, with his partner, Lester Sill, finishing up their version of the song with the Crystals. When Tommy heard the Crystals' version, which eventually became a huge hit, he said, "I don't think you guys have anything to worry about.. Have you heard what's going on across the hall?" He was basically betting against his own record.

The next day Tommy was in the unenviable position of walking into KFWB to try to get Vikki Carr's version on the air first. A half hour after he dropped it off, Tommy was downstairs at Aldo's when

Bobby Dale came in. He slid into the booth next to Tommy, put his hand on his shoulder, and said, "Sorry, Scooter. No way." Tommy had gotten there first, but Phil Spector's version with the Crystals had the style, hands down.

To add insult to injury, Tommy had to escort Vikki to a sock hop in San Bernardino the next night. She was going to lip-sync the song, and while she was waiting to go on, there was another group onstage wearing lumberjack shirts and singing 'Let's go surfing now, everybody's surfing now . . ." They sounded pretty rough. When they finally got off the stage and Vikki got up to pretend to sing her version of "He's a Rebel," these guys started shouting at her, "Boo, hiss, get off the stage . . . She's a piece of shit." Tommy walked up to them and said, "Hey, guys, give this broad a break here, you know," and they said, "Oh, fuck her and fuck you."

The band in the lumberjack shirts turned out to be the Beach Boys, shortly before they had their own first hit, doing one of their first public gigs. A few months later, when their record came out, they sounded like a completely different band. Because in fact they were. By then, they were employing a group of LA session musicians known as "the Wrecking Crew" to cut their records, and they had developed the falsetto voices and the clean sound that became their signature.

One day Tommy was up at KFWB when two guys appeared "from out of the shadows." The shorter of the two said to Tommy, "Excuse me, are you the new promotion man for Liberty?" When Tommy said yes, the guy said, "My name is Lenny Waronker and this is my friend Randy Newman." Lenny was in his last year at USC and Randy was in his last year at UCLA, and Sy Waronker, Lenny's father, who was the chairman of Liberty Records, had given the boys a chance to make a record together. Now they were trying to hustle it at radio, and they wanted Tommy to help get it played.

It never did get on the air, but from that point on, he, Randy, and Lenny became inseparable, the three musketeers, Tommy pushing records, Lenny developing his production chops, and Randy starting to compose the songs that would eventually make him a music business legend. Being so close to the source and the people who wrote and produced the music got Tommy thinking that maybe he should be more hands-on too. He started considering moving to the publishing side of the music business. Publishers signed writers, went into the studio to cut demos, and worked with the best musicians around. He had the sense that being a record promoter for the rest of his life wasn't his destiny. Too, he hadn't been playing his saxophone since he came to LA, and he missed the excitement and creativity of spending time with good musicians.

This was on his mind when Dick Glasser, who was running Liberty's publishing company, Metric Music, asked Tommy to go to New York as a promotion man. It was a big job and a big promotion and Tommy said, "Okay, I'll go. But the first job that opens up in publishing, I want it." Glasser told him, "Okay, you got it."

New York was the number one market in America. For Tommy, it was not just a trial by fire; it was a trial by ice.

Tommy arrived in Manhattan in the middle of winter. He had purchased what he thought was a warm coat at a shop on Hollywood Boulevard, but when he landed in LaGuardia it was eminently clear that the coat was "Hollywood warm"; he was freezing.

His first day in the city, the regional guy for Liberty, Ted Feigin, took him around to the various radio stations. The first stop was WINS, the big Top Forty station, and they walked from Tommy's hotel at Seventh Avenue and Fifty-ninth Street to WINS on Columbus Circle. It was a two-block walk, but by the time they got there, Tommy couldn't move his fingers and his feet were numb.

Ted wanted to introduce him to Pete Myers, who was the most powerful disc jockey at WINS; Pete had the drive-time shift, 6 to 9 a.m. When they arrived, Ted and Tommy entered a kind of holding pen, an area about fifteen feet square with a waist-high wooden barrier. Inside the pen were about twenty guys stacked up against the barrier, all tough-looking New York guys, like Juggy Gayles and Julie Rifkin, hardcore veteran promotion men, all sweating it out in their winter coats, waiting for Pete to come through the door.

When Pete walked out of the studio, all twenty guys started shouting at once—"Pete! Pete!"—and waving their records in the air. It was like the hog futures pit at the Chicago Board of Trade. At one point Pete stopped and took a record from one of the outstretched hands. There was a little turntable up against the back wall and he put the 45 on the platter and played about three seconds of the song. Then he wound it forward another few seconds and played another ten seconds or so. He did this a couple of times, then he took the record off and threw it back at the group in the bullpen. Didn't say anything, just walked off ignoring the screaming throng. It wasn't just the arrogance of the man but the raw power that got Tommy's attention. Welcome to New York!

In those days, the music business was small enough that it could be very explosive; things could happen fast. Disc jockeys had a lot of say over what got played, and when a record got played, if it was a hit, you would know it within hours. A record that was played on WINS or WMCA could sell fifty thousand copies in the New York area alone in the first couple of weeks. Of course the listeners had the final word—if a record got played and it *didn't* sell, well, that was the end of that subject—but back then, in the early sixties, people listened to the radio all the time, and when they heard something they liked, they went out and bought it. Period.

The disc jockeys acted as though they knew what the listeners wanted to hear, but the truth was nobody did. The only way to know was to get the record played on the air and see what happened, so the disc jockeys were the gatekeepers. They held the keys to the kingdom.

Naturally, it was more than difficult to get a record played in America's number one market. If you didn't have personal relationships in New York, you could forget it. For a while Tommy didn't know if he was sinking or swimming, just barely staying afloat in these troubled waters. Finally, one day, some guy from Liberty was trying to get a record played at WMCA, and when he called the station, the music librarian told him, "Don't worry, you got a great guy [Tommy] working for you here; he'll take care of you. When it's time for the record to go on, it will go on." The story got back to Tommy and for the first time, he knew he was keeping his head above water. By then, he had been in this shark tank for over six months.

New York had a lot of important disc jockeys to get to know. At WINS, there were Murray the K, Jack Tracy, and Pete "Mad Daddy" Myers; at WMCA, B. Mitchell Reed, Harry Harrison, and Cousin Brucie; at WABC, Scott Muni and Sam Holman. And out in Queens, there was an R&B station with a great disc jockey who called himself the Magnificent Montague. He was a total wild man who eventually wound up at KGFJ in LA later in the sixties and coined the phrase "Burn, baby, burn" during the Watts riots.

He and Tommy became good friends, and Montague started pitching *him* on a record. "I got this cat," Montague told him, "you gotta meet this cat. You gotta tell your record company to sign this guy. He's unbelievable." He finally played Tommy the record called "If You Need Me" by an unknown artist named Wilson Pickett. Tommy flipped and set up a meeting between Montague, Al Bennett of Liberty, and Pickett's man, a tough black dude from Harlem named Harold Logan. The opening meeting at Liberty was classic—everybody sat around a huge glass conference table with all the black cats on one side and all the white guys on the other side—and in the end, it was Wilson's first big hit. Tommy was getting closer to the source.

During the early sixties, New York was still the geographic center of the music business—that wouldn't shift out to LA until later in the decade—and there was still a "Tin Pan Alley" located between 1650 Broadway and the Brill Building, where teams of hip young (mostly Jewish) songwriters wrote the hits that pop musicians sang. These two buildings housed dozens of music publishers, record companies and producers all under one roof. Just as Seventh Avenue was about fashion, this corner of New York was the music business. And in the early sixties, it was still a relatively small business. The entire annual gross revenue of the recording industry was less than $200 million. A decade later it would be in the billions. Back then, if you were looking for somebody in publishing or promotion, you could find them on that corner or around the block at either Al and Dick's Bar or Jack Dempsey's restaurant. Everybody knew everybody.

The business was so "inside" that at 1650 Broadway there was some sort of signal system by which the elevator guy knew when somebody important walked in and sent the word out immediately. One day Tommy walked in with Snuff Garrett and the elevator guy said, "Hi, Mr. Garrett." By the time they reached the fifth floor, every publisher was out in the hallway yelling "Hey, Snuff, I got something great for Bobby Vee," or "Snuff! Got a minute? I got a smash for Gene McDaniels." Some way or other the elevator guy put the word out. They would probably give the elevator guy a taste, but that still doesn't explain how the word got out so fast.

Tommy's old friend from Cleveland, Ernie Farrell, was the one who introduced him to Alan Freed. Ernie had become the national promotion man for Reprise Records in LA, which was basically Frank Sinatra's company. They were housed in a small office off Melrose Place—it was just Ernie and Mo Ostin—and they recorded Frank and his friends Sammy Davis Jr. and Dean Martin.

Of course Tommy had grown up with Alan, "the Moondog," back in Cleveland—he would listen to him on the radio religiously—but he never knew him personally, and he had no idea that after he left Cleveland, Freed had made a bunch of jive teenage rock and roll movies and then been busted for payola. Subsequently, Freed got divorced and moved to California, where he was basically broke.

When Tommy first moved to LA, Alan was married again, this time to a lovely woman named Inga, and they were living in Palm Springs. When Ernie told Tommy he was going out to Palm Springs to visit Alan, Tommy said he'd love to meet him and went along for the ride. It was a ride that lasted several years and took him to some of the wildest spots he'd ever been.

With Tommy and Alan, there was nothing but laughs; Alan loved his vodka and he loved telling stories about the old days. Sometimes Tommy would drive down to Palm Springs and spend the entire weekend with him. And when Tommy moved to New York for the year, he would hang with Alan there too. Alan would come to town every so often to work for Morris Levy, the hoodlum who ran Roulette Records. Morris would give Alan little projects to do just to take care of him. It was a loyalty thing; Alan had helped Morris sell a lot of records along the way, and they took care of their friends.

During Tommy's year in New York, Alan showed him the underbelly of the city, the raw side that few straight folks get to see. Alan was a small man, but he had a powerful voice and a huge presence; he was so well known in New York that he could actually get in a cab and the driver would say "Where to, Mr. Freed?"

He knew all the scenes. He once took Tommy to visit some of his friends in a third-floor walk-up, and when they knocked on the door it was opened by a flaming queen who said, "Alan, darling!" The place was all queens. Tommy remembers a billboard campaign for Smirnoff Vodka featuring a beautiful woman lying on her side, only it wasn't a woman, it was this guy who opened the door, a cross-dresser, flat-out gorgeous as a woman.

Another time, Alan took Tommy to the Page Three Club, which featured lesbian strippers. That night, Tommy saw "the weirdest guy I had ever seen, very tall with long strings of hair hanging down over his shoulders, walk out onstage and shake a ukulele out of a potato sack. He looked at it like he was surprised to see it, and then he started singing 'Tip-Toe Through the Tulips' in a high, warbling voice." It was Tiny Tim, years before he became famous and got married on *The Tonight Show with Johnny Carson*.

Another night, Alan and Tommy ended up at a place called Dante's, an old showbiz hangout, and Johnny Carson himself was at the bar with his sidekick, Ed McMahon. They were both legendary drinkers, and this night was no exception. Somehow, Tommy, Alan, Alan's wife, Inga, and Carson all wound up in a cab going to PJ Clark's. When they arrived the bar was packed, and in the crush of people they wound up sitting next to Richard Boone, the actor who played Paladin on the television program *Have Gun, Will Travel*.

Johnny was a bad drunk, and when he was stoned he could go from maudlin to vicious in a flash. He started talking to Boone—who was also a serious drinker, his nose looked like the craters of the moon—and Boone wanted nothing to do with Carson. Carson said, "I wanna have you on my show," and Boone said, "Fuck you, I don't wanna go on your show. Fuck you and fuck your show." Humiliated, Carson turned on Alan. He said, "Fuck you, Alan, you're a fucking has-been." Before it went any further, Alan, his wife, and Tommy ducked out the side door; Inga missed the first step, fell, and hit her head. "Now there was blood everywhere," remembers Tommy. "Suddenly it was like a scene from *Barfly*."

But Alan still wasn't done. He put Inga in a cab and he and Tommy went to the Copacabana—not downstairs to the showroom but upstairs, where there was a private bar. They were sitting there having a couple of drinks when Alan put his head down on the bar and went to sleep.

"I started trying to wake him up," says Tommy, "shaking him a bit, saying, 'Alan, Alan,' and the next thing I know these two huge guys show up. Being Sicilian I can spot a hood a mile away, so I knew these guys were connected. I say to them, 'I tried to wake him up,' but they totally ignored me, like I was invisible. They said, 'Alan, let's take you home.' Finally they got him to raise his head and he said something that sounded like 'Awwwwrrrgh.' They asked him where he was staying and I volunteered, 'He's staying at the Warwick.' They still didn't pay any attention to me, like I wasn't even there. They said, 'Okay, Alan, come on let's get you home.'"

They got Freed up from the barstool and he pointed to Tommy and said, "Gotta take my friend home too." So they all went outside and got into a large black sedan, Tommy and Alan in the back, the two hoods in the front; they drove to the Warwick and one of the guys helped Alan out of the back and then disappeared into the hotel with him. "He must have walked Alan all the way up to his room," Tommy remembers, "because it took a long time for him to come back. Meanwhile, I'm sitting in this car and it's dead silent. No radio, nothing. The guy driving doesn't say one word to me, and by this time I knew that if I asked him how his day was, it was not going to be a productive conversation."

Finally the guy comes down, gets in the car, and says to Tommy, "Where do ya live?" It was the first time that either of these guys acknowledged his existence. Tommy told him "Fifty-seventh and Third" and they drove to the corner of Fifty-seventh and Third, pulled over, let him out of the car, and drove off. Not another word was spoken.

These guys were part of the Gambino crime family, and because Morris Levy was connected with the Gambinos, they were simply making sure that Alan Freed was okay. By coincidence, they happened to be at the Copa, saw what was going down, and like the good soldiers that they were, no instructions or explanations were necessary. That was how it worked, and that was how well respected Alan was within the New York criminal community. Of course that community was equally important to the record business; the jukebox take alone covered a lot of largesse.

Morris Levy was one of the last of the old-school gangsters in the record business. After he was indicted by the federal government for tax evasion, he had to sell his publishing company, and Tommy's good friend Chuck Kaye (the son of Lester Sill) went to see him, hoping to buy the company. At the time, Morris was living on a huge horse farm in upstate New York, like Hyman Roth in *The Godfather*. To get there, Chuck had to drive up a long winding road. When he got to this enormous mansion and rang the bell, a butler answered the door. "Chuck Kaye to see Mr. Levy." "Oh yes, Mr. Levy is waiting for you."

The butler led him through a beautifully appointed home with expensive paintings on the walls and gorgeous rugs on the floors, all the way back into the kitchen where there was a small door off the pantry. The door opened and there was Morris Levy sitting in a little room with a small television on a folding table, eating a steak like he was back in the Bronx. It was like a safe room where he could hide from his own life. That room was the only place in this huge house where Levy felt comfortable.

Gangsters were part of the scenery in the record business. But one day while living in New York, Tommy got a surprise call from Dominic Sospirato, the bagman from Cleveland. Dominic said he was staying at the Waldorf—all the hoods would stay at the Waldorf when they were in the city—and he asked Tommy to have a drink with him. "Now when a guy like Dominic says 'Let's go have a drink,'" says Tommy, "you know it's not just because he's thirsty."

Dominic was friends with Ninfa's family, and they had sent him to check up on Tommy because Tommy was still talking to their daughter about getting together. Tommy met Dominic at a bar near his hotel and they had a totally sociable conversation; Ninfa's name never came up. But it was clear the only reason he was in town was to see what Tommy was up to and report back to the old man.

Altogether, Tommy spent about a year in New York working as a promotion man. Then Liberty bought Imperial Records, and along with the record company came the publishing company Travis Music, which owned hundreds of great New Orleans songs by writers like Fats Domino, the Neville Brothers, and Alan Toussaint. As soon as that happened, Dick Glasser honored his promise, and Tommy moved back to LA to go into the publishing end of the business.

Imperial was known more as an R&B label, going back to the 1940s. Eventually, they bought The Aladdin label—which had a wealth of material with artists such as Amos Milburn, Louis Jordan, Clarence "Gatemouth" Brown, Wynonie Harris, Johnny Ace, and even Lester Young—and a small New Orleans label called Minit Records, which had great product from a record producer and writer named Dave Bartholomew. So Imperial was a treasure trove of songs, the very songs that Tommy had listened to on his little portable radio while lying in his sickbed.

His first job back in LA as a publisher was to go through dozens of reel-to-reel tapes, listening to the music of his past, everything that was in the expanded Liberty catalog. "I couldn't believe they were paying me to do this," says Tommy. "I would stay at the office until one o'clock in the morning, just listening to this music. I was living and breathing songs and records. It was one of the happiest times of my life."

In the early sixties, LA was a company town and the music business was still an intimate affair; everyone would hang out at a few favorite places. One was Martoni's in Hollywood. On just about any night, the action could be unbelievable. LA was redefining the hang, and there was an encroaching dark undertone.

One night, Tommy was sitting in a front booth and noticed the singer Keely Smith and her brother Piggy sitting in the next booth. A few moments later, Jimmy Bowen, Keely's husband at the time, walked in and sat down. Soon a fight erupted at Keely's table. And when Tommy turned around to see what was happening, there was Keely Smith on the floor, flat on her back, with Jimmy on top of her, his hands around her throat. Finally, Jimmy picked Keely up in his arms, almost lovingly, and walked to the door. He got to the door, kicked it open—because of course he had his arms full—turned around to the room and said very cordially, "Good evening, folks!" and walked out. They didn't call it show business for nothing.

Another night Tommy was leaving Martoni's in Hollywood just as singer Sam Cooke was walking in with Al Schmitt, an A&R man from RCA Records. Tommy knew Al and as they stopped for a minute to talk, out of the corner of his eye, Tommy saw an interesting-looking Asian woman eye the group. "I couldn't help but notice her," he says, "because she was checking us all out."

A few hours later, he was listening to the radio at home when the announcer broke in with a news flash: "Sam Cooke has just been found shot and killed." The mysterious Asian woman had taken Sam up to her room in a seedy motel in Watts, and when he went to take a shower, she disappeared with all of his clothes and all of his money. The story is that Sam flipped out, wrapped a towel around himself, and went downstairs and started banging on the office door. Maybe he thought the motel owner was in cahoots with the Asian woman; maybe he thought the Asian woman was inside the office. In testimony, the manager of the motel, a black woman, said Sam was screaming," If you don't let me in I'm gonna kick in the door," and when he did, he and the woman struggled, and she shot him dead. To this day, many believe dark forces were involved in the shooting of Sam Cooke, that the Asian woman was working with the Mafia or the FBI or who knows what. But most agree that dark forces were present in the business all along and that they just caught up with Sam Cooke that night.

In yet another corporate turnover, Dick Glasser left Liberty to take a gig as an A&R man for Columbia and Liberty brought in an old-line publisher named Mike Gould to run the company, a suit-and-tie guy out of place in the emerging hippie world. Gould got his start plugging big band songs, and he was still mentally hanging around the bandstand. Tommy referred to Mike as "the world's foremost authority on number three pencils." He and Mike were like oil and water—they didn't mix at all—which was demonstrated one day when Mike got a call from Vernon Duke's publicist.

Duke was a classic old-school composer who had written great songs like "Taking a Chance on Love," "I Can't Get Started," "April in Paris," and "Cabin in the Sky." Apparently he had a bunch of songs that had never been published, and the message was that he would now be interested in entertaining some offers for the publishing rights. Mike arranged for himself and Tommy to go by Duke's house for dinner and hear these songs.

When Phil Skaff, who was still the head of Liberty, heard about the dinner, he invited himself along to meet the great man. So the three of them, plus Duke's publicist, arrive at this beautiful Mediterranean mansion in Beverly Hills. They ring the doorbell and the door is opened by an impeccably turned out Filipino houseboy, restraining two large boxers on a leather leash. He escorted the guests into the den, made them martinis, and told them their hosts would arrive soon. About twenty minutes later, Vernon Duke and his wife came downstairs.

Duke was a White Russian, very formal with a thick accent; back in the old Soviet Union, his mentor had been the great composer Prokofiev. He considered himself an aristocrat, and like many highly educated European composers who fled during the thirties, when he came to Hollywood he started writing film music. His wife was matronly and quite formal. After an elegant dinner had been served—"I had never tasted wine like that," recalls Tommy—Duke said, "Shall we go to the library and have a cigar and a cognac?"

As they walked through the house they passed a small study featuring a pedestal on which sheets of music from hundreds of years ago were displayed, old liturgical charts from back in the day when the notes were square instead of round. Then the group arrived at a huge library with twenty-five-foot ceilings, solid walls of books, and a grand piano. Mike Gould and the publicist sat on a couch facing the piano and Phil and Tommy sat in leather chairs facing each other. Cigars and cognac were passed around, and then Duke said, "Would you like to hear some of these songs?"

"Now on the way there," Tommy recalls, "we were saying, 'Gee, I wonder what kind of guy he's gonna be,' and I said, just joking around, 'Watch, his wife is gonna sing these songs.' Sure enough. He sits down at the piano and his wife stands up in front of the piano and he starts to play this intro and she starts singing and it's like Jeanette McDonald or Margaret Dumont. Phil and I look at each other and Phil just lost it. He started laughing and he can't stop. He's trying to hold it in so he's kind of snorting. So then I lost it too. Nobody appreciates the absurdity of life more than me, but nobody could have kept a straight face listening to this." With Phil and Tommy sputtering into their cognacs, Vernon Duke soldiered on, while Mike Gould was silently outraged.

Finally, gathering that the presentation wasn't going well, Duke was about to put the keyboard cover down—"It's amazing he didn't throw us out the door right then," says Tommy—when Gould said, "Vernon, please, would you do us the honor of playing 'April in Paris?'" And gentleman that he was, Duke played it. Five minutes later the party was over and the guys from Liberty were out the front door. "I guess the point is," says Tommy, "that Mike Gould and I had come to an impasse."

Tommy started looking around for another job. He went to see Mickey Goldsen, who ran Criterion Music—they owned all of the publishing in the Martin Denny catalog, with hits like "Quiet Village" —Mickey even had a terrace behind his office with a Hawaiian tiki shack built out of palm leaves, just to keep the tropical theme going—but Mickey was also a friend of the great songwriter Johnny Mercer, one of Tommy's heroes, and he owned a lot of Charlie Parker's compositions. Working with him could have been a good fit for Tommy. But then something happened that changed the game completely.

When Tommy went to Phil Skaff to tell him he couldn't work for Mike Gould anymore, Phil said, "Hold on. What do you really want to do?" Tommy didn't even have to think about it: "What do I really want to do? I want to produce records." Back when he had been a promotion man, if he wasn't at a radio station pushing the product, he was at a recording studio watching Snuff Garrett or Phil Spector producing hits, sitting in the back, keeping his mouth shut, and thinking to himself, "I could do this!" And he had been thinking about it ever since. So when Phil Skaff asked, it just popped out of his mouth. He hadn't planned on asking for it; he had gone in to resign.

But Phil said, "If I give you a job as a staff producer, will you stay?" And Tommy said, "Absolutely." And that was it. His fate was sealed.

Naturally there were a few initial missteps. For one thing, Tommy didn't really have any idea what it meant to "produce" a record. Other than having made some publishing demos with Randy Newman, P. J. Proby, and Jackie DeShannon, he really didn't know what a producer was or did. Back then, the credit "producer" didn't appear on the back of many record albums. Of course people were doing it, running recording sessions, but everybody had to invent what it was for themselves. So when Phil gave Tommy his shot, the first thing Tommy did was try to figure out how to load the gun.

It's hard to describe in today's world of unlimited access to all things technical and musical that there was a time, not that long ago, when some aspects of the music business were mysterious. Making records was one of those things. Today every kid has a program on his computer with more recording power than a full-blown studio used to have. Today hundreds of thousands of students are learning record production at colleges and trade schools all across the country. But in the early sixties, the number of people involved in the record business was counted in the hundreds, not thousands, and everybody had a personal style that they had developed on their own. The way they developed their own style was they made their own mistakes.

The very first record Tommy produced was for the guitarist Tommy Tedesco, a well-known LA session musician, a jazzman who knew his way around commercial music. Tommy had booked all the "A" players: Emil Richards on vibes, Pete Jolly on piano, Hal Blaine and Jimmy Bond on drums and bass. He had his old partner Nick

DeCaro do the arrangements—Nick and Tommy had developed a musical radar over the hundreds of gigs and thousands of miles they had shared, and Tommy subsequently persuaded Nick to move to LA. So far so good.

Since it was the first session that Tommy was actually in charge of, with the clock on the wall counting down the money being spent, he was visibly nervous. Perhaps it was the clock thing—the same reason he was no good at taking tests in school; he hated clocks. Whatever the cause, things started to go south. At one point, he froze, like a deer in the headlights. He remembers, "Guys were making mistakes. I could hear it but I didn't stop them. I was inside my head, second-guessing myself and letting a lot of things get away." In the studio, you have to react in the moment; you can't be thinking too hard about what you should or shouldn't be doing. In a way, being a producer is like being another musician; it's not about being right or wrong as much as it's about being *there*. The engineer, the great Bones Howe, got on the talkback and said to the musicians in the studio, "Okay, guys, we're on the honor system today." Which was code for "Nobody is in charge." When he said that, Tommy woke up. "I realized that it was up to me and if I wasn't present I shouldn't be in the room." This was his first real lesson in record production: *Pay attention.*

Not long thereafter, Tommy stopped producing records from inside the control room altogether and joined the musicians in the studio while the music was being recorded. Traditionally, producers stay inside the control room, close to the engineer and the telephone and all the action. But that's exactly why Tommy chose to go inside the studio: all the action, the phones ringing, the chatter between engineers, the clocks!—it distracted him. He couldn't focus unless he was literally one with the musicians.

On the particular date when he made the transition from inside the booth to inside the recording studio, Tommy was wanting to point something out to the piano player and was frustrated by having to get his attention over the talkback system. So he asked the second engineer to set up some earphones and a chair and a music stand out in the room, and when he settled in, he thought, "Man, it's so much nicer out here with the guys who are actually playing the music." Talk about finding your comfort spot; he was back in the band.

Even the term "control room" seemed to describe what Tommy didn't like about the traditional production arrangement. You don't control the music; you set up an environment in which the music and the performance just naturally arrive in the moment. If there was a music room and a control room, there was no question which side of the glass Tommy was going to be on. Tommy would always be that guy who played saxophone with Sammy Dee, and he was not going to have another glass wall between him and what he loved.

The next record Tommy produced was *Coming Through* by the O'Jays. They were a hardworking group from Cleveland who took their name from a deejay named Eddy O'Jay who worked at the local R&B station. Their being a rhythm and blues group from Cleveland made it a natural for Tommy.

They cut a song called "Lipstick Traces" that Tommy found when he was logging tapes from the Imperial catalog. The record became a regional hit in Detroit, Chicago, and, of course, Cleveland. For Tommy, in baseball lingo, it was a solid single. Lesson two of record production: *Find a great song.*

Pay attention, find a great song, and learn from the masters.

When Tommy first retuned from New York, he and Lenny Waronker and Randy Newman all worked for Metric Music, Liberty's publishing company. They spent their days listening to new songs and to the new recordings that were being released. When they went out, it would be to visit A&R men to pitch songs or to go to demo sessions to get a sense of how records were constructed. If they took a break, it was usually to have lunch at the La Brea Inn and then go back to the office to listen to more music until midnight or one in the morning. In short, they were totally immersed in popular music.

The composer Burt Bacharach was just hitting the scene then, first with Chuck Jackson's "Any Day Now," and then, in quick succession, with all the classic hits he wrote with Hal David for Dionne Warwick. Tommy studied these records thoroughly, unraveling the production techniques and examining the musical nuances. When he got his hands on an advance copy of the Bacharach/David production of "What the World Needs Now" with Jackie DeShannon, he wore out several test pressings, playing it over and over and each time hearing something new.

Bacharach was changing the form of the Great American Songbook both melodically and rhythmically. Up to that point, the typical form for a standard song was thirty-two bars—an eight-bar verse, usually repeated for another eight bars, then an eight-bar bridge, and then the last eight-bar verse out. Burt would change that. He would also write in different time signatures, and if he did write a ballad in 4/4, like "A House Is Not a Home," he would make sure to throw in a 5/4 bar at a certain spot, something fresh and original. And he would also have the piano or guitar play his signature eighth-note figure that made it feel like the time was in 6/4. You could always tell a Bacharach song.

Tommy was lucky enough to attend a few of Bacharach's recording sessions. "He would play piano, of course," says Tommy, "and at the same time, he would be singing the melody to explain where he wanted the emphasis or a crescendo to be. Sometimes he would rise up from the piano bench in a dramatic way to emphasize a passage." Bacharach was inspired, and he inspired Tommy. It was all about communicating your passion to the musicians in the room.

After his "regional hit" with the O'Jays, Tommy was approached by Jerry Moss to become the first staff producer at A&M Records. He had met Jerry when they were both promotion men driving to radio stations together. "We'd split the gas money so we could plug our records in Bakersfield and San Diego," Tommy recalls. "And then the year I was in New York, Jerry would come in, and even though he was originally from the city, he didn't know any of the radio people there, so I would take him around to the different stations. We became tight."

Jerry formed A&M Records with Herb Alpert after Herb had a huge hit with "The Lonely Bull" for Herb's group, the Tijuana Brass; this one record funded the company. Then they released a Tijuana Brass album called *Whipped Cream & Other Delights* with a cover picture of a naked woman smothered in whipped cream, and that album sold more than two million copies; the cover alone probably sold a million.

At the time there were only four people working at A&M—Herb was the music guy, Jerry was the promotion guy, Gil Friesen was the business guy, and there was a secretary named Joline. Tommy became employee number five.

It was October 1965, and Tommy was still pretty green in the studio. He was learning the ropes and hanging out with other younger record men. One of them was Sonny Bono. Sonny was a songwriter and a promotion man, not the pop singer he would become, and he was pitching his music just like everybody else. "Sonny stood out," remembers Tommy, "because he had a Beatles haircut, and this was before the Beatles broke on the American scene."

Tommy and Sonny hung out at Martoni's. One night Red Baldwin, a promotion man for Atlantic, pulled out a picture of a gorgeous naked girl and said to the two of them, "Man, check out this chick I just met; she's staying with me." He said her name was Cher. A few nights later, they were all back in Martoni's and there she was. And that was the night that Sonny met Cher.

Sonny often worked with Phil Spector, and he started bringing Tommy around to Phil's recording dates at Gold Star Recording Studio. Watching those sessions was another crash course in record production for Tommy because he was seeing someone who really knew what he wanted, who had a musical vision and was totally committed to it.

"I saw how his tracks were put together," says Tommy. "They called Phil's productions 'a wall of sound,' because the arrangements and instrumentation sounded so massive, but part of that was created by the great echo chamber they had at Gold Star. Anything you put into that chamber came back at you sounding like it had gained another dimension or two."

"Another part of the sound was the way Phil used multitracking. In those days we were recording on three-track machines, and to get a bigger sound, you would have to go from one three-track machine to another to 'double' something, to give a little extra weight to the part. But in the process, you would lose a little because you would 'go down a generation.' After a while the process would produce diminishing returns. So instead of always doubling a part electronically, Phil would hire three or four guitar players to come in and record the same part live. That way he would get that weight without losing fidelity. And the parts would naturally be slightly different, because they were being played by different guys, and that's where you would get that out-of-phase kind of thing that would build his 'wall of sound.'"

Phil was a meticulous guy and he would have musicians playing their parts over and over again, forty, fifty, sixty times, until he was satisfied. "Naturally, the musicians would become tired and bored," says Tommy, "but Phil had a great sense of humor and a way of keeping the pace going so that the players hung in there with him. He kept the rhythm of the date going. That made a big impression on me, seeing somebody create an atmosphere where the musicians wanted to give him what he needed." Production is a personal thing but it is also a social thing; you have to communicate a vision, and you also have to make others care about that vision as much as you do.

Phil was clearly a character with a dramatic style, both in his manner of working and in the way he lived. But when he was alone with Tommy and the few friends that he felt comfortable with, he acted much different, almost reserved. Tommy got the feeling that at bottom, Phil was a very shy guy and simply wasn't comfortable with his rising celebrity.

"One day he asked me to take him to the airport and hang with him until his plane left," remembers Tommy. "This would have been right around when Tom Wolfe came out with his book of essays called *The Kandy-Kolored Tangerine-Flake Streamline Baby,* which included a piece about Phil and, among other things, his fear of flying. Wolfe described how he had freaked out on the runway while waiting for a plane to take off. There was a heavy downpour and all the flights were backed up and there was the usual paranoia you get when you're in a small enclosed space. Suddenly Phil yelled out, 'Man, this plane ain't gonna make it,' and he demanded to get off. The pilot had to turn the plane around, at great inconvenience to everyone, and when they finally got back to the terminal, Phil was banned from ever taking another United flight.

"When we arrived at the airport this time, by the time we got to the desk to check in, the Valiums Phil had taken started to kick in. He was kind of wobbling. The first thing he did was check out the other passengers that were taking his flight, and what they looked like. When he saw a few infants being checked in, that made him feel more secure—he figured the flight wouldn't go down with babies on board. Not that I understood that logic."

A few months later Phil moved into a huge mansion. It was his baronial phase and he had hired an English couple to be part of his staff. The butler's name was Albert, and to break him in, Phil invited Tommy and Bobby Dale as his guests for a formal dinner. It was just the three of them at this long dining table, with lots of silverware, lighted candles, and two maids in little white caps. The butler told Phil, "Here's a bell. If you ever want any help, you just pick it up and ring it." So every two minutes Phil was ringing that bell and calling, "Albert! Albert!"

The next day Tommy sent Phil a housewarming gift to say thanks for the dinner, a beautiful silver coffee warmer. After a couple of days, he still hadn't heard whether the gift arrived, so he called and asked. Phil said, "Oh man, that was you!" And he told Tommy a story that connected some dots but left a lot of the ends loose. It turns out that Phil was being threatened by the mob; the reason wasn't clear, but whatever it was, he was afraid for his life. He was upstairs the afternoon a plain-paneled truck showed up with Tommy's gift. Albert, who had been working for Spector for only a couple of days, answered the front door and took the gift. From the upstairs window, Phil saw the truck pulling away and he shouted down to Albert, "Who was that?" When Albert said, "Oh, Mr. Spector, you just received a gift," Phil came down, saw the box, and immediately assumed the mob had sent it.

He said to Albert, "Man, get rid of that fucking thing! It's gotta be a bomb," and Albert ran out the back door with the box and threw it into a ravine behind the house. The two of them stood there staring at it for about twenty minutes, waiting for it to blow up, and when nothing happened, Phil told Albert to get a hose and hose it down. Finally the box fell apart, revealing something shiny and metallic. They stared at it for another ten minutes and then Albert went down, dragged the muddy box back to the top, and of course, they discovered the coffee warmer.

Phil was nuts, but he was an experienced record producer and he gave Tommy little tips that improved Tommy's studio routine. Once Phil stopped in while Tommy was putting a mix together. Tommy was listening at a very high decibel level, and when the playback finished, he asked Phil what he thought of the balance between the rhythm section and the vocalist, and Phil said, "Have you listened to it at low level?" He was the first person to tell Tommy that if you listened to a playback at a lower level you were better able to hear the relationships between musical elements. From that day on, Tommy mixed soft.

At this point, Tommy still hadn't signed anybody to A&M and he was getting antsy. He was working with people who were already on the roster, people like Chris Montez—Herb Alpert had cut one record with Chris and then he handed Chris over to Tommy. The first thing Tommy cut with him was "Time After Time." And then they did "The More I See You," and that really made some noise. But Tommy was still searching for somebody to sign, to make his own statement.

One day, a guy named Charlie Underwood played Tommy a single he was trying to sell called "Ju Ju Man." "I never heard anything like it," says Tommy, "and I immediately agreed to release it, but I wanted to make a few changes. So Charlie said, 'Well, the guy who did it is in town. He's from New Orleans but he's living here now. If you're interested, I'll put you guys together.'"

Tommy went over to the studio where he found this very thin guy with a scraggly beard sitting on the couch in front of the recording desk; Tommy gave him some feedback on the recording and Mac seemed to like what he heard and went into the studio and did a few things on the organ. As he was playing, Tommy thought, "This guy's really great. He's really unusual." Maybe he had found his first major signing to A&M. But when they finally put the single out, it bombed, and that was the end of that. As Tommy would later say, "A failure is anathema to a record company. If they put their hopes in something and it doesn't happen, they are not likely to go back to that well." But that's how Tommy met Mac Rebennack (aka Dr. John), who would remain one of his go-to guys.

So when a couple of months later, in early '67, Tommy needed an organ player for a session he was doing, he called Mac to make it. After the date, he and Mac went outside to smoke—in those days, it was an outside thing, you didn't smoke in the studio—and as they were standing in this little alley passing a joint and Mac started telling him about this record he was going to make for Atlantic. "Man," Mac said, "I'm changin' my name. I'm gonna be Dr. John."

And sure enough, a few months later, Bobby Dale came over to Tommy's house and put a new release on the turntable, and said, "Tommy, you gotta hear this. You won't believe it!" Tommy looked at the cover and saw "this insane-looking guy with feathers in his hair and paint on his face." The record was called *Gris Gris* and the sounds coming out of the box just blew him away. He had never heard anything like it, and of course neither had the rest of the world. And it was Mac. He was "Dr. John the Night Tripper" now, and his record was a phenomenon. From this we learn a fourth commandment of production: it's often not what you know but when you know it: *timing!*

Tommy was still struggling to find his feet as a producer. He had assembled a first-rate production team, including an eighteen-year-old engineer named Bruce Botnick and his old pal Nick DeCaro doing the arrangements, but he needed an act. And then, finally, he got lucky. It came, as most good things do, from out of the blue. Herb had signed a group called the Grads. They were nothing special, but they had the ability to sing phonetically in four or five languages and at the time, vocal groups were popular. Herb asked Tommy to see what he could do with them.

One night, Tommy was trying to come up with something for the Grads and he happened to be listening to a Pete Seeger recording of the song "Guantanamera." It occurred to him that the Grads could do it: it was in Spanish, it wasn't too complicated, and it was really catchy. So the next day he brought the group in, played it for them, and said, "Guys, this is it. This is the song we're going to do."

By the time they went into the studio, Tommy had listened to the song dozens of times and it was so ingrained in him that he knew every part. "As I was putting this whole thing together," Tommy remembers, "I realized that when Pete Seeger did it with the Weavers, it started off with everybody singing the chorus, then the verse came in, and then there was this little interlude with a recitation. And as Pete Seeger was reciting this middle section, Ronnie Gilbert of the Weavers was singing the verse behind him, and it was a magical moment." Every hit song needs one magical moment. For Tommy, his goal was to recreate this one.

They got a great take of the song. They were recording on a four-track machine, so he had the singers double the backgrounds to make it sound bigger. He had the best session players in town—the Wrecking Crew, as they were called, including Tommy Tedesco playing guitar—and instead of a regular upright bass, he used a guitaron, the Mexican version of the bass, to give the song an authentic feel. He had all the pieces he needed except for who was going to do the recitation in the middle to create that magical moment. He knew this was going to be the key to the whole thing.

First he asked Herb Alpert to do it, but Herb declined because he has a small lisp. Then, he asked Michael Nesmith from the Monkees, who was a good friend, and Nesmith came in but he couldn't get serious about it. He just thought it was a joke. At the time, Tommy was living with Johnny Hayes, a great disc jockey with a huge voice, so he had Johnny come down and give it a try, but when Johnny stepped in front of the microphone, it sounded like he was reading a commercial. In frustration, Tommy stopped everything and said, "Look, John, let me go out there and you listen to how I am saying it, just to get a sense as to how it sounds, and then you can do it."

Tommy went into the studio, Botnick started the tape, and Tommy did the recitation. When he came back into the control room, Bruce said, "Hey, you should hear what you just did." In his infinite wisdom, Bruce had recorded Tommy's performance. And it was perfect. "When you're making records," says Tommy, "you just want to get it right. You don't care how it happens or who does it, if it's you or him or whoever. I said, 'That's it! We got it.' Johnny didn't talk to me for six months. But when it's right, it's right."

And it was right. A&M changed the name of the group from the Grads to the Sandpipers. By lucky coincidence, the record was released at the moment that thousands of Cubans were coming to Miami, and because the song is based on a poem by José Martí, a famous Cuban freedom fighter, the day the record hit the air the distributor in Florida called A&M and ordered twenty-five thousand copies. And it spread from there. That record was another huge turning point in Tommy's career.

A&M was really like a family company. They say you can't choose your relatives, and there was some truth to this insofar as Tommy couldn't always choose who he was being asked to produce.

For example, Herb and Jerry were very close with the singer Andy Williams, who was then married to a French chorus girl named Claudine Longet. She was trying to be an actress and she sang a little—she had done a nice version of the Antonio Carlos Jobim song

"How Insensitive," and Herb thought that because Astrud Gilberto was having a big hit with "The Girl from Ipanema," Claudine, who also spoke with an accent, had a shot. Tommy was assigned to find another song and produce the record.

He found a song called "Hello Hello" by an obscure group called Sopwith Camel and thought it would be cute to do it with Claudine. And it worked; the combination of this kooky song and her singing in a thick French accent—"Hello hello, could you please have some of my tangerine"—became a huge hit. The album sold over seven hundred thousand copies. But the good news became the bad news: he had to do another album with Claudine. "She was a sweet chick," says Tommy. "I really liked her, and thank God she knew as well as we did that she wasn't really a singer—but artistically, the experience made me question what it was I had signed up for at A&M."

Between the Sandpipers and Claudine Longet, Tommy was starting to make some real money, but he wasn't making any real music. The only record he did during this period that he thought was any good was one called *Rock Salt and Nails* by the singer Steve Young, but it didn't sell at all and nobody heard it. Other than that, it seemed like it was always time for him to do another Sandpipers record.

He was frustrated, being stereotyped as a producer of middle-of-the-road records, having success with music he didn't particularly dig. By this time, he hadn't played the saxophone for almost five years and it was starting to feel like he was losing a limb, being disconnected from the music that he loved. When he first moved out to LA, he had his mother send him his horn, and when he started working at the publishing company, he would occasionally play it on demos. But now the horn rarely came out of the case, and pretty soon he stopped playing it altogether.

"It was a great loss," Tommy says. "I'm really sorry that I didn't keep playing because it's a form of self-expression for which there is no substitute. Knowing you can express yourself through an instrument is unlike any other musical or financial reward. Of course when I finished a project I would feel good about it. But it wasn't the same as knowing you can play and having the sense of self-satisfaction and accomplishment that comes with self-expression. But of course, at this point, it's just a dream." It's like remembering your first real romance; sometimes the sense of loss can be overwhelming.

Along with his growing sense of frustration, producing middle-of-the-road music and being estranged from jazz and his saxophone, a powerful new element entered the picture: LSD. There were times in 1967 when he was taking acid several times a week. The first time he took it was with Bobby Dale. "Talk about tripping the light fantastic," he says. "Suddenly it was 'Where is this and where have I been?'" LSD became a way for Tommy to reflect on his life, and it caused him to do some deep soul searching. He knew something important was missing: he was having fun but he wasn't moving forward. He just didn't know how to put all the pieces together.

"Taking LSD was the most sobering thing I ever did," says Tommy. "Not that I didn't also get hung up on my shoes or whatever, just wandering through the Disneyland of my mind like everybody else. But I found the experience was always sobering because it sat you back on your heels and made you realize that just about everything you were taught was not necessarily the case. And then, when you heard somebody say something that you knew was jive, you'd say, 'This is bullshit.'" Acid raised the curtain and showed Tommy that the great and mighty wizard was also in show business.

Then, in 1967, Bobby Dale moved to San Francisco. KFWB, where he had been working in LA, had a sister station in Oakland, KEWB, and he landed a job there. In San Francisco, Bobby was hanging out with Tom Donahue and Bob Mitchell, two influential disc jockeys who were changing the sound of popular radio in the Bay Area, and even though they worked at different stations, they gravitated to each other because of their deep intellectual love for the music. They were definitely not about show business; San Francisco was all about authentic American culture: rhythm and blues, jazz, Lenny Bruce, bohemians, and that nascent thing called rock and roll, and these guys were starting to put the pieces together.

Donahue was another brilliant individual who read voraciously and had a photographic memory. Physically, he was a huge guy, but, like Orson Welles, he "wore his fat well." You never thought of him as being obese, although he was. He had a large beard and powerful eyes and the ability to size people up instantaneously. He also had a larcenous streak; he was one of the deejays who had been fired in the payola scandals.

In 1967, Donahue wrote a piece for *Rolling Stone* titled "AM Radio Is Dead and Its Rotting Corpse Is Stinking Up the Airwaves," which trashed the Top Forty format and became a sensation around the country. He had taken over programming for a small FM station in the Bay Area, KSAN, and had changed it into America's first alternative "free-form" radio station. This was "the format of no format," built on album tracks chosen by the disc jockeys rather than singles prescribed from a playlist, and it changed how people listened to music for a long time.

Since it cost only $12 to fly to San Francisco from LA on PSA, Tommy jumped on a plane and spent three days in the Bay Area that completely opened his eyes. He fell in love with the city, particularly North Beach; it reminded him of Greenwich Village in the early sixties, plus it was primarily an Italian scene, with Ferlinghetti's City Lights bookstore just across the street from the Condor and the Jazz Workshop and Enrico Balducci's place, and above Enrico's was the infamous Swiss American hotel where all the cats stayed.

He started going up to San Francisco most weekends and fell in with a bunch of characters who would have a profound effect on both his sense of humor and his sense of the possible. Red Baldwin, for one; he had been the road manager for Lester Young and Billie Holiday, so he knew all the bebop musicians and all the bebop stories. Red was inherently funny, and humor was one of Tommy's main modes of travel.

He and Red hung at the Condor—this was before it became Carole Doda's strip club and was still a dark, quasidegenerate venue with many redeeming qualities: Sly Stone had the house band and Hervé Villechaize, the guy with dwarfism everybody knows from *Fantasy Island*—"Boss, the plane, the plane!"—was working at the door on weekends.

One day, Red and Tommy were standing at the bar talking to this great-looking chick and Red started hitting on her. The two were getting along marvelously until Hervé came over. Being a small person, his face came up to the woman's crotch, and the first thing he did was put his arms around her hips and bury his face between her legs. Then he whispered something to her and she just turned to Red and said "Excuse me" and disappeared out the door with Hervé. Red turned to Tommy and said, "How about that? Beat out by half a motherfucker."

Abe Kesh was another character whose sense of the possible made a huge impression on Tommy. Abe had an apartment close to North Beach where Tommy would occasionally crash. When they first met, Kesh was still dressing like the promotion man he once was, wearing checkered sports coats and ties. He had been the hipster who broke "Walk on the Wild Side" for the jazz organ player Jimmy Smith, and like Bobby Dale he was another guy who had all the records in his collection and would go from playing Albert King to Beethoven or *Tosca*. "It was one of the brain-openers of all time," Tommy remembers. "Abe had a very dry but deadly sense of humor. I used to have this nervous habit where my leg would start going up and down a hundred miles a minute; after he saw me doing it for a while, he started calling me Thumper."

"One time, there was this big chick who was hanging around, six feet tall and a little chunky, and she wanted to be a singer in the worst way. And like the joke goes, that was the only way she could be a singer. At one point, she joined Abe and me at New Joe's Bar, and she said, 'Excuse me. I have to call my manager.' Abe looked up at her and said, 'Manager? When's your next fight?'"

Humor was the glue that held these hipsters and this scene together, and it was also the quality that had spelled survival for Tommy since his days in the hospital. Tommy gravitated to humor and good times like a heat-seeking missile.

By this time, Tommy had become very good friends with Bob Krasnow, another legendary record man. Tommy was sitting in the studio with Bobby Dale when Krasnow, a promotion man for Del-Fi Records, came up to KFWB to pitch a record. Dale introduced the two of them, and from that moment on, they became lifelong co-conspirators. Again, humor was the bonding agent.

Tommy remembers, "One night, I was sitting at the bar in Peppone's with Casey Kasem. I had known him since he was a customer of mine at the barbershop in Cleveland, and in walked Krasnow. Casey started talking about how he was on a diet and Bob said, 'If you're on a diet you shouldn't be drinking.' Casey said, 'Scotch isn't that bad. But you know what really puts the weight on you? Watermelon.' And without missing a beat, Bob said, 'Jesus, I'm gonna have to call Roscoe.' Now Roscoe was a black disc jockey who was also a good friend of Bob's. When that line popped out of Krasnow's mouth," says Tommy, "I fell in love with the guy."

Tommy had been telling Bob, "Man, you got to come to San Francisco with me and try this acid," so one weekend they flew to San Francisco together and got with Bobby Dale and a flamboyant young woman named Deirdre La Porte. Deirdre was not one of those "love and peace" hippies—this was well before the hippie movement anyway—but she took a lot of acid and you never knew if she was high or not. She was the same all the time: "just great," says Tommy.

They met at the Villa Roma Hotel and dropped the acid, and within the hour, everybody got off . . . except Krasnow. This was not uncommon for someone's first time; they didn't necessarily know the signs to look for and didn't realize when the trip had begun. Bob was saying, "What's the big deal? Hey, you got any more? No? Where can we get some?" and so Deirdre, being a very agreeable person, said, "I think I know where we can get some more." Tommy felt fine so he offered to go with her.

The next thing he knew, he and Deirdre were in Bobby Dale's huge black Cadillac two-door sedan, one of those land yachts you had to pilot around the hills of San Francisco very carefully, and he was behind the wheel. The minute he pulled into the street, a set of headlights hit him directly in the eyes and he realized he was in trouble.

But it was too late. They were on the road, and Deirdre was giving him directions. "Take a right here, take a left there, go down two blocks." They wound up on a very steep hill and she said to Tommy, "Make a right," and Tommy looked over and said, "Make a right on what?" Because he could no longer see the street; the hill was so steep he thought she was telling him to drive over the edge of the world. She said, "No, there's a street right here, do it," and so he turned in that direction, taking it on blind faith that there was a street. In fact, she was taking him down one of those steep side streets that runs into Broadway in North Beach.

The next thing he remembers, they were at some kind of communist meeting. Deirdre had gone inside to ask around and came back with bad news: "No, man, they don't have anything. Let's try the Committee." The Committee was a comedy improv group that used a little theater further long on Broadway. There Deirdre went in and scored in a matter of minutes.

It was a harrowing trip getting back to the Villa Roma where Bobby and Krasnow were waiting, and of course, by the time they got there, Krasnow was completely whacked out and doing the things everybody does: looking at some small object for a minute and then laughing hysterically, or getting hung up on the bedspread, a pattern of squares and triangles that suddenly started dancing. Bob spent the rest of the night discovering the synesthesia of human sensory experience, how colors can bring on sounds, how music can dim the lights, how voices in the room can be a symphony.

Around six in the morning they all decided to go out to a restaurant in Chinatown for some fresh pork buns. The only people out and about in Chinatown at that hour were the street crews hosing down the remains of the night's revelry. The sound and smell of fresh running water suggested a brand new day to the group, and the pork buns were the best things they had ever tasted. They didn't want the adventure to stop, so they all went to one of those hardcore bars on Broadway, directly across the street from Enrico's, and started drinking with a bunch of serious alcoholics. Just another San Francisco weekend in 1967.

Tommy never had any trouble with the dysphoric aspect of LSD until the weekend of the Watts riots in LA. He was in San Francisco, high on acid, watching the war go down on television. This time, Tom Donahue was in the other room having a bad trip, and for the first time, Tommy was starting to experience negative energy himself. "It was the only time I can remember having any suicidal thoughts, which fortunately left me, but they were certainly real at the time," he remembers. Bobby Dale saw what was happening and said, "Come on Scooter, let's take a ride."

They got in Bobby's car and drove through the Presidio. They were listening to all this great music on the radio, and when James Brown's "Papa's Got a Brand New Bag" came on, Tommy's trip changed from a stairway to hell to a stairway to heaven. Listening to music with Bobby was like that for Tommy. The man was a 50,000-watt transmitter all by himself; when they were together, just hearing a song on the radio could be a hallelujah experience.

Bob Krasnow, Bobby Dale, Abe Kesh, Red Baldwin, Tom Donahue—they were all street guys, but they were street guys who dug everything from Puccini to Otis Redding and spent every moment coming up with new schemes. They lived from moment to moment, not knowing what was coming at them from around the next corner. One minute they could be totally broke and the next minute they could get a check for fifty grand. Their lives were improvised, and maybe that was on account of their connection to the music.

These guys had serious fun. You either laughed at the situation you were in or you flipped out, and these guys, with their foxhole humor, were survivors. Like Tommy, they were misfits who, in Tommy's words, "if it wasn't for the music, would all have been complete failures." But they just happened to come along at a time when having this particular love proved to be an asset, not a liability. Their saving grace was that they loved music at just the right time and in just the right place.

"To me," says Tommy, "these guys were bigger than life, and one of the reasons I respected them was because they were able to call a spade a spade. They could tell somebody to their face 'That's bullshit' if that's what the situation required.

"I was always the nicest guy in town. But these guys brought out something in me that hadn't been there before. I found a kind of comfort zone in the darker side of things. I mean, I already had this anger because of what I went through as a child—I eventually spent hundreds of hours with a shrink about this—but it wasn't anger toward other people that I felt; it wasn't bitterness. But I would not be truthful if I said there weren't times when I asked myself, 'Why me?' These guys helped me see it for what it was."

As Lenny Bruce said, you can't know the good about yourself if you don't know the bad about yourself. There's something comforting in confronting the facts of life and seeing them as they are, laughing at them instead of getting angry or bitter. It makes the human situation more bearable, if not more believable. They were all still in show business, and the slope was getting slipperier by the day.

In 1967, Tommy was living in LA in an outrageously luxe apartment on Hollywood Boulevard that he shared with deejay Johnny Hayes. During the forties, Tyrone Power had rented the same apartment. You'd walk up a long flight of stairs that opened on a huge room with thirty-foot ceilings. It was like a movie set. Then there was another staircase that went up to a second floor where there were three bedrooms and three baths off a spacious landing. Tommy paid a little more to have the master bedroom, which had a terrace overlooking Hollywood Boulevard.

Johnny Hayes was an interesting character. Originally from Macon, Georgia, with a fantastic radio voice, he had trained himself to cover his Southern accent, but he was still a Southerner through and through. "Like a character out of Tennessee Williams," says Tommy.

"He was a gun nut and he kept a loaded .357 Magnum pistol in his room." Plus he had a drinking problem, and one night he put a bullet through the ceiling of the apartment. But Tommy wasn't put off by Johnny's weirdness or eccentricities. He could always meet people halfway and, most important, Johnny had a fantastic sound system with a Fisher power amp and wonderful speakers. It was set up in the living room, and this room became a gathering spot for music freaks throughout Hollywood. Since the apartment was centrally located between La Brea and Laurel Canyon, people would stop by at all hours of the day or night because they knew it was a place you could always go to hear music, get loaded, or do whatever you wanted. Open door.

"You would never know who might show up," says Tommy. "People would be at Martoni's at two in the morning and they'd say, 'Hey, let's go to LiPuma's.' Randy Newman, Lenny Waronker, Reb Foster, Chuck Kaye, B. Mitchell Reed, pretty much everybody in the business crossed that threshold at one time or another. Every night you could find a bunch of guys sitting around talking shit, digging music, and taking drugs."

This was the place where one night Tommy went to wash his face in the powder room and saw his face going down the drain with the water.

Suffice it to say, a lot of music history went down in their Hollywood Boulevard pad. Back when the Rolling Stones first came to town, Charlie Watts and Keith Richards, along with their manager, Andrew Oldham, had come to Metric Music looking for songs. Tommy started playing them some things from the Minit Records catalog. One by one they all split except for Andrew, who finally said, "Hey, do you know where I can get some smoke?" Tommy said, "Well, I don't know where you can get some, but if you want some, I've got some." He and Oldham drove to the pad on Hollywood Boulevard.

Tommy pulled out the smoke and he and Johnny Hayes started playing records for Oldham. Hayes had a great collection of 45s, every record in its own individual green sleeve. They listened to dozens of classic and obscure R&B songs. The next day, Johnny called Tommy at work and said, "Hey, man, I'm putting all my 45s back in their sleeves and there are like two empty sleeves here with no 45s." Tommy said, "You think that maybe Oldham took them?" He said, "I don't know, man. All I know is I can't find them."

About a month later, Johnny called and said, "Hey, man, I know at least one record he took." It was "Time Is on My Side" by Irma Thomas. And that was the breaking hit that made the Stones in the States. "He didn't have to steal it," says Tommy. "He could have simply asked for it. I had the whole catalog."

Tommy wasn't there the night Lenny Bruce fell—or jumped—out a window at the Swiss American hotel in San Francisco. The place was a dive; back in the days of the Barbary Coast it had actually been a jail, and then sometime around the 1920s it was turned into a hotel. But when they took out the bars and put in the windows, instead of using dowels to secure the frames, they apparently just glued them in, so at any point, with a little pressure, the window could fall right out.

Lenny had this "suite" on the second floor right above New Joe's club and there was an orgy taking place in his room. Everybody was bare-assed naked and high on acid and Lenny was going through some routine where he stood up on the windowsill to make his point. As he was leaning up against the frame, ranting, he lost his balance and the whole thing just gave way. Lenny fell naked right onto Broadway at three in the morning. His body was broken in many places.

A few months later, back in LA, Lenny was convalescing from his fall in a rented pad in the Hollywood Hills. Phil Spector had signed Lenny to his label and asked Tommy if he wanted to meet the legendary comic. Tommy said, "Absolutely!" Lenny was his hero; he spoke truth to power. Everybody on the cutting edge knew his routines by heart. Going to meet Lenny was like going to meet the hip oracle.

Lenny had rented a brand-new house on the extension of Hollywood Boulevard up above Laurel Canyon. You had to walk up a flight of stairs to get to the first floor, and when Phil and Tommy made the climb they discovered there wasn't a stick of furniture; the whole place smelled of cheap new carpet. Phil said, "Gee, I wonder where he is?" Turned out Lenny was in the basement sitting in a wheelchair.

Since he knew that Phil was coming he had managed to get out of his hospital bed and set himself up in the chair; one leg was in a cast and one arm was in a sling, and he was surrounded by piles of legal books. He had been arrested for obscenity so many times that he had finally decided to fight the most recent case. He was obsessed with the law, and most of the conversation they had that day was about civil justice and the lack thereof.

The bit that had started his legal troubles was called "To Come Is a Verb." In one of his routines, he talked about how he was having to defend himself against cops who came into the club where he was working and wrote down some of the words he said, like "fuck, shit, fuck you, motherfucker, cocksucker," and then, in court, he was forced to defend himself against *their* act, not his.

"Lenny seemed like a very sweet guy," says Tommy. "At one point, his daughter walked in; she was twelve years old at the time, and you could see that she was crazy about her father. Then his mother came in. Her professional name was Sally Marr, and she was like your typical Jewish mother except that she was very hip. She hung around and listened for a bit and then she split."

And then Lenny was alone in his wheelchair, raging against the authorities and the hypocrisy of society, cracking jokes, quoting Justice Brandeis, planning his future. About a month later, Tommy went to see him at a theater at La Brea and Hollywood Boulevard. "It was one of the most amazing performances I have ever witnessed," says Tommy. "He walked out onstage wearing one of these car coats that were popular at the time, like he had just come in off the street, and he was carrying a copy of the *LA Times*. He walked up to the microphone, opened the newspaper, and started turning the pages. Every now and then he'd stop and say 'Oh, here's a good one,' and he'd spend the next twenty minutes riffing on this headline or that story. That was the whole act. He was like a jazz musician." Years later Lenny explained he always went onstage wearing a coat so that he was ready to go when the cops came in and arrested him.

"To see somebody's mind move the way his moved, you realized that this was the real deal; he was blowing like Lester Young," says Tommy. Lenny Bruce was a clarion voice of the time, a living example that school was open and it was all around you, all the time, and most of the time the rest of society was part of the problem, not the solution. He made you realize that all you had to do was show up, be present when attendance was being taken. His drive for a ground level honesty would also show up later in Tommy's productions.

Track Four:

Blue Thumb

Tommy's father died in the spring of 1966. That was the summer that "Guantanamera" became a hit and Sam LiPuma lived long enough to know that his son was doing well. "A&M paid me fifteen thousand dollars a year," says Tommy, "That was a lot of money then. It was at least five thousand more than Sam was making as a barber. But he didn't really know from good, because when I got my first royalty check I couldn't believe it. It was for eighty thousand dollars. I had never seen so much money in one place in my life. My father averaged seven thousand a year. When you think about it, it would have taken him twelve years to make what I made in that one year."

In those days the royalty rate for producers was 2 percent of $4.98, or about ten cents per record. So if you sold a million records it would mean $100,000. And then the following year he had the hit with Claudine Longet, and suddenly it was like funny money. One of the first things he did was buy a house.

Right after Tommy moved into the house in Studio City, he got another call from Dominic Sospirato. This time, Dominic said he just happened to be out in LA and could they have a cup of coffee or something. "I hadn't seen him since that time in New York," says Tommy. "So I said, 'Sure, where are you?' He said he'd gone to see a friend who had a pizza place out in Encino. It must have been a good friend, because it took a long time to drive out there and pick him up."

Once again, Dominic was doing Ninfa's parents a favor, checking Tommy out. Because Ninfa and Tommy were still talking about getting together, and at one point they had actually decided, over the phone, to get married.

In fact, Tommy's family—his brother and his parents—had gone to Ninfa's house, in the old Sicilian fashion, on Tommy's behalf, to give her the ring. Ninfa's parents didn't want this to happen, and her father would not come out of his room to see them. At the last moment, when they were having coffee and dessert, he finally came to the table, sat down, and said, "Look, I just been through one of these things with her and I don't want anything to do with another marriage. What she's gonna do she's gonna do." A few weeks later, Ninfa called Tommy and said, "I can't go through with it."

Years later, Ninfa told him Dominic had come back to Cleveland after this particular trip to California and told her parents, "Forget about him. He's in another world. He's in never-never land."

Good Italian girls listened to their mothers and their fathers, and when Ninfa's parents looked at Tommy, they had to be thinking, "What is he gonna make of his life?" And there was another fear, a darker one, that nobody spoke about: Down deep, Tommy feels, they saw him as a cripple, and they were afraid that whatever was wrong with his leg could be passed along to his children. It was a superstition, it was based on ignorance, but there it was; they saw Tommy as damaged goods.

A few months later Tommy and Bob Krasnow were going to Europe and they made a stopover in Cleveland. Ostensibly, Tommy wanted to show Krasnow where he came from. "It was really the first time I realized how different my life had become," says Tommy. "When Kras saw the barbershop where I worked on Fleet Avenue, in the middle of the steel district, the look on his face said it all. Not only was the shop still there but some of the same customers were still there. Kras could see what I had been doing ten years before and he simply couldn't believe it."

But there was another reason to make the trip. While in Cleveland, Tommy called Ninfa and went to see her. "It's not something I'm particularly proud of," he says, "but, as people say, 'Don't get mad, get even,' so I went to see her in a limo. Both the father and the mother were there, and I can't say I didn't get a sense of satisfaction pulling up in a long black car. Because being back in the old neighborhood made it very clear to me that if we *had* gotten married it would have been a disaster: my life had already changed a hundred eighty degrees."

Tommy met Gill Kleiner on a blind date set up by Gary Klein, Gill's boss at the time, and his wife, Bonnie. Tommy picked up Gill at her place in Glendale. "I couldn't believe she lived there," he remembers. "I had been living in LA for five years and I had never even *been* to Glendale. It was all the way north of the 405, totally goyish. The street she lived on, Brand Boulevard, was nothing but a string of car lots. But one of the first things she told me was that she had heard 'Guantanamera' at this coffee shop where she and her friends used to hang out back in Queens—she was a doo-woppin' rock and roll freak—and she told her friends at the time, 'I love this record. Just listen to the voice in the middle.'" For Gill, it was love at first sound.

In New York, she had been working for the composer Bert Berns (at 1650 Broadway, across the street from the Brill Building), and then in 1966, when she moved to LA, she took a job with the music publisher Charlie Koppelman. So she and Tommy had mutual friends in music publishing.

Their blind date was nothing remarkable—Tommy showed Gill the house he had just purchased in the Valley, they stopped at Monty's Steak House for a drink—but a few weeks later they were both attending a film screening for one of Coppola's early movies, a counterculture film called *You're a Big Boy Now,* and even though Gill was there with one of Tommy's friends, something happened that would bond the two of them together.

Tommy was standing, talking with some "very straight people" ("they looked like they were right out of an Omaha insurance center,"), and as he went to get a match to light a cigarette, a half-smoked joint fell out of his matchbook. It landed on the floor next to his shoe. From across the room, Gill saw the whole thing happen and very casually walked over to where Tommy was standing and put her foot over the joint to cover it up. Tommy casually bent down, Gill moved her foot, and Tommy picked up the joint. That was it. "That," says Tommy, "is how I knew she was the one for me."

But the real moment of clarity came several months later when, one evening, Tommy found himself at a party along with the usual suspects, but at this particular event there was also a naked woman strapped to a door in the middle of the room. The creepiness of the scene triggered something in him. He had seen enough. He immediately went into a quiet back room, called Gill, and asked her to marry him. Two weeks later they made it official and she became his log in the flood, his ship on the ocean, his rock, for more than fifty years.

The Monterey Pop Festival was a long time coming and a long time gone. Planned for the weekend of June 16, 1967, designed by several music industry insiders, everybody knew it was going to be a major event as soon as they heard about it. Not just because the timing was right musically—all these nascent bands without record deals—but because it was a celebration of an industry about to explode. You could feel it; it was in the air. It was the beginning of the end of innocence.

Tommy and Krasnow got there the day before and settled in. They weren't alone: Janis Joplin came early and stayed late, sitting at the edge of the stage with a bottle of Jack Daniel's in her hand and watching the entire show for three solid days.

The new music was one thing, but the showdown between freedom and responsibility was something else. Tommy remembers witnessing the Who smashing their instruments, "and what I remember most about that," says Tommy, "was watching Wally Heider, the engineer from San Francisco who was hired to record the festival, frantically running around trying to save his microphones. He must have had twenty thousand dollars' worth of gear onstage and Pete Townsend was going berserk. If you look at the film of the concert, you can see this heavyset guy coming out of the wings and grabbing the mics. He thought these guys had gone off their heads, which of course was the point of the whole thing."

And then of course there was Jimi Hendrix. He came onstage just as dusk was falling. As soon as he came out of the wings, Tommy got out of his seat and stood close to the stage. He was only a few feet away when Jimi had his magic moment, squirting the lighter fluid and torching his guitar. It was one of the strangest things, like something you might see on an acid trip. And then, out of the corner of his eye, he saw, "a tall thin guy standing right next to me at the edge of the stage. He was holding a guitar in his hand and watching really intently. It was Chuck Berry. And his eyes were fixed on Jimi

Hendrix burning his instrument. It wasn't like he got emotionally moved by it at all. He just stood there and watched the whole thing go down." Talk about the torch being passed.

At the time, you didn't really think about these moments as timeless images. You didn't think about history being made at all. It was just what was happening—in fact, they called it "a happening." But the energy on that stage during the weekend was transcendent. On their way back to LA, Tommy and Krasnow stopped off in Carmel for lunch at Nepenthe, a hip little restaurant originally built by Orson Welles as a getaway pad for his lover, Rita Hayworth. When Tommy and Kras walked in, it seemed that everybody in the place had that thousand-yard stare on their face; they had seen the future and the future was black and white and in technicolor, Otis Redding and Jefferson Airplane and Eric Burdon, soulful and funky and British and trippy all at once—like a San Francisco free-form radio set come to life.

"I found myself sitting at Nepenthe," says Tommy, "and realizing that right now Bob Dylan was shooting bullets of verbal truth like 'Subterranean Homesick Blues,' 'Mr. Tambourine Man,' 'It's Alright Ma (I'm Only Bleeding),' and 'It's All Over Now, Baby Blue,' and the Beatles' *Rubber Soul* was running up the charts and don't forget that *Sgt. Pepper* was only months away, and then add to it Otis Redding and Jimi Hendrix, and some great bands like Funkadelic and Buffalo Springfield, and there was this musical explosion happening, all this great music was going on all around me, and I'm sitting there thinking that when I get back to LA, I'm booked to go into the studio with the Sandpipers again."

Obviously, Tommy knew this couldn't last, and he knew he had to do something about it.

Bob Krasnow was running Kama Sutra Records and his offices were on La Brea Avenue just across the street from A&M where Tommy had his office, so the two of them would have lunch together often. In the summer of 1968, Bob walked across the street one day, sat down in Tommy's office, and said, "Man, I've got to start my own record company," and he painted an elaborate verbal picture that ended with asking Tommy to leave A&M and go with him. He said it was going to be a small, hip label, able to outmaneuver the big guys, and he was asking Don Graham, who was A&M's vice president of marketing, to come along too.

As tempting as the idea might have been, it was anything but a sure thing for Tommy. He was making a fortune at A&M and he had access to all the great music and musicians in LA. But he knew he was getting typecast, producing music he didn't care about, and that if he didn't make a change, he was going to be producing the Sandpipers or some equivalent for the rest of his life. After a brief period of reflection, a matter of hours, actually, he told Krasnow, "I'm in." And from that moment on, things just got further *out*.

Like Tommy, Krasnow was a dyed-in-the-wool record man who had cut his teeth on rhythm and blues—Krasnow had been promoting James Brown before he came to LA—and, aside from his love of black music, he also shared Tommy's appreciation for the absurd. And when it came to the absurd, the combination of the two of them, along with the historical moment, was beyond ripe—it was incandescent.

A single example: One day, for no apparent reason, Krasnow decided they should go to Las Vegas. He and Tommy jumped on a plane and arrived at the Riviera Hotel a couple of hours later. They checked in to a suite, and before they even unpacked, Bob pulled out some "windowpane" acid—these little squares that felt like plastic, but when you put them under your tongue they dissolved. He poured this stuff out on the table, and the two of them started wetting their fingers and picking it up, and naturally they were picking up more than one at a time so there was no telling how much acid they actually ingested. After a little while, when it still felt like nothing much was happening, they were confident enough to go out for dinner.

Somebody had told them about a great seafood restaurant at the Desert Inn called the Aegean of the Sea. They had made a reservation there before they dropped the acid, so they got in the elevator and went down to the casino level. When they got into the elevator, everything seemed normal, but by the time the doors opened onto the casino floor, it was like the scene in *Fear and Loathing* in which outrageously horrible designs in the carpet turn into dragons and Hunter Thompson and his attorney are strangers in a strange land. They just kept walking, but by the time they got to the cab stand, they were absolutely flying.

They asked the driver to take them to the Desert Inn, and at the hotel they made their way to the Aegean of the Sea restaurant. It was a cavernous, multitiered space with seating on several levels, and the maître d' started to lead them around the top tier to get to their table. The place had what looked like aquariums built into the walls, but up close these turned out to be curved plastic panels with fish painted on them and moving lights behind them to make it look as if the fish were swimming. Nothing was what it appeared to be; it felt like they had been walking through this bizarre landscape forever. And way down at the bottom of the room, many levels below, there appeared to be a large pond in the shape of a figure eight, and floating in this pond was a large white wooden swan with a harp on it.

At the time, Bob had an outrageous Jewfro and was also wearing a large crucifix around his neck, so he and Tommy were getting a lot of looks. Then, just as they finally got seated, a woman in a strapless evening gown mounted the swan, sat down behind the harp, and hit a switch, and the swan took off swimming around the figure-eight pool while she started playing "Smoke Gets in Your Eyes" on the harp. For some reason that just did it for Bob and Tommy. "We just lost it," says Tommy. "We were practically on our knees laughing and pointing at this tableau, and of course the maître d' was looking at us like we were out of our minds, which of course we were."

In a way, this entire scene—flying to Vegas for vague reasons, ingesting inordinate amounts of chemicals, making their way to a fabulous venue where out of the blue a musical moment that no one could have predicted is served up in front of their eyes—pretty much captured what Blue Thumb (that's what Krasnow had named his company) was going to be like for the next several years.

When they started Blue Thumb Records, it was a once-in-a-life-time chance to do it their way, to take their fun more seriously. The outrageous party continued, but it became a party with a purpose: to make art out of chaos, or simply to beat the chaos into product, but in any case, to make a business out of the ongoing hang.

The Blue Thumb operation was anarchistic but focused: If *this* was the way something was usually done by the major labels, they were determined to find a different way. Starting with their headquarters: Rather than renting a straight-up corporate space in a Hollywood zip code, they set up shop on the second floor of a funky little pink stucco office complex on Canon Drive in Beverly Hills.

To reach the Blue Thumb suite, you had to cross an outdoor courtyard, squeeze into a small wrought-iron elevator, go rattling up to the second floor, and then walk down a long open-air corridor. Once inside, there was a reception area and two offices: Don Graham was in the one on the right and Bob was in the one on the left. In those days, Tommy lived in the studio.

Bob's office was painted dark gray with a floor-to-ceiling mural of Jimi Hendrix on the far wall. He had mounted rotating stage lights in the corners of the room, and every now and then, when the spirit moved him, he would turn the room lights down and let these stage lights play across Jimi's face. It was his own little Fillmore Auditorium. He would be sitting in the large antique chair behind his desk, usually wearing his fringed leather vest, and visitors would have to take the antique barber's chair across from him. The barber's chair was a nice touch, an *hommage* to Tommy's roots and a possible reference to getting your psychic hair trimmed.

There was no A&R policy at Blue Thumb. It was simply eclectic. Tommy and Bob signed what they wanted to. They were great friends and listened to the same kinds of music, and basically, while the major record companies were paying big bucks to artists, Blue Thumb didn't have that kind of money, so they had to take a different approach. "We didn't have the funds," says Tommy, "but we had the fun." They had to find the acts that were too far out for the major labels, acts that were on the fringes of the business, artists that were *unique.*

The first band they signed was Captain Beefheart and His Magic Band. In fact, Beefheart originally came up with the name Blue Thumb. He was going to start a blues band and call it that until Krasnow heard about it and said, "I don't like it for a blues band, but I love it for my record company."

Right after they signed Beefheart, Bob and Tommy took the band to London. The whole trip would be an eye-opening experience. When they met the band at the LA airport, the drummer was dressed in a child's bathrobe, with a rope knotted around his waist and shower clogs on his feet; on his head he wore a sandbox sifter with Porky Pig and other cartoon characters dancing around the side of it. The guitar player was wearing a yellow plastic raincoat, the kind a five-year-old kid might wear, with plastic clogs and a red plastic cowboy hat. And Beefheart was dressed in his usual Mad Hatter outfit. When Bob asked them about their luggage they said they didn't have any. Not even a toothbrush. All they had were their instruments. That's how the band was going to Europe.

In London they were booked to play at a club called Middle Earth, located in "the Docklands," an area right on the Thames River. The venue was literally in the middle of the earth: one entered and walked down three floors of stone steps to get to a massive underground area where the music performances took place. The club had three stages situated around this cavernous space, and acts rotated stages throughout the night. It felt like an enormous World War II bomb shelter, which in fact it had been.

In LA, Beefheart had been associated with Frank Zappa, and the word across the pond was that this was a show you shouldn't miss. The place was mobbed with people wanting to see this new musical phenomenon they had read about in the rock and roll press. Beefheart walked onstage playing his weird saxophone, wearing his Mad Hatter's outfit, "singing and doing all his stuff," says Tommy, "and the crowd was digging him, and he was walking around when suddenly he just disappeared. He stepped back and fell off the stage. The audience loved it. The place was so packed that they just broke his fall; they grabbed him and passed him back onstage." This could have been the birth of crowd surfing.

On that same trip to England, Bob took Tommy to the famous Portobello Road flea market, where Tommy bought the first piece of art that, unbeknownst to him, would start his decades of collecting, a passion that would come to rival his obsession with music. "We were just wandering around when I happened to see a Jean Cocteau drawing," says Tommy. "It was of a flirtatious women knocking a hat off of a handsome gentleman. I had just been turned on to the writings and films of Cocteau by Bobby Dale, but I really didn't know anything about him as a person or as an artist. I thought it was a nice image, and not knowing anything about art, I bought it for five hundred dollars. At the time, that was three months of mortgage payments, but something told me I had to own it. That simple little drawing was what ignited my interest in things visual, which would blossom into a full-blown passion."

Meanwhile, Bob, who was known as "the king of the hang," was continuing to explore new levels of enjoyment. While in London, he signed the band T. Rex to Blue Thumb. The band was really just two guys, Marc Bolan and his partner, Steve Peregrin Took, and it was Steve who gave Krasnow his first Mandrax, a soporific pill that created euphoria in those who ingested it. "When he found Mandrax," says Tommy, "Bob found his personal heaven. I think the reason we ended up signing T. Rex was because Steve Took turned Bob on to Mandrax."

This drug wasn't about enlightenment, it was about oblivion. It was just one small sign that the naïveté of the sixties was about to come undone, that the social experiment was starting to unravel. This was right around the time of the Manson murders in LA, and the paranoia there was rising like heat off a baking highway. People were taking harder drugs and carrying guns. Peace and love was looking more like "lawyers, guns, and money." In 1969, when the murder at the Altamont festival happened just months after the love-in at Woodstock, there seemed to be a kind of inevitability about it; it was just a matter of time before reality bit the hippies in the ass big time. And then the Sylmar earthquake hit.

That night, Tommy came home late from a recording session, around three in the morning and was finally falling asleep when, he says, "he felt like he was in a maraca." He and Gill jumped up and ran out the back door—they were afraid the house was going to fall down—but when they saw their big white German shepherd (Ofay) running back into the house through the dog door, they had second thoughts; the ground was shaking so violently that all the water had leapt out of the swimming pool and was turning the backyard into a sea of mud.

So between Mandrax, Manson, and the mudbath, the party was getting more than interesting; it was getting real.

Blue Thumb was the little engine that could, a small record company that relied on one-of-a-kind artists and a radical image to get the attention of the press. One of the first ads they took out in *Rolling Stone* read, "Are you now or have you ever been a member of Blue Thumb?"—a takeoff on the old anticommunist question of the fifties; the implication was you were either on the bus or you were off the bus.

The label also started a newspaper called *Thumbin' It,* which they gave away free at record stores, basically a collection of articles pilfered from everywhere and anywhere—*National Geographic, Sunshine & Health, Popular Mechanics, Billboard,* whatever—interspersed with stories about new Blue Thumb releases. Pretty soon, people were sending them articles. A lot of people wanted to get on the bus.

Around the same time Leon Russell and Denny Cordell started a label called Shelter Records and struck a distribution deal with Blue Thumb. The first ad that Shelter ran was a picture of Leon sitting on a recording console next to a naked woman with her legs spread. When Bob Krasnow saw this, he immediately became inspired to run his own ad for Blue Thumb showing a group of naked women fleeing with large blue thumb prints on their asses; the text read HERE COME THE BLUE THUMB. Nobody was going to outshock these guys. And when they signed the "Butts Band," which was basically the Doors minus Jim Morrison, they held a party at Chasen's in Beverly Hills, a very chic restaurant, and at a key moment in the evening they had three naked guys streak the place with BUTTS BAND written prominently on their asses.

"If it couldn't be done or shouldn't be done," says Tommy, "we probably did it. Basically, that was our philosophy. And it was so foreign to the way the record business had been run before that, which was normally a bunch of people sitting around in offices waiting for other people to come in for appointments." It was like being the first men in space. Nobody had ever been that high before. But they just kept pushing the limits, running into people wherever they went and signing them up. Blue Thumb was as much a movement as a record label, one of those instances where somebody's instincts ran right into history. In the meantime, there was financing to consider.

Naturally, as the record business was exploding, a lot of large corporations wanted to get a piece of the action. One of those corporations on the road to becoming an entertainment conglomerate was Gulf & Western. It was originally founded in the 1930s as a company that stamped out metal car bumpers, but eventually it morphed into ABC Paramount. David Judelson, one of its founders, explained to Krasnow, "I was in my garden tending to my bees and I had a vision. I realized that just as bees have a queen surrounded by lots of little workers, I had this image of a big company surrounded by lots of smaller satellite record labels."

Bob and Tommy had gone to see Judelson because they desperately needed financing, and as Tommy quickly learned, there's no honey without a sting somewhere in the picture. They found their way to G&W through Artie Ripp, one of Bob's old partners from Kama Sutra: Artie set up the meeting and in return, Bob promised him a piece of Blue Thumb Records. Only Bob forgot to mention this part of the arrangement to Tommy. Eventually, Blue Thumb made the deal with Gulf & Western and Artie came looking for his piece.

It happened late one night, when Tommy found himself sitting at a table at an industry convention with Artie. Artie said, "I'm the guy who made the connection with Judelson," and then he got to the part where he was supposed to get a piece of the company, and Tommy said, "Hold on. What does any of this have to do with me? This is between you and Krasnow."

"The next thing I know," says Tommy, "Artie threatens me, in a not so subtle way, saying maybe he'll call his friends in the Mafia. I said, 'Look, Artie, I'm Sicilian. You call your friends, I'll call mine.'" Artie never got his piece of the company, but he did eventually discover Billy Joel and took a quarter from every record Billy ever sold. Like they say, where there's a will, there's a lawyer.

The fate of Blue Thumb was often entwined with Bob and Tommy's social life. It's where they made their contacts, had their connections, and got a foretaste of the future. For example, one night at Alan Pariser's place—Alan was one of the guys behind the Monterey Pop Festival—Tommy remembers walking in and immediately gawking at a young Gracie Slick from the Jefferson Airplane. "She was gorgeous," he remembers, "an absolute stunner. She was wearing this Indian band around her head; you couldn't take your eyes off her."

Suddenly these other two guys walk in. One was a hip-looking black dude wearing shades, and the other was a hip-looking white dude wearing a plaid double-breasted suit and sporting the wildest hair Tommy had ever seen. "It looked," he says, "like he had just put his finger in a wall socket." The duo were South African trumpet player Hugh Masekela and his producer, Stewart Levine. "These guys really made a first impression."

Stewart was a record producer with a small stable that included both Hugh and the Jazz Crusaders, a hip jazz/funk quintet out of Texas. The group's pianist, Joe Sample, would ultimately become one of Tommy's first call guys. Before they left Pariser's party, Bob, Tommy, and Stewart all started thinking about going into business together; Stewart would continue producing and Blue Thumb would distribute his productions. "We had a lot of common interests," says Tommy. In the end, it was more than a business deal; it was a lifestyle decision. "But of course," he says, "music was always the main thing."

The three often traveled together, both physically and metaphysically. One weekend, for example, they all went up to the Fillmore Auditorium in San Francisco, where you literally didn't have to get out of your chair in order to score psychedelics. This night they found organic mescaline. Mescaline was different from LSD—it wasn't as deep or as steep—and it was closer to laughing gas than truth serum.

At the Fillmore, they ran into Stan Marcum, Carlos Santana's manager, who invited them back to his house in Sausalito. They all jumped into the stretch limo Bob had rented and headed across the Golden Gate Bridge. Tommy remembers, "Stew was so wired that he kept changing seats the whole way. Finally, I said to him, 'Hey, man, relax. You don't have to walk all the way across the bridge.'"

When they got to Stan's house they were greeted by "a very strange-looking dude" who turned out to be a professional opium chef. There is an art to smoking opium, and this guy prepared the pipe for the new arrivals. Soon they were all floating with both feet on the ground. Then somebody put on an album by the pianist Alice Coltrane; Tommy had never heard Alice Coltrane before, and the combination of her music and everything else going on created a magic space "just somewhere left of seventh heaven. It felt like the world had opened up." It was one of those peak moments that intimated even greater things to come. Suddenly Tommy became obsessed with Alice Coltrane.

When they got back in the limo, Tommy decided he was returning to LA immediately. He was on a mission. Bob and Stewart said they would leave the next afternoon, but Tommy said, "No, man, I'm going back now," and he dropped them off and took the limo to the airport. "When I finally got on the plane," he remembers, "I looked down the aisle and saw a sea of dead faces. It felt like all these people wanted to be anyplace but on this plane. I thought they all looked like they were wearing the mask of death. And I'm still feeling this transcendence from Alice Coltrane's music."

Tommy landed in LA and went straight to Tower Records, where he bought every Alice Coltrane record he could find. Then he went home, woke Gill up and said, "You have to hear this," and started playing all these Alice Coltrane tracks. And of course it was clear she wasn't really hearing it.

"Looking back," says Tommy, "it's amazing that we survived the period. But what's also amazing is the power of music at that particular time and place." More than the influence of the chemicals involved or the dissolution of social norms on all fronts, it was the opportunity to participate in a world where music was not only the means of transportation but the destination as well. The level of engagement one had with the music—popular music, everyday music, radio music—and the potential transformation of the human soul and the unfolding of human potential—would never be more powerful nor more profound than it was at this particular moment in history.

One has to keep in mind that the music business was a special case of a special case: Not only were the times changing, but music was the catalyst of the new frontier and these music men were the outliers; all the previous rules were being broken but nothing firm had yet taken their place, and so what used to be firm ground was now fluid. Many routine, mundane events were spinning out of old orbits.

Like the wedding of Tom and Rachael Donahue. They got married at the Jefferson Airplane mansion in San Francisco. "We were standing in the garden," remembers Tommy, "when somebody came around with hors d'oeuvres. I was talking with this guy Victor Moscoso, the artist who designed all those wild psychedelic posters for the Fillmore, and he said 'I wouldn't take that if I were you.

Everything in this house is laced with acid.' So we didn't eat a thing. And then at the last minute they brought out the wedding cake and we all figured the cake came from a store so it couldn't possibly be dosed with LSD. But no. There were people who walked away from that wedding, including members of Rachael's family, that nobody heard from for three days. People just thought they went off their rockers."

It was a time of anarchy, but somehow at Blue Thumb they were able to harness it, make great records, and make some musical history as well.

Their first real success came with the British singer/guitarist Dave Mason. Dave had been with the group Traffic and Tommy had been a big fan of the band and, particularly, of Dave's songwriting, like "Feelin' Alright" and "Hole in My Shoe." Traffic was long gone and Dave was now signed to Island Records as a solo artist. The word was that his contract was for sale.

Blue Thumb had been contacted by Mason's representatives, Group Three Management, three guys well known to Tommy: Alan Pariser, Barry Feinstein (a wild, funny photographer who would loom large in the development of Blue Thumb Records), and Sid Kaiser, a friend and coke dealer of Peter Lawford and the Rat Pack and the gentleman *consigliore* of the Group. The asking price was only $15,000, which was not a lot of money even then.

Tommy's only question was why Chris Blackwell at Island Records would want to sell Dave Mason's contract for so little. It turned out that Dave was a pain to deal with and Chris had had enough. With Group Three's encouragement, Blue Thumb signed Mason, and Tommy started putting the recording sessions together.

This was a first-time challenge for Tommy, who didn't have a reputation as a rock and roll producer—he had been doing mostly the

Sandpipers and Claudine Longet—and he knew he had something to prove. He took his time putting together the hippest band in town: drummers Jim Keltner and Jim Gordon, pianists Leon Russell and John Simon, and Carl Radle on bass. These were not just some of the greatest session players in LA but also sophisticated guys who could play any kind of music with an authentic feel. This record was going to be a statement about Tommy LiPuma's production chops as much as a first-class presentation of Dave Mason's compositions.

The first song they recorded, "Only You Know and I Know," took barely an hour to get down on tape, and it became the album's biggest hit. The way they put it together might seem haphazard at first. Dave played bass along with Jim Gordon on drums, then over-dubbed several guitar parts. Next he sang the vocal and then doubled it, and finally he added some harmony parts. But what really made the song happen was Jim Gordon's drum part. "The rhythm pattern he came up with," says Tommy, "which was like a march, just opened the door to the song. When I heard it, even though it was just bass and drums, I knew I had the goods."

At the time of Mason's signing, most hit records were from groups—Traffic, the Beatles, the Stones—and Dave was one of the first to step out of a hugely successful band and attempt a solo career. His album *Alone Together* became Blue Thumb's first gold disc.

"It was one of the highlights of my career," says Tommy, "because it gave me a sense of confidence and it made the case for my ability to produce all kinds of music." And, through a twist of fate, it connected Tommy with Al Schmitt, who would go on to record and mix virtually every record Tommy subsequently produced, a relationship that lasted more than forty-five years. Al became like a director of phonography, translating Tommy's musical visions and aural landscapes into reality.

"I often think being a record producer is like being a film director," Tommy says. "The songs are like the script; you have to make sure the songs are great, like the script has to be great. You cast the musicians like you cast the actors—you can get a great musician, but if he's wrong for the part it just won't work. And finally, whereas in a film it's the cinematographer who captures the image, in recording, it's the engineer who's responsible for the sound. And the sound of the record is very important to its success."

Tommy had known Al for years, but as an A&R man and record producer at RCA, not an engineer. They first met back when Tommy was plugging songs for Liberty, pitching songs by Randy Newman and Jackie DeShannon and Al was producing big acts like Sam Cooke, Henry Mancini, Eddie Fisher, and the Jefferson Airplane. But Schmitt was also one of the first true modern recording engineers in the record business; when he started as an apprentice at New York's Apex Studios back in 1947, many records were being recorded in radio studios with engineers who were not necessarily expert at recording music. By the time he moved to LA in the late fifties, Al had recorded Charlie Parker, Duke Ellington, and a killer's row list of top artists and pioneered the invention of modern recording techniques (he was the first engineer ever to put a microphone on a kick drum).

In 1970, when Tommy called him about Dave Mason, he was working with both Eddie Fisher and the Jefferson Airplane, the Airplane all night, dodging the LSD that people were putting into his food and drink, and then waking up to record Eddie Fisher at ten o'clock the next morning. And he was burning out.

Al had spoken to the head of A&R at RCA, a guy named Ernie Altschul, to get some relief. He said, "Ernie, I can't do this. I can't do sessions all night long and then come in and do dates at ten o'clock in the morning." Ernie said, "What do you mean you can't do it? Truck drivers do it all the time." Al said, "Then get yourself a fucking truck driver," and he quit.

He kept working with the Airplane as an independent producer and wound up making a lot more money than he had as a staff A&R

guy. When Tommy called, he was independent and interested in mixing the Dave Mason project, but with reservations. "I haven't mixed an album in eight years," Al said, but when Tommy pleaded with him—"Look, man, it's like riding a bike. It will take you a couple of hours, maybe a couple of days, whatever, but you'll get right back into it"—Al said, "Okay, I'll do it on the condition that if I don't like the way it's going I can split and if you don't like the way it's going you'll break it to me soft."

In the end, not only did Al do a great job, but it turned out to be a pivotal moment in his life as well, because when he heard how great the album sounded he realized that what he really loved doing was recording and mixing records, not all the politics of producing them. And soon, Jackson Browne was calling him and asking him to record and mix the album *Late for the Sky,* which became a huge success. And Al never turned back. Today, Al Schmitt has twenty Grammys for engineering, thanks in part to Tommy's fortuitous phone call.

Blue Thumb pulled out all the stops to make sure the Dave Mason record got noticed. Another big factor was the packaging. This fell to the genius of Barry Feinstein and his design company, Camouflage Productions. Camouflage was the de facto art department for Blue Thumb, and Blue Thumb records not only sounded different from other labels, but they looked different as well.

For example, for *Alone Together,* Barry invented the "kangaroo pack," a three-fold album jacket that turned into a poster with a pouch at the bottom. And in every pouch they put a one-of-a-kind multicolored disc. It was Barry's idea, and it was completely unprecedented: every Dave Mason record actually looked different from every other one, because Barry had gone to the manufacturing plant and convinced the plant manager to drop colored pellets into the boiling plastic before the records were stamped. Hence each disc literally looked like its own spin painting.

It cost 14 cents more per album to do this, and the guy at the manufacturing plant thought they were all nuts, but when the record arrived in record stores, it had a serious impact on the hipsters. One big store on Broadway in New York City actually displayed the record going around on a turntable in the window with mirrors behind it, like a spinning Rorschach test; there were people standing outside staring at it and they couldn't even hear the music.

Barry Feinstein was a very macho guy with deep experience. He had, for example, taken the iconic photos of the prescription drug bottles on Marilyn Monroe's nightstand the morning after, and he was also the guy who drove Bob Dylan across the country for Bob's manager, Albert Grossman. (When asked what Dylan was like on the ride, Barry said, "You can get the best of Bob in stereo for $4.95 in any record store.")

During the Blue Thumb years, Barry became one of Tommy's closest friends. Physically they were as different as chalk and cheese: Whereas Tommy was diminutive in size with a humorous aura, with Barry, "you knew by looking at him," says Tommy, "that you didn't want to mess with him. He was like one big muscle, totally bald with a very thick handlebar mustache. He rode a motorcycle and he was very attractive to women; he loved them and they loved him."

He was tired of doing location shoots, with hours of driving and setup to accommodate some corporate art director's fantasy of a far-out concept. Instead, he set up a big roller suspended on metal poles in his studio and hung backdrops over it so you could pretend to be anywhere you wanted to be. He changed backdrops like you change sets on a film—you could have your picture taken in the desert or in the mountains, wherever you liked, and you never had to leave his room. Subsequently, his office was ground zero for some of the most far-out and creative packages in the business, including those for Janis Joplin, Ike and Tina Turner, the Rolling Stones, and George Harrison.

Barry always had the best weed. All sorts of odd characters would come and go—actors, hipsters, art world aficionados—while clients would be waiting for their photo shoot. Tommy had developed the habit of dropping by the Camouflage offices to relax and partake of the inspiration. Typical was the day Seymour Cassel popped in. (Seymour was one of the stars of the film *Minnie and Moskowitz*, but at the time he was "between pictures.") Barry was in the photo studio taking somebody's picture while Tommy was hanging outside in the office when Seymour came running in wearing a beret with a red star in front, like he was Che Guevara. He was completely wired from blow, convinced he was being followed by the cops. Peeking out the window, he said, "I've been driving around these fucking hills all day trying to lose these motherfuckers." They all looked outside and of course there was nobody there.

But even Barry, a rock-solid guy, was beginning to succumb to the growing paranoia of the times. He carried a loaded .38 because he was afraid that the television producer Burt Sugarman was going to send somebody to kill him because his former wife—Carol Wayne, the zaftig actress who played "the Matinée Lady" on the Johnny Carson show—was now dating Sugarman. The notion was convoluted and made little sense, but the times were getting crazier, and since everybody was slipping into it together, it was often hard to notice.

Barry did the cover for the Gábor Szabó *Magical Connection* album on Blue Thumb. He used a canvas backdrop from a 1930s jungle movie. As a lark, he leaned a broom against the set so it appeared that there was a broom in the jungle. It was an arresting photo, and Barry fell in love with it to the extent that when it came time to design the album cover, he decided he wanted to use this photo but he didn't want to put anything on top of it, not the artist's name, not the album title, no type whatsoever. He told Tommy and Krasnow, "I can't put type on the front. Let's put it on the back."

Tommy reminded Barry they were in business to sell records and this idea was crazy. "Look," he said, "you don't want people to have to go on a hunting expedition to find the album. You have to figure this out." Barry figured out a way to print copy on the cellophane wrapper so they could print the cover with no copy on the photo itself and instead put "Gábor Szabó, *Magical Connection*" on the shrink wrap. An inspired solution to a crazy idea.

But the Gábor Szabó project was also a good example of how fine the line could be between crazy and inspired. It was recorded at the Record Plant in LA, and the dynamic in the room was bizarre from the beginning. On the first day of recording, the engineer, who was also part owner of the studio, handed the guys a joint when they walked in and then a few minutes later casually mentioned, "By the way, that was Angel Dust." The entire room wound up on some other planet, even as the tape was rolling. This set the tone for the sessions.

When it came time to do the album cover, Barry arranged for all the musicians to come to his studio at ten o'clock in the morning. Gábor and the band arrived looking pretty rough because they'd been up all night. To get back in the mood, they turned to the hair of the dog that bit them. At one point, while Barry was loading film into his camera, everybody started pulling out little bottles of cocaine, hash pipes, joints, whatever they had. Barry came back and started taking pictures and so, along with some nice cover shots, he also had the photographic evidence of the band getting high.

Everybody laughed and moved on. But two weeks later, when the finished album design was presented, there was one of those pictures on the inside of the package. The cover was still the great jungle shot with the broom; the back was a nice shot of all of the musicians standing around casually; but when you opened the gatefold, there was this wild picture with one guy smoking a joint, another guy taking a hit from a hash pipe, every kind of everything. Obviously Barry thought it was great. Krasnow agreed. But Tommy went nuts.

He tried to talk them out of it, but in the end Krasnow said, "Oh, man, nobody's gonna know what you guys are doing," and they went with it.

The album came out on a Tuesday, and that Friday, Leonard Feather, one of the most influential jazz critics in the United States, reviewed it in the Weekend section of the LA Times. His entire review was focused on the inside photo and the fact that it showed the musicians *in flagrante delicto.* He wrote almost nothing about the music itself. Tommy said to Krasnow, "See! 'Nobody is gonna see it,' right?" And Krasnow pulled out one of his favorite expressions: "Ah, man," he said, "tomorrow they're gonna wrap fish in it."

There was a kind of courage in following an idea or an attitude to its logical—or illogical—conclusion. And they were selling records.

The next person signed to Blue Thumb was Dan Hicks. Dan Hicks and the Hot Licks was a fantastic vocal swing group Tommy had heard on one of his trips to the Bay Area. Hicks's songs, especially "Canned Music" and "I Scare Myself," knocked Tommy out. He was also taken by the contrast between Dan's offhand style of delivery and the ferocious musicianship of the guys in the band: Sid Page, the violin player, was a technical monster, and the guitar player, John Girton could swing like crazy. The whole act was hot and cool at the same time, and to top it off, Dan had two sexy chicks he called the Lickettes, Naomi Eisenberg and Maryann Price, singing backup. It was a total package.

Tommy and Krasnow went up to San Francisco to meet with Dan, who was living on a houseboat in Sausalito. They got to the boat and discovered they had to walk a plank to get from the pier to the deck, but the plank was bent from years of use, and in the middle it was actually underwater. And right beyond this dip in the plank was a big dog turd. In order to make the deal, they were going to have to jump over the dip in the plank and avoid the dog dropping. Normal people might have objected; Tommy and Bob thought it was hysterical. They were convinced Dan had done it on purpose; Dan denies it.

Tommy knew he wanted to record Dan live, and he chose the Troubadour on Santa Monica Boulevard in LA, a classic venue and home to all the singer-songwriters of the day. Ultimately, he recorded five shows so that he had many different takes to choose from, and he pulled together the best takes from each night for the final album. He and Al had two 16-track machines in the truck running in parallel so they didn't miss anything. They also recorded a wild track with all of the audience applause split out separately so that when they went to compile the album, they could run a big loop of this applause to cover edits between one take and the next. The album, called *Where's the Money?*, came out sounding like one totally great live show, an example of how studio production is a kind of lie that tells the truth.

Dan Hicks and the Hot Licks was one of Blue Thumb's most successful acts, and they were constantly touring. Unfortunately, practically everybody in the band wound up hooked on heroin. First of all, it's hard to live out on the road, and heroin smooths the edges; and second, there was a lot of heroin in the Bay Area. Even Tommy and Al had a little run-in with it when making the next Dan Hicks album, *Last Train to Hicksville*.

One night they had dinner with Hicks's bass player, Jamie Leopold. After a great meal and a quick stop at a jazz club they all went back to the hotel and smoked a couple of joints. Then Jamie pulled out a small bottle of white powder and said, "You guys want a pop? It's pharmaceutical." It was dilaudid, synthetic heroin.

That's all Tommy had to hear—"pharmaceutical"; what could possibly go wrong? In a few minutes he was flying, but Al was turning green. The drug made him sick as a dog. Jamie got up to go and before he left, he said to Tommy, "You want another pop?" Tommy was so high that he was reading the sports page; he said "Sure."

"As soon as Jamie split," recalls Tommy, "I had this feeling and I knew I was in trouble. And then both Al and I were hanging over the toilet. This went on till six in the morning, when we finally called the front desk and said, 'We have food poisoning. Do you have a house doctor?' He connected me to a guy and it turns out the hotel had its own pharmacy, so the doctor called in a script. By 9:05, there was a knock on the door and within ten minutes we were cool."

They canceled their session for the day and then, around eleven that morning, Jamie came back to the hotel, and when he saw how sick they both were, he said, "Listen, I know this sounds crazy, but if you take another hit it will help you feel better." Tommy thought he was nuts, but that's how it starts, because heroin will make you feel better—for a minute.

Tommy had known pain his whole life. "The pain in my hip has always been there," he says. "It never goes away completely. There was a point, early on, in 1964, when I had a bad relapse but I just dealt with it. No medication at all.

"I had another major relapse in 1972 and that's when I met a Japanese doctor who did the first hip replacement and he introduced me to pain relief in the form of Percodan. He was way too casual about it and eventually I was taking fourteen pills a day. It got to the point where I didn't know what day it was; it was just one long floating moment.

"Then, when it came time to give me my pre-med for the hip replacement surgery, they were giving me methadone, which is synthetic heroin. I was so high that I must have smoked a pack of cigarettes waiting for them to come and get me, and I called half of the country on the phone. When they took me downstairs strapped in a gurney, a guy walked by and I was so high I asked him if he had a cigarette. And my arms were strapped in.

"As a kid, when I was in the hospital, I don't remember ever having anything for the pain. They must have given me something, but I don't remember it. But that's the way they dealt with pain back then. I remember having dental work done as a kid without Novocain. Back then a little pain was supposed to be good for you.

"But of course I've always remembered that first euphoric feeling of looking down at myself when I was in that coma, and there is a definite connection between that particular memory and my desire to recapture that feeling of release again through drugs. I really didn't connect the two until many years later, but I think once you feel your body coming to your rescue like that, you want to feel it again and again. We are hardwired to respond to that emotion like Pavlov's dog.

"I eventually did get off the pain meds after I went to see Dr. Newman, Randy's father. He asked me if I was hooked on anything and I told him I was taking Percodan for my hip. He said I had to get off of it and the best way to do it was to delay my intake one hour at a time. It took two years to get it down to two pills a day, and then another year to get off of it entirely. And I never went back to it. Every operation I've had since, I've never taken anything for the pain. I just deal with it." Anybody who has ever had major surgery knows what incredible willpower that requires.

Over the years, a lot of very good people got blown away by drugs. Back then, drugs were everywhere and often seemed to be a reasonable response to an uptight, repressed society. Like they used to say, "Free your mind and your ass will follow." It may have been excessive, but the sixties was the epoch of excess—even the war in Vietnam was an example of this—and nobody had really been down this particular road before.

"At first it was pretty tame," says Tommy, "smoking pot and taking acid, but later, when cocaine entered the picture, it got serious, both financially and psychologically: It became something you didn't want to be without. The word on the street was that cocaine wasn't addictive, and we all thought of it as kind of a benign thing. It became an important part of the enhancing paraphernalia of the period. But it was an evil drug nonetheless, and when it was used in excess, it could literally change your personality.

"By the time I stopped using cocaine in the late seventies I had come to the conclusion that all you were ever trying to do was get back to the first high you ever experienced."

By the late seventies, Red Baldwin was strung out, living out of a VW bus with his dog. Every so often he'd stop by Tommy's house for a shower and some food. He was flat broke. (One day he saw a kumquat tree in Tommy's back yard and got really excited because, as he said, "Kumquats, man they're like four dollars a pound.") Another time, he was on the ground looking for something and it turned out to be a filling from his tooth, so Tommy sent him to his dentist. And then one day he stopped showing up and they found him dead in his bus.

Abe Kesh, too, became a drug addict. It started when he had back problems, but once he found heroin, he used it whether he had pain or not. At one point it got so bad that he went in for a back operation, and of course he didn't tell them he was already a junkie, and somehow, after the operation, he suffered a stroke. He had been an important disk jockey—he was "Voco" on KSAN, the voice of San Francisco—and he ended up a vagrant in Sausalito, believing he was the goalie for the Detroit Rangers.

Pain is a rolling horizon, but addiction is a constant companion.

"Over the years," says Tommy, "we had some real success at Blue Thumb. Dave Mason, Dan Hicks, The Pointer Sisters, The Crusaders, Ike and Tina Turner. There were a lot of lesser-known things that were just great too, like Ken Nordine's *Word Jazz,* João Donato's *Bad Donato*. It was just a fantastic roster. But every time we would get an act going and it started making some noise, some bigger company would swoop in and grab them.

"The first time it happened was with T. Rex. They had a song called 'Ride a White Swan' that they recorded for Blue Thumb. Then Warners came along and apparently found some loophole in the contract and ended up signing them. So Warners put out 'Ride a White Swan' too." Blue Thumb had already pressed up singles and so we put out the album with a bonus single inside. Warners flipped out and it wound up in court. Warners won. Then something similar happened with Dave Mason: Columbia came along and offered Dave a million bucks and he took it.

"It just became very difficult to be a small label," says Tommy. "First of all, as a small company, we were starting to have trouble getting paid by the distributors. They simply held on to the money they owed us until we had something else that they wanted. Then maybe they'd send half. And second, because the record business was exploding, all the major companies had bushels of money and there was no way we could afford to fight them."

In a way, Blue Thumb was the end of the beginning; by the mid-seventies, small companies were being swallowed up by big companies and it was no longer possible for a couple of music driven guys to get together and start a company out of their love, expertise, and passion. There really wasn't another company like Blue Thumb before or since. They were their own competition.

In 1972, Gulf & Western bought the label outright. In 1973, having become aware that Krasnow was still operating Blue Thumb out of his own pocket, as if corporate accounts were his private check-book, they fired Krasnow. Tommy was collateral damage; he too was out of a job. The next year, G&W sold the label to ABC Dunhill, and they either absorbed or abandoned the Blue Thumb titles into their own catalog. Either way, the great experiment was over.

The ultimate irony was that Blue Thumb was about to become highly profitable due to a new release by The Pointer Sisters burning up the charts.

In the end, the competition won.

Track Five:

Breezin'

In 1974 Tommy got a call from Columbia Records asking if he would be interested in doing an album with Barbra Streisand.

Barbra had just completed the film *The Way We Were* and Marty Paich had already done the single on the title song; now they were looking for somebody to produce the rest of the album. Barbra was a big star. She had made *Funny Girl* and done Broadway and one of the things that Tommy loved was her tragic version of "Happy Days Are Here Again"; it was a thrill just to think about working with her. When he got the call, he said, "Are you kidding? Absolutely."

Barbra was right in the middle of preparing for the film *Funny Lady* so she didn't have a lot of time to devote to the recording. In fact, they were scheduled to record all eight songs in one long day. That's like a gourmet chef turning out a hundred meals in an afternoon. You can do it, but there is literally no room for error. So preproduction was very important.

Before the session, Tommy went to her house to go over some songs. He brought the composer Barry Mann along with him because he wanted to do one of Barry's tunes and the idea was Barry would demo this and several other songs for her. Barbra was living on one of the most prestigious streets in Beverly Hills in a Mediterranean-style home. It had a grand hallway and a magnificent staircase going up to the second floor, twenty-foot ceilings, big Palladian windows, and gorgeous Matisse oil-on-paper drawings on the walls. Everything about it was elegant and cordial.

At one point, Barbra left the room "for a minute" that dragged on for more than half an hour. Barry, being a very funny cat, and humor being so important to a musical situation, spotted a plate of candy on the table and started putting pieces into his pocket, a silent riff that just let the air out of the balloon a bit. Then he turned to Tommy and said, "Hey, man, let's just take the whole plate," and he picked up this exquisite silver candy dish and pretended to put that in his pocket too. The joke served its purpose, lightened the mood, and when Barbra came back, he and Tommy were able to go through the songs with good humor.

The next time they all met was the day of recording. The sessions were done at Western One, a classic old Hollywood studio, with a full orchestra and Nick DeCaro conducting his arrangements. Barbra was in great voice. "It's always impressive to be in the room with a spectacular talent like that," says Tommy. "From the moment she opened her mouth, she sang so good she made the microphone sound good!"

Since they had only one day to do eight songs, the vibe in the studio was intense and nerves were stretched tight; everybody was being ultra cool. Just before the first song was to be recorded, a small glitch in the wiring of the control board brought things to a halt. Barbra had casually asked, "Can I have some echo in my earphones?" Tommy said, "Sure, Barbra," and turned to the second engineer and said, "Give her some echo." The engineer said, "Gee, I'm sorry but we can't put echo in the earphones." These days, this is like saying your car doesn't have windshield wipers. It just doesn't happen. But this studio was so "classic" in some ways it was still back in the fifties. Tommy hit the talkback and said, "Barbra, I'm sorry, but for some reason or other we can't put echo in your earphones." And that was it: She went nuts. It took the better part of a half hour to get back to a place where they could begin to work again.

When they eventually got going, they kept going. All the way past midnight. This is where the men and women get separated from the boys and girls. The stress and effort required to stay focused for that amount of time, to deliver inspired, sensitive performances one after another, really made all the participants—musicians, technicians, Barbra herself—draw deep down for inspiration.

Tommy became so involved in the process that he broke a cardinal rule of record production: Give the musicians a break! Obviously he knew how important it was to call a time-out every now and then—keeping the musicians on your side was one of the first rules he learned from Phil Spector—but here he was, going way past midnight, and he hadn't called the first rest. Finally, from the back of the string section, he heard a woman say, "Hey, how about a fucking break here!" The room went silent. Then they all cracked up. The voice belonged to Eleanor Slatkin, a small but tough woman and a fantastic cello player, speaking up for the rest of the men and women in the room. Again, laughter defused the situation, and after the break, the recording was completed.

Barbra was a perfectionist, and the whole process had been as exacting as a ballet, performed by and for some of the greatest artists in the world, with Barbra as the prima ballerina and Tommy in the role of choreographer. In the end, the collaboration had been perfectly balanced.

However, a few weeks later, Tommy called Barbra to say he wanted to remix the one song that Marty Paich had done—the hit "The Way We Were"—so it would sound more like the rest of album, and she agreed. The original session tapes for the song were sent over from RCA studios, where they had been recorded, but they arrived with no accompanying logs to tell Tommy and Al what was on the various tracks and which parts of which vocal performances had been used. It took hours to pull everything apart and put it back together.

A month after the album came out, Tommy got a call from Barbra. She had noticed that there were a few spots in the vocal on the album that weren't exactly the same as those she had chosen for the single, and she was upset. It turned out she had an uncanny ability to remember every note of every performance she had ever sung—total musical recall when it came to her own work—and of course there was nothing that could be done about it. To this day, if you listen to the version on the album, there are differences in the vocal performance compared to that of the single; "The Way We Were" isn't the way it was.

As he started to make money, Tommy began collecting art seriously. At first, his interest had been casual: he bought some things by local artists just to put on his walls. Then, while on a trip to New York, again with Bob Krasnow, they happened to walk into a gallery on Madison Avenue, and that's where Tommy saw the work of an artist named Louis Lozowick, one of the premier precisionist artists of the 1920s. His paintings could look like photographs. As they perused the gallery, one piece in particular struck Tommy, not just for its execution but for its subject matter: It was a picture of the Merck pharmaceutical plant, the originators of commercial cocaine.

That print, regardless of what originally piqued his interest in it, got his visual juices flowing; he couldn't get over the masterful execution—it was an aerial view of the plant—and the more he looked at it the more he loved it. He bought it for $500, and by the time he got it home, he had forgotten all about the original reason it had caught his attention and had fallen in love with the artist's vision, technique, and emotional message.

In the gallery, he had also picked up a copy of *Artforum* magazine. One day Gill was looking through it and saw a color reproduction of another painting by Lozowick, a semiabstract painting of New York City, with the skyscrapers and the elevated trains intermingled in the image. Tommy liked it and called the gallery and asked how much the painting was. He was told $3,500. In 1974 that was a lot of money, much more than he had ever paid for anything except maybe a car, and when he hesitated, the gallery owner said he would send it out on approval. When it arrived, Tommy fell in love with it too.

"I had never seen anything quite like the way the artist had painted the trains and the skyscrapers to make them look like they passed through one another," says Tommy. "The way it expressed the motion and intensity of New York through different layers and planes of reality. I called the dealer and was able to work out a payment schedule: five hundred down, and a thousand a month for three months. Just like that the painting was ours.

"That picture completely changed the way I looked at art, and I discovered how a great work of art could move you. I suddenly saw, qualitatively, something that made me look beyond the surface of a picture. It was as if a window opened on a world I never knew was there.

"The longer this picture was in my presence, the more I loved it, and of course I started looking to buy another. The dealer was happy to send them to me on approval, and some months later I found another one that I liked, and bought it. Then I started searching out galleries in LA that handled American art."

One day, reading the *LA Times*, he saw an ad for American modernist art; it mentioned some names that sounded familiar to him from books he was reading, so he called the number and went to meet the man who placed the ad. He was a retired dry cleaner from

New Rochelle, New York, who had moved to LA and was buying and selling pictures out of his home in his retirement. This chance meeting started Tommy's interest in American modernism, at a time when the work was still affordable, and it became his passion.

"I started going over to his house where he had pictures everywhere, on the floor, on the walls, and over a period of a few months, I bought several things from him. Soon he was telling me about books to read and I started discovering the artists and finding out about the stories behind their paintings.

"The next thing you know, every time I went to New York I started going to galleries and finding these pictures on my own." The real breakthrough for Tommy came when he bought the Marsden Hartley painting *Aztec Legend* in 1974. "Suddenly," says Tommy, "everything that wasn't worthy cowered before this picture." Today one would have to pay $5 million for this Hartley. At the time, Tommy was able to buy it for $35,000. Again, it took him a year to pay it off, at three grand a month.

"I don't know where the attraction to art came from," Tommy says. "The music is kind of obvious; it was part of my birth. But when it came to art, I never even looked at a picture until I was already in my mid-thirties, when I saw a particular painting and thought, 'Gee, I would like to have that in my living room.' But then it became a passion, which is the reason that I suddenly got a knack for it, or perhaps I had a knack for it and that's why it became a passion. Either way, I have often been as passionate about art as I am about music."

Why American modernists? Perhaps because it was an alternative dialect of an idiom he already understood intimately. "Most of these American artists had spent the first part of the century, before the war broke out, in Paris and were influenced by the European modernists like Matisse, Braque, and Picasso," says Tommy. "They had also been influenced by the impressionists and postimpressionists like Van Gogh and Gauguin. But all of them, Europeans and

Americans, were influenced by Cézanne, particularly his late paintings, in which he started breaking up the picture plane into cubist compartments. Within their visual simplicity, they were highly complicated. A famous American modernist once said 'Matisse isn't the problem, Cézanne is,' by which he meant someone had created a new path, and now the problem was to build on this within his own style. It was no different than Charlie Parker and Dizzy Gillespie having been nurtured on Coleman Hawkins, Ben Webster, and Lester Young, and then taking that style to bebop.

"There are many interesting parallels between painting and music," Tommy says. "A great artist has a style to the way he paints. Even if you know nothing about pictures, you'll know a Picasso, a Matisse, or anyone who has a distinct style. The same is true with music. The first thing you recognize is an artist's *voice*. And whether you are painting a picture or arranging for an orchestra, you have to think about volume and shades of color. The great Russian modernist painter Wassily Kandinsky referred to his paintings as 'music for the eyes,' and thought of them as 'improvisations' and 'compositions.' He believed that all forms of art were equally capable of reaching a level of spirituality and he also believed that music was a key to the birth of abstract art."

A month after the demise of Blue Thumb Records, Tommy got a call from Lenny Waronker at Warner Bros. offering him an A&R position. The timing couldn't have been better. Tommy had pulled his production chops together at Blue Thumb, and Warners was the kind of place where they could be put to good use. It would be the first time that Tommy worked for a major company, with all the resources and funding that went along with it. If he had a hit, they could sell twice what a label like Blue Thumb could sell. He had gone from Liberty to A&M to Blue Thumb, all second or third tier companies, so going to Warners would be a big change. Plus Warners was a company that really trusted their A&R department. The invitation from Lenny opened a road in front of Tommy that he would travel with great success for many years.

Not long after Tommy joined Warners, label president Mo Ostin called him into his office and asked him his opinion about hiring Bob Krasnow to head up a new black music division. Mo knew that Krasnow's Wild West operating style had cost him Blue Thumb, but Krasnow was acknowledged to be a savant when it came to black music, and Warner Bros. desperately needed to do something to counter its lily-white West Coast image; they weren't being competitive in the urban market, and Krasnow had his ear to the street, his deep connections in the business, and the credibility of having once worked as a promotion man for soul singer James Brown. In fact, back in the day, when he was pushing records for the King label, Krasnow once opened his briefcase and showed Tommy a loaded .38 pistol, a stack of James Brown 45s, and a pile of cash, and said, "This is my office."

When Mo asked, Tommy said, "He's great at what he does but just remember one thing; while you're sleeping, he's thinking." In other words, Krasnow could be trusted to be Krasnow. Bob was offered the job, took it, and over the years brought to Warners acts like Chaka Khan and Parliament Funkadelic, increasing the company's urban profile and bottom line by many factors.

When Tommy and Bob joined Warner Bros., the company was in a state of transition, physically as well as conceptually; not only was Warners looking to branch out into black music (disco was raging through the airwaves and nightclubs), but the company was also moving into new offices. At first, A&R was shoehorned into an old building on the Warner Bros. film lot and it was all pretty knockabout, but within the year, they had built a new structure and the A&R department was a self-contained unit on the bottom floor.

Warner's A&R was basically Lenny Waronker, Russ Titelman, Ted Templeman, and Tommy, with support staff. This small group of talented producers would produce literally dozens of million-selling records. But what really made Warners special was its president, Mo Ostin. During the sixties, the initial era of corporate take-overs and consolidations, Warner Bros. Records had been owned by Seven Arts, but in 1969, Steve Ross's company, the Kinney Corporation, bought Seven Arts and renamed it Warner Communications. When Steve made the deal, he also got Reprise Records and its president, Mo Ostin, in the package. Mo joined Joe Smith, who was already acting president at Warners, and it became "the Joe and Mo show," and Warner Bros. Records was off and running, with Joe as the comic and *bon vivant* and Mo as the brains of the operation.

Mo had great confidence in Lenny Waronker, his first A&R man. One of Lenny's early signings had been Arlo Guthrie, who had a modest hit with "Alice's Restaurant," but what was more important to Warners' growth was that Arlo connected the company to a lot of great musicians. That's how Warners got Maria Muldaur, for example. These musicians in turn connected Warners to their friends and associates, and so Mo was inclined to give the A&R department a lot of discretion in building this extended family.

Another person who hadn't sold many records at the time but who became a major asset to the company was Randy Newman; other musicians all respected him and wanted to be on the same label he was on. But the big breakthrough at Warner Bros. was Joni Mitchell. She was a magnet for important talent, like Neil Young, who followed her over. So Warners was building its artist roster from the inside out, not just trying to cut hits and then disposing of the talent, which is how many other companies operated.

Aside from artists' recommendations, the best way for record companies to find new talent during the sixties and seventies, when the business was expanding like a supernova, was from the lawyers that represented the artists. It could be like one-stop shopping.

Record companies would look up a lawyer's client roster and see who they had. And then when they got a relationship going with that lawyer, he or she would be inclined to take their next great act to Warners. It was a people business, and Mo Ostin was a people person.

He also knew what he didn't know. "It's so important for both producers and executives to know what their strengths are but also what their weaknesses are," says Tommy. "A lot of people walk into these big jobs and think, 'Well there's a hit record, and I like *that*. So if I like *this* other record, it's going to be a hit too.' People just assume that they know what a hit record is. But often, when you hear a song in its infancy, it doesn't sound much like the final product; maybe the rhythm isn't developed or the harmony hasn't been fleshed out. But that's the whole point; you need to recognize a hit from the song's *potential*. And that's the job of a producer. Anybody can hear a hit record when it's finished."

Lastly, Mo understood how important the artist's career was to the whole picture. During the seventies, Warners would stay with an artist for three, four, five albums if they believed in them, without any return; Warner Bros. was one of the first companies to have an "Artist's Development" department. Two guys, Bob Regehr and Carl Scott, ran that shop and made a big contribution to the success of the label because they weren't just putting out records, they were actively building careers.

There was a big difference between this operating climate and that of other companies. For example, at Columbia, which was very much from the old school, employees would have to be there at 10 a.m. and go to meetings. "At Warners we'd have an A&R meeting once a week with everybody coming together and talking," says Tommy. "Other than that, nobody ever told you what time to come in, or that you even *had to* come in. You made your own fate and you were either going to sink or swim based on your ears. If there was pressure in the job, it came from yourself, because you knew you had to deliver. But it was very conducive to creative things happening.

"There was so much more emphasis on the person back then," recalls Tommy. "Not necessarily whether this person was going to deliver hits, but was this person in tune with what was happening."

Not long after he arrived at Warner Bros., Tommy went out to dinner with Lenny to discuss his future at the company. He was feeling there was something missing in his work flow, and that something was jazz: He wanted to start using his jazz background more because it was such an essential part of who he was and where he came from.

"I had been brought up on pop music," Tommy recalls, "and the blues and R&B of course, but when I started playing saxophone, I became a complete jazz nut, and that never left me. And then when I became a promotion man I found myself back in love with pop music, but the jazz thing was always there. Jazz is at the core of how I hear music, so I had this sense that I needed to utilize my love for jazz in the productions I was doing."

At the same time, he was hearing the records that Creed Taylor was producing for his company CTI, which were basically jazz records based on pop songs with jazz artists. Creed had a huge hit with Wes Montgomery on "California Dreaming," and he also had a hit for Grover Washington on the Marvin Gaye song "What's Going On." Tommy had been a fan of Creed's records going back to Ray Charles's *Genius + Soul = Jazz* on Impulse. So this was on his mind when he sat down with Lenny.

Tommy started right in, telling Lenny that he needed to use more jazz elements in the artists he worked with. That he was drawn to them. "I told him," said Tommy, "'It's who I am.' But I don't think I was really able to translate to Lenny where I was going with this.

Lenny basically told me he didn't think Mo would go for it. But from that moment on I started thinking of ways to incorporate my love for jazz into my productions."

And then he found Michael Franks. Somebody had given Tommy a record Michael made for a fragrance company that had ambitions of entering the record business. It wasn't a great record but the material was unique and Michael's delivery had both jazz and pop elements. It seemed like a natural.

They got together at Tommy's house; Michael played guitar and sang him some of the songs that would become iconic a year later, "Popsicle Toes" and "Monkey See Monkey Do." "Talking to him," says Tommy, "I discovered that he was deep into his inner world. Like the title of the album we made said, he was devoted to *The Art of Tea*. And he was going with a woman who was also very interested in psychedelics. It was kind of a small, intimate situation and it wasn't going to be a large deal, it wouldn't cost Warners a lot of money, so I just went ahead and signed him."

Not all jazz musicians understand the simplicity of pop music, and many pop musicians—maybe most pop musicians—do not understand the nuance of jazz. Choosing the musicians for the Michael Franks project was an important first step for Tommy, and he was fortunate that he had known and worked with the members of The Crusaders, pioneers when it came to playing groove jazz, sophisticated music that often had the simple, focused aura of pop music.

"As far as I'm concerned," says Tommy, "it's all about the rhythm section, regardless of what genre of music you're recording: if you pick the right rhythm section you'll come out with a decent record." For *The Art of Tea*, there was Joe Sample on piano along with Wilton Felder on bass and Larry Carlton on guitar, all three members of the

Crusaders, a solid, experienced rhythm section. Tommy brought in John Guerin to play drums, another master at refining a jazz concept into a simple groove. (John was married to Joni Mitchell at the time; in fact, it was John who introduced her to jazz, which spun her work into a new direction.) So again, what Tommy called "casting" a record became of primary importance. The sound and emotional feel was established before they even went into the studio.

When *The Art of Tea* was released, it took a month or two to get noticed, but finally the song "Popsicle Toes" broke out of Philadelphia, and within six months Warners had sold more than two hundred thousand copies; in the end, the album went gold. After that, nobody at Warner Bros. talked to Tommy about wanting to combine jazz and pop anymore. "Whatever I had mentioned to Lenny about wanting to go in my own direction was never brought up to me again," says Tommy. Suddenly, the feeling around Warner Bros. was "Maybe LiPuma is on to something." And that's when Bob Krasnow walked in with George Benson.

People often ask what is record production; what does a record producer actually do. It's a fair question because it's not always obvious and every producer has their own style. The short definition is that a producer does everything that needs to be done, from the beginning to the end, to make the record a success. Every time is different but every time is the same; you keep living with the voice of the artist in your head, fashioning and refashioning the music that you chose, until finally your musical vision is realized. The devil, as they say, is in the details. Then, if you're fortunate, it ends up reaching an audience. The George Benson album *Breezin'* is a good example of what Tommy would go through again and again as a producer.

It began when George was still on CTI and, on one of his trips to San Francisco, Tommy caught one of his sets at a jazz club there. When he heard George sing "Summertime" it blew him away: "I had never heard him sing before," says Tommy, "and I never forgot it." The next time the name George Benson came up was when Krasnow called him to say, "Man, I have an act that was made for you: if you want George Benson, I can get him on Warner Bros." They set up a meeting.

George showed up at Warners with his manager and the first thing Tommy asked was why George didn't sing on his records. The manager was silent, but George said, "Because Creed Taylor wants to make me the next Wes Montgomery." Wes Montgomery did not sing. Tommy said, "Well, if we find the right thing for you, we have to do a vocal." Years later, long after the record they made together had become a huge hit, George told him that was the reason he decided to put his fate in Tommy's hands—because the first thing Tommy had said to him was "Why don't you sing more?"

They made the deal and got busy picking tunes. Tommy remembered a song from the Gábor Szabó session back in the Blue Thumb days, a catchy thing called "Breezin'." It was written by the guitar player Bobby Womack—another Cleveland guy (who had actually gone to the same barber's college as Tommy before he, too, escaped into the music business). It was a really simple tune, but it stuck with you long after you heard it.

Another song that stuck with Tommy was "This Masquerade," written by Leon Russell. "After Blue Thumb ended," says Tommy, "Leon went with EMI and made an album called *Carney* which is where the song came from. When I first heard it on that record, it didn't really jump out at me because he sang it through a graphic equalizer to make it sound like he was talking on the telephone. I just didn't realize how strong the melody was. But right around the time I was picking songs for George, somebody sent me a demo tape of a young saxophone player—turned out to be David Sanborn—and the song on the demo was Leon Russell's 'This Masquerade.' When I heard David's version, I said, 'Yeah, this saxophone player is great, and we'll definitely sign him, but this song—I know this song from somewhere.' When I heard Sanborn's version, I really *heard* it, like for the first time."

When they started rehearsals for George's record, Tommy brought in a couple of musicians from New York who had been touring with George, Ronnie Foster on keyboards and Jorge Dalto on piano, and also Ralph McDonald to play percussion. He filled out the band with several LA players, including the drummer Harvey Mason and Phil Upchurch on rhythm guitar.

But when they cut "Breezin'" he wanted Bobby Womack to play rhythm guitar because it was his tune. At the time, Bobby had a bad cocaine habit and was pretty messed up. The first day they started recording, his wife came in and said, "Oh Bobby's gonna be here any time." In fact, he didn't show up for another thirty-six hours.

In the meantime, they kept going with other tunes. They were just about to record "This Masquerade" as an instrumental and were listening to the original version by Leon Russell when George started singing along with it. It sounded absolutely great as a vocal, so, at the last minute, Tommy sent Phil Upchurch's wife over to Tower Records to buy a copy of the album. She came back to the studio and copied out the lyrics, and that's how the song wound up on the record as a vocal and became a number one hit single.

When something just falls into place naturally it always seems inevitable in retrospect. They ran the song down once or twice and then decided to try a take. "The version you hear on the record," says Tommy, "is that take. There was only one take. And we were in the middle of recording it, and it was obvious that it was a magical moment—you could just tell that everybody was blown away—and out of nowhere, just as we got to the top of the fade, the door to the studio opens up and in walks Bobby Womack. He just walked right into the studio, unannounced, with all the mics live and the tape rolling. I started making these frantic signs for him to be quiet and thank God he saw me. His wife had fallen asleep on the studio couch so he tiptoed over and sat down next to her. And that was it; we got the take. It was really an extraordinary moment to be in the room when that happened."

Next, since Bobby was there, they decided to record "Breezin'." Bobby was still pretty messed up, and since he didn't know any of these New York musicians, he was nervous. Ralph McDonald, the percussionist, was sitting behind the drum kit—he was not really a drummer, he was just fooling around—and Bobby, probably thinking this guy was going to play drums on his tune, began to get anxious. He was saying, "Hey, drummer man. You gonna have to do a lot better than that." The situation became tense. The real problem was that Bobby was dissembling to keep the attention off his own physical condition. "He sounded terrible," says Tommy. "Like he had rubber bands on his guitar instead of strings. Totally out of tune. It was an enormous comedown after the magic moment of 'This Masquerade.'"

They got through a take of "Breezin'," and Bobby was so messed up he just left. The first thing Tommy did was wipe his guitar off the track. But even though his playing was unusable, Bobby had managed to come up with one of the musical hooks that really made the song work. Tommy went to work repairing the track. "If the drums are right," Tommy says, "you can always find a way to make it work; if the drums aren't happening there is no way to repair a track. Fortunately, Harvey Mason was the drummer and he played great."

"I told Phil Upchurch I wanted him to replace Bobby's guitar parts but that I wanted him to keep the great hook Bobby had come up with and really hang it out there. I also wanted to replace the bass part, and fortunately Phil Upchurch is one of the great bass players of all time. He listened to the track and first he replayed the bass and included Bobby's guitar hook in the bass track. After we got the bass, Phil got out his guitar and doubled the bass part on the low string to reinforce it. It just gave the part a little more weight. And then Phil, being the studio master that he is, said, 'I got an idea,' and he played that answer hook you hear on the record that really makes the track happen. And that was it; it was perfect."

In the end, there were six cuts on the album, and five of them were first takes. The rhythm tracks for the album were finished in just three days. In the world of multitrack pop records, that is virtually unheard of. But when Tommy got the rough mixes home, he knew he had something very special.

"A record has a life of its own," says Tommy. "You don't always come up with everything in one fell swoop. One night I was sitting in my studio at home listening to the tracks and in my head I kept hearing strings. I knew I wanted to put strings on the album, but the question was who to use to do the arrangements. There were several people that came to mind, including, of course, Nick DeCaro, but for some reason I thought of Claus Ogerman."

Claus, a brilliant German arranger, and Tommy had been friends since Tommy was a song plugger in New York and Claus had an office in the Brill Building. Claus had done string arrangements for a lot of pop music, from "It's My Party" by Lesley Gore to the outrageously romantic charts on the Antonio Carlos Jobim album *The Composer Plays*; but the work he had done with pianist Bill Evans (*Bill Evans with Strings*) was something Tommy held in the highest regard. Claus never got in the way of the main attraction. "He would write these unison string lines that sat behind the voice or the instrument and always added a sensual mood," says Tommy. With Claus, what sounded simple—his voicings, the way he inverted chords— was marvelously sophisticated.

He called Claus in New York and pitched him on doing string arrangements for the George Benson album. Claus told him he was leaving for Munich in a few days, and Tommy said, "How about if Al Schmitt and I come to Munich?" Within a month Al and Tommy were on a plane to Germany to record the string charts with the Munich Philharmonic.

Munich in 1976 still felt like an old storybook town. Looking out the window of the Four Seasons hotel the night they arrived, Tommy saw the little trolleys go by and it felt like the twenties or thirties. "That first night," Tommy remembers, "Claus took us to a famous beer hall that went back to the era of Bach and Wagner, where the waitresses were all these portly women with rosy cheeks wearing lacy flowered dresses. Claus told us that if the patrons got rowdy, these women had a special technique where they would grab you by the ear and march you right out the front door."

The next day, a free day in the schedule, Tommy and Al decided to fly to Paris for the day. It was a lark—they heard some music and ate some great food—and the following day they returned to start recording. Claus picked them up at the airport and took them directly to the studio. It looked great. It was one of those fabulous old rooms from the thirties, and they were using the Munich Philharmonic Orchestra, so what could possibly go wrong?

"The place was fantastic; wonderful high ceilings and the greatest collection of microphones you have ever seen," says Tommy. The Germans pioneered the development of recording microphones prized around the world, like the Neuman U 47 and U 69 models, and the place was stocked. Tommy and Al were looking around the room and Tommy happened to look over at the tape machine and noticed the speed control said "7 ½ and 15ips" (inches per second). This got his attention: "I had told Claus before we left the States that we were recording this project at 30ips," which means the machine has to run at twice the normal speed because, even though you use more tape, the fidelity can be a lot better. "I told Claus, 'Make sure that you got it set up for 30ips,' but either he didn't know what I was talking about or he forgot, because when I looked at the machine, I knew immediately we had a big problem."

It turned out this classic old studio didn't have a single 30ips machine. Tommy and Al had traveled five thousand miles and were expecting an orchestra in a couple of hours and there was no machine that could play the tapes they brought with them. The engineers started calling the factory to see if they could switch out the motor in the machine while Claus got on the phone and started calling around for alternatives. At one point, he said, "There's someone I know here in town, Giorgio Moroder. He's got a studio. Let's go see if you think it would work."

They got to Moroder's place and it was clear that there wasn't really enough room for a symphony orchestra. Moroder was making electronic dance hits for Donna Summer at the time, and since he mostly used synthesizers instead of live instruments, he didn't need a very big space. But he had a machine that ran at 30ips. Al Schmitt, knowing they were running out of time, said he would make it work. He got busy trying to figure out how to pack forty musicians into a space for ten. In the end, he literally had musicians sitting on top of each other.

And then, of course Moroder didn't have forty sets of earphones—he rarely had more than four musicians in the studio at one time—so there was no way for everybody to hear the playback. They tried setting up two little monitor speakers in the room but there was too much leakage—there were more than thirty live mics in the room. "I was really starting to sweat," says Tommy. "It looked like after coming all this way, there was no way to record."

In a moment of frustration, Claus said, "Forget it. Just give me a set of earphones and I'll conduct." This meant that only Claus would hear the music; the string players would be "flying blind." And that's how they ultimately did it: the orchestra playing the charts without hearing a single note of the music they were accompanying while

Claus conducted them. It was masterful all around, like an aerial ballet.

But by the time they had it all figured out—where to place the musicians, how to conduct the session—they had run out of studio time. It was eleven o'clock at night and they still had one more song to do. But the musicians had been on the clock for more than twelve hours and they were worn out. Tommy tried to arrange to come back the next day, but the studio was already booked.

Warners had an office in London, and Tommy had the home number of somebody who worked there, so even though it was around ten o'clock on Saturday in London, he got the name of a "fixer"—that's what they called music contractors in England—and said, "We need a full orchestra tomorrow and we'll fly in on the redeye tonight from Munich." The fixer said no problem. Tommy couldn't believe it. The only thing, said the fixer, and it might be a small problem, was that not all of the "A" players would be available. At times, if you don't get the "A" players, you could be in real trouble, especially when it comes to reading rhythm notation, because not all classical string players know how to swing.

The next day, at ten in the morning, Al, Claus, and Tommy arrived at a beautiful studio in central London; the string players turned out to be wonderful musicians, and in half an hour they were finished recording.

The next day they were on the plane home, flying back to the States with several large reels of tape. They were carrying them by hand—they weren't letting those tapes out of their sight. A single roll of two-inch tape weighs approximately ten pounds and they were each carrying two rolls. When they finally got the precious cargo stowed in the overhead compartment and settled into their seats for a drink, the captain came on the speaker and said, "Welcome aboard. And by the way, the flight to Boston was canceled so in order to accommodate the Boston passengers, we're going to stop there first and then go on to LA." Eight hours later, when they got to Boston, they discovered their flight to LA required changing planes and now they had to take a connecting flight through Chicago. More schlepping of tapes through the Boston airport. In Chicago, they had to change terminals; again, still more schlepping of tapes. It was turning into a physical marathon.

Then they discovered they would have to make another stop before landing in LA, this time in St. Louis. By now, reality had morphed into a kind of dream mission, not unlike *The Lord of the Rings*, in which two mortals had to deal with odds and forces of mythological proportion. Jet lag was taking over. Finally, they got back up in the air, had another drink and, just as they were about to land in LA, well into the second day of their adventure, the captain got on the PA and said, "I've got good news and bad news. The bad news is that the fog is so thick we can't land in LA. The good news is that we're *all going to Las Vegas!*" And so they did.

They landed in Las Vegas at one in the morning, still carrying four heavy boxes of tapes.

Their next flight was supposed to leave in the morning from the same gate, gate 20, so they checked the tapes in to a locker and checked themselves in to a hotel to get a few hours of sleep. At the hotel, the crew from the flight was in line right in front of them and the pilot told Tommy, "You know, it was a funny thing, the next flight after us landed with no problem because when we tried to land, we blew all the fog away."

Tommy and Al went to sleep, but they were so destroyed by the adventure that they missed their wakeup call—or perhaps it never came. In any case, they had missed their flight, and the next flight to LA was leaving from gate 10; more running through the airport with tape boxes, "and I'm thinking," says Tommy, "that if we would have waited for the plane that left London the next day, we would have gotten home sooner."

And people want to know what a producer does.

After the whole experience, London, Paris, everything, the total cost of that album in 1976 was $52,000. Today it would cost ten times that much. Of course, in the end it didn't matter; George Benson's *Breezin'* sold more than eight million copies.

It was helped by the fact that when the single of "This Masquerade" was released, a station in San Francisco started getting calls for "the new Stevie Wonder record." The reason, says Tommy, "was that George Benson is a kind of musical chameleon; he can sound like Nat Cole or like B. B. King or whoever he wants to sound like, and at the time, he was being influenced by Stevie." When the station in San Francisco played the record, both the station and Tower Records were inundated with people asking for the new Stevie Wonder single. Within two weeks the song was Top Ten across the country and wound up number one on every chart: pop, R&B and jazz.

Having a hit record like *Breezin'* made it possible for Tommy to relax a little. In fact, he relaxed a lot; for the next couple of years he spent more time collecting art than working in the studio. The years of trying to prove himself were over; a hit the size of *Breezin'* changed every part of the equation. All the tension he had been carrying around inside, after his years of struggle in Cleveland and the trials of hustling in LA and New York, finally let go and he returned to appreciating the human side of the music; life was no longer strictly about capturing or manufacturing tracks, he could now—even in the face of his enormous financial success—go back to a more innocent time of simply loving the music. It started when Claus Ogerman introduced him to Antonio Carlos Jobim and João Gilberto.

Claus was living in Munich six months a year and in New York the other six, and every time he was in the city, he and Tommy would get together. Warners had a great brownstone on Fifty-second Street, with their offices on the second and third floors right above a nice little restaurant. So "going to work" meant hanging out in a great space with great friends.

"A couple of times, Claus brought Jobim by the office," says Tommy, "and we wound up hanging out all night. And to hang out with Jobim and Claus was really a mind-bending event for me. They were intellectuals and they were interested in such a wide range of topics, they would cover everything from politics and art to music and history. I'd sit there in awe, with no sense of time passing."

One night, Claus and Tommy were doing a string date and Jobim came down to watch. After the session, they left the studio together and got as far as the bar on the corner. They started drinking and talking and wound up staying there until five in the morning. The bartender kept the place open just for them. "I remember looking out the window as the sun was coming up," says Tommy. "It was an amazing feeling. Transformational. Like time was suspended. We went out into this pale dawn and made our way to this twenty-four-hour restaurant on Fifty-first and Park called the Brasserie and continued to hang there.

"And a couple of other times, Jobim invited us over to his apartment at Eighty-fifth and Fifth. We'd buy a couple of bottles of scotch on the way and that was it. He would tell stories all night long. It was a lesson in learning to take life as it came, to live it at its own pace."

Inevitably, Tommy signed Jobim to Warners, and they did an album called *Urubu*, the Brazilian word for "vulture." It turned out the vulture would become a key image in Tommy's experience with Jobim and Brazil. These vultures hung out in the mountains near Corcovado, home to a lot of great Brazilian music. At the time there was a military government in Brazil that was despised by the people, and Jobim wrote the song "Urubu" as a reference to the government as vultures because they were feeding off the Brazilian population. But he did it cleverly and carefully so that they couldn't bust him for it.

Tommy was about to do another record with Michael Franks, and since Franks was also a big fan of Jobim, they decided to go to Brazil and do some of the recording there. Neither one of them had any idea what that entailed, but Tommy had gotten to know the great Brazilian drummer João Palma, and he also knew João Donato, a piano player who had been on Blue Thumb, so he called Palma and told him to set up the session, that he wanted Palma to play drums and Donato to play piano, and then Al Schmitt, Michael, and Tommy all flew down to Rio.

Tommy's vision of Brazil came from records like "The Girl from Ipanema," so he was expecting nothing but beautiful beaches, beautiful women, and beautiful weather, the whole scene languid and elegant. But when they landed in Rio at six-thirty in the morning, they jumped into a car to the city and ran smack into morning rush hour traffic. It was bumper to bumper for miles. Tommy's first discovery about Brazil was that they mixed sugar in their gasoline—apparently because they had a lot more sugarcane than oil—and so there was a sickly sweet smell in the air. "We were stuck in traffic for an hour," says Tommy, "and it could have been Secaucus, New Jersey."

They checked in to their hotel to find their suite was a luxury alcove directly above Copacabana Boulevard and the traffic sounded like it was in their living room; it ran day and night. In 1977, a dollar went further in Rio than practically anywhere else in the world, and the place was jumping with people doing black market deals around every corner; even the bellman offered a better exchange rate than you could get at the front desk.

Palma had arranged to pick them up at one-thirty the day they arrived, so they all took a brief nap and went downstairs at one-thirty to meet him. And they waited. They waited for over an hour and still no Palma. Tommy couldn't reach him on the phone, and then it started to dawn on him that he "was not in Kansas anymore. I was gradually getting the first faint glimmer of the thought 'What have I gotten myself into?' And then I realized, 'Hey wait a minute; this is Brazil.' So instead of getting uptight, I started to relax." He and Al went back upstairs and took another nap. They just got into the rhythm of life in Brazil.

Palma showed up around four and they all piled into his car and went to meet Jobim in Leblon, a hip area of Rio where Jobim lived. They met up at a small restaurant there and had a lunch that lasted until eight o'clock that night. Jobim was just getting started. He suggested they all go to the steam baths; at midnight, they were still at the baths, drinking quart bottles of beer and eating sticks of grilled beef. Day one.

Day two, Palma picked them up around one; he had Donato with him and they drove straight to another great little restaurant. It didn't look like it was open, but Palma went inside to talk to the owner. He came back and said the place was theirs: When the owner heard that João Donato was part of the party, he unlocked the doors. Donato had just made a new record, which he brought in to play for everybody and when he put it on the house system suddenly there was a party in progress: great music playing and all the waiters dancing as they served the food. "Everybody was moving," says Tommy. "Even the cooks. I never experienced anything like it. We were eating and the place was grooving.

"At one point a song came on that had an absolutely haunting chorus. It had this heavy, infectious bossa nova beat but the melody was from somewhere else. Absolutely hypnotic. I couldn't get it out of my head. I asked João about it and he said he had gone into the jungles to a *macumba* ceremony where the music was designed to promote trance. That's where he heard the melody and he used it as the chorus of his song." Good food, good friends, good music, trance: transformative.

The party then moved to the house of a friend of Palma's who was serving *feijoada*, the Brazilian version of French cassoulet (a peasant dish made with leftover pieces of sausage, chicken, and duck mixed with beans and cooked in a rich fat stock.) There they ate and drank and talked for hours more.

Day three, Jobim took everybody to an Argentinean steak place where they kept bringing you small pieces of sliced meat until you couldn't eat any more. Finally the jet lag caught up with Al Schmitt and Michael Franks and they both went back to the hotel. But Tommy and Jobim kept going long into the night. "I have no idea how much more we drank or when we left this joint," says Tommy, "but at one point I finally said to Jobim, 'Look I have to get back to the hotel.' We were going to be recording the next day. So Jobim offered to drive me back.

"We got into his car and it was pretty clear we were both totally juiced, and we were driving down Copacabana Boulevard, he was talking to me and every so often he looked at the road. He was kind of going from one side to the other, and then he went through a traffic light, and the next thing you know, there's a flashing red light behind us. At the time, Brazil had a military government, and my first thought was they were going to lock us up and throw away the keys. People were being 'disappeared' down there regularly.

"Antonio pulled over and the cop walked up to the car. The cop was so big that I couldn't even see his face in the window. Jobim rolled the window down and started speaking to him in Portuguese. After a few minutes the cop walked back to his car and I said to Jobim, 'Man, that was close.' But Antonio just smiled and rolled his window back up and the next thing I knew, the cop had pulled around in front of us and was giving us a police escort back to the hotel. After they dropped me off, the cop took Jobim back to his house. Turns out Jobim was so revered in Rio that they eventually named the airport after him: Antonio Carlos Jobim International Airport."

Day four, finally time to do some recording. In the early evening, everybody met at the studio. It was a small, casually thrown together room, more like a musician's rehearsal space than a full-blown recording studio. For example, they had only three reels of tape in the whole place, which meant if they recorded at 30ips, they could get only about fifteen minutes of music per reel. Normally Tommy would do two or three takes of each song—recording four or five songs could conceivably take up to ten reels—but they got around the tape shortage by listening to everything they did as soon as they did it, choosing the best take, removing it from the reel, and then recording the next song over the remaining tape. This made the three rolls go a long way, but it also meant they were recording master takes over tape edits, something that would never be done in the United States. And since the studio was wired in such a way that you couldn't listen to playback in stereo, they were never really sure what they had on tape. Clearly the lesson being given was to live life as it came and turn problems into opportunities.

The best example occurred in the song "Bwana He No Home," which featured João Donato on piano. In the middle of the take, the sustain pedal started to fall off the piano. But João didn't stop playing and he didn't miss a lick: When he got to the piano solo portion of the song, he was trying to figure out how to get the effect of a working sustain pedal by hitting a note, holding it down, and then going on to another note. It created a brilliant, original-sounding solo, and they kept the take as a master.

Around midnight, the manager of the studio came in to say he was going home, but not to worry, his assistant would stay around. Then, about an hour later, the assistant came in to say that he was going home too and not to worry, they could just lock up when they were done. At two o'clock, they took the three reels of tape they had used and closed the door behind them.

Day five, they were scheduled to leave Rio, and Warners had arranged a car to drive them to the airport; the plan was to go up to Corcovado on the way to the airport because, Palma said, there was a great hotel there where they could have lunch. Around noon, a guy wearing blackout shades and driving a black 1965 Chevrolet with tinted windows pulled up to the hotel. On the rear windshield of the car were two circular decals: one was a skull and crossbones, and the other one was a black panther's head, mouth open, fangs exposed. Tommy and the others jumped into the car and went to pick up Palma. When Palma saw the car and driver, he went white; when Tommy asked him what was wrong, João said, "Ixnay! Ixnay!"

Halfway up to Corcovado, the driver pulled over for the view— Tommy was hoping to see some of the *urubu*, the vultures that Jobim had written about—and when they got out of the car, João said to Tommy, "Man, where did you get this driver? He's a fucking killer!" It turned out the panther decal identified him as part of the Brazilian paramilitary, exactly the kind of bad guy Jobim had written his song about. A vulture was their driver!

When they got back into the car, Tommy, with Joao translating, casually asked the driver, "Say, do you know where we can find any of the vultures we heard about?" The driver said, "No, you don't want to see them. They're filthy, disgusting animals, and that isn't the Brazil we want you to see." He kept talking about how wonderful the country was and how the government took such great care of its people. It was as if Jobim's song had come to life.

It reminded Tommy, as he was getting out of town, that earlier in the week, when they had all been sitting around Palma's friend's place, an animated cartoon had come on the television depicting children dressed in different ways, one in a business suit, another like a native with a band around his head, the others decked out as various types of people, happily dancing around in a circle. It was an advertisement promoting the government's policies and suggesting that all Brazilians were happy. Palma's friend watched it with bitterness and then turned to Tommy and said, "Look at what these sons of bitches show us. They treat us like we're children. This is what they think that we are. Like we can't see what they're really doing."

The last record Tommy produced for Warner Bros. before he quit working there the first time, was for the pianist Bill Evans. "It was a very moving experience for me," recalls Tommy, "his playing was very special and some of the records he made—like *Conversations* and *Bill Evans with Strings*—were among the most beautiful jazz records ever made. He redefined the art of the jazz trio, and he influenced virtually every other jazz musician, including Miles Davis, who could not have made *Kind of Blue* without Bill's help." Another reason the project was special for Tommy was that it was clear Bill was not well. He had been a heroin addict for some time, and when Tommy met him, even though he said he was clean, it was clear he was not.

Bill had made several recordings for CBS prior to signing with Warner Bros., and both he and his manager, Helen Keane, had been disappointed in how he had been treated there. They said that Clive Davis, the president of CBS, had "fallen out of love" with Bill and was no longer taking his phone calls. In fact, they were not wrong: CBS had started moving away from jazz, even as Warners was starting to have real success with it. Tommy had negotiated large production and marketing budgets with Helen so that Bill would finally have, for the first time, a shot at wider acceptance.

To that end, Tommy was thinking about getting Johnny Mandel involved to do the string arrangements. His work was hip and very commercial. In fact, his theme song for the film *M*A*S*H* had become something of a hit. When they spoke, Johnny was very cordial and candid; he said he was going through some problems and had just started attending AA, and he said, "To tell you the truth, Tommy, I just have no ideas right now. I'm like a blank slate."

Tommy had already suggested to Bill that they record the theme song from *M*A*S*H*. It was called "Suicide Is Painless." But what Tommy didn't know was that Bill had just divorced his wife, who had been straight when she met Bill but then had become an addict because of him. When Bill left her to go with a much younger woman, she found out about it and killed herself, leaving behind a letter blaming Bill for ruining her life.

"I didn't know any of this when I played that song for him," says Tommy. "It was just a pretty song to me. When I found out later, I was speechless."

Two years later, Tommy ran into Bill at the Vanguard in New York and could see how frail he was. Bill died a couple of months later.

Keith, Andrew, and Charlie visit Tom looking for tunes for the Rolling Stones.

With the Sandpipers.

With the O'Jays.

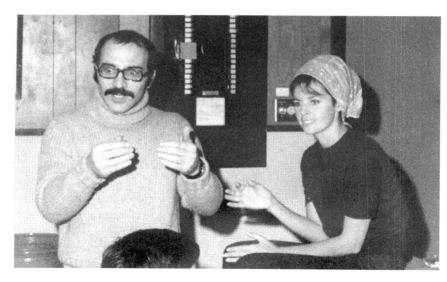

With Claudine Longet.

Tom doing a percussion overdub back in the day.

With distribution executive Sal Iannucci (l) and
Bob Krasnow (r) admiring the new Dave Mason spin disc.

Clowning with Al Schmitt in the studio.

With Dan Hicks.

With Michael Franks.

Track Six:

The Blue Horizon

In 1978, Herb Alpert and Jerry Moss persuaded Tommy to return to A&M and offered him his own record label, Horizon Records. If he could deliver one album as big as the George Benson record, he would be fabulously compensated. There was nothing wrong with his situation at Warner Bros., but he wasn't even a vice president there, just an A&R man, and going from A&R man to the presidency of his own label was a very attractive proposition. "In hindsight," says Tommy, "I can see how Herb and Jerry appealed to my ego, and I guess maybe I let my ego get away from me a little bit."

His first day back at A&M, as he was about to leave his house for the office, the phone rang. It was a William Morris agent calling to pitch a tape. Word had spread fast; Tommy had his own label and was looking for talent. Tommy told the agent he would stop by and pick up the tape on his way to the office.

"Bobby Dale was staying with me," remembers Tommy. "I had hired him as a consultant, so he went with me to this guy's place. The guy plays me this thing, whatever it was, and I wasn't crazy about it. I was about to leave and I asked if he had anything else I could listen to. He said, 'Well, as a matter of fact, I got this tape of this girl. Maybe you'd be interested in listening to it?' I said sure, let me hear it.

"He put on this ridiculously great song by a girl playing guitar and singing, with a voice that was just stunning. Dale and I looked at each other like, 'What is this?' It turned out it was Rickie Lee Jones's demo tape and she was singing everything that would eventually be on her first album: 'Chuck E's in Love,' 'China White,' 'The Moon Is Made of Gold.' I said, 'Could you set up a meeting with *her*?'"

Two days later, this guy walks into Tommy's office with a young girl with dirty blond hair and a black eye. It was Rickie Lee; she had gotten into a fight with her boyfriend, Tom Waits, and he had knocked her out cold. The whole side of her face was swollen and she could barely talk. "I sat back and checked her out," Tommy says. "She looked like she had walked right out of a Charles Bukowski book. But it comes with the territory, and her tape was great, so I pushed on."

Tommy said, "This tape is just great and the songs are great," and Rickie Lee said something that sounded to him like "Arrrrgh." "And that's when," he says, "I realized she was a junkie and she was completely junked out." He told her he wanted to sign her, and that's when he also discovered that the guy who had brought her in didn't actually represent her.

It took about a month for her to lose the black eye and the swollen jaw, and during this period, she came by the office a few times and she and Tommy sat together and talked about the recording they would do, the musicians to use and the timing of the project. During this period, Tommy introduced her to Mac Rebennack and they quickly became an item. Everything was feeling cozy and it looked like Rickie Lee would be his first signing for Horizon. A brilliant start.

Then one day, kind of offhand, she said, "I'm doing this showcase thing at the Troubadour tonight." Tommy, surprised, said "Great. I'll be there." When he got to the Troubadour, Tommy discovered that Columbia had given Rickie Lee the money to put the band together for the showcase—she had never mentioned to him that Columbia was in the picture—and as soon as he walked in and saw Lenny Waronker he knew that Warner Bros. was in the mix too. He and Lenny were still great friends but they both knew this was going to be war.

Rickie Lee came onstage wearing a glittering black dress, a cheap white fox stole wrapped around her neck, and a red beret, and she just killed it. "She was absolutely great," says Tommy. "The next day, Warners started getting real aggressive, pushing to make the deal with her. Her lawyer knew that I had been there first and I believe he really wanted to make it work for me, but a deal is a deal and I had a problem."

Tommy's problem was that Jerry Moss, the financial boss of A&M, wouldn't match Warners' offer. Jerry had a rule at the time that he wouldn't pay a new act a royalty greater than 10 percent on 90 percent of the records sold. This was called "ten on ninety," and it was pretty standard in the record business at the time. The missing 10 percent was called a "packaging deduction," and nobody in the business was ever able to explain why this clause was still in the contract, because it originally came from the time when 78 rpm records were made and often broke in shipping. Obviously, this was no longer true with LPs, and it was pretty obvious that it was just a way for record companies to shave points in their own favor. Rickie's lawyer was not having it. Warners agreed to waive it but Jerry Moss wouldn't budge.

"Probably the biggest mistake I ever made in my professional career," says Tommy, "was not telling Jerry Moss about the gig at the Troubadour and not insisting that he come along with me. I begged him to reconsider. I told him this girl was the real deal and I wanted to sign her, but he said, 'Hey man, this is what I do. The Carpenters started at ten on ninety.' Well, maybe they did, but the day after 'We've Only Just Begun' was a hit, that deal changed real quick."

To this day, Tommy believes that if Jerry had only seen her that night, his whole experience at Horizon—and his entire career path—would have gone a different way. But Warners won, and Tommy, in his own words, "just went nuts. I couldn't believe I had lost this chick. It was like the gold ring had slipped out of my fingers. Of course, her first record came out on Warner Bros. and boom! It was huge."

So the first thing that happened at Horizon was what *didn't* happen: Tommy *didn't* get to sign Rickie Lee Jones. And an artist like that doesn't come around every day or every year. That set the tone for the whole Horizon experience.

"Looking back, I know we did some nice things at Horizon," says Tommy. "The first record I made for them was called *Jungle Fever* by Neil Larsen. It was all original material with Buzzy Feiten playing guitar and he was on fire. I remember Herb called me and said 'This is really a great record,' but nothing happened with it. Maybe I was a little early with this jazz/pop thing; it didn't really sound like what was on the radio at the time."

Next he signed Mac Rebennack. He had seen Mac in Scorsese's film *The Last Waltz* and knew he wanted do something with him; now he reached out and it was as though they had never left each other. Mac had been writing with Doc Pomus, so the first album they did together on Horizon, called *City Lights*, was all Mac and Doc Pomus songs. But again, there wasn't anything that put the album over the top. Tommy was starting to tread water.

Next, he signed a band called Seawind, which was the hottest band in LA at the time. They were all great players—particularly Jerry Hay, the trumpet player, who went on to do arrangements for Quincy Jones and Michael Jackson—but their songwriting was lackluster. The problem here was that the drummer and his wife, who fronted the band, were born-again Christians, and the rest of the band didn't want to hear about it, so it was already a group on its way to splitting up. Again, nothing happened with the album.

Tommy actually had a bit of a hit record in Japan with Ryuichi Sakamoto's Yellow Magic Orchestra, but he was never able to get paid for it. He had gone to Tokyo on a business trip, and the last night he was there, somebody played him the record. "It blew me away," says Tommy. "I said, 'I'll put it out.' We put the thing out in the States and nothing happened with it. But in Japan it was like the Beatles."

When A&M pulled the plug on Horizon Records, it was simply down to the money, caused in part by a coincidental shift in the record business. A&M had been with independent distributors since the beginning, and independent distribution had become very precarious; it was difficult to get paid. Unbeknownst to Tommy, Jerry Moss had decided to leave the independents and to switch to RCA distribution. He literally changed horses in midstream a week after Tommy arrived at Horizon.

Feeling guilty about leaving all these independent distributors high and dry, Jerry gave them all a thirty-day return policy. That meant the distributors had thirty days to return everything they had ever bought from A&M for a full refund. "Well," Tommy says, "these guys started going around to Pick 'n' Saves everywhere and buying A&M product for twenty-five cents and then selling it back to Jerry at full value. They made a killing and Jerry had to eat forty million dollars in returns. It almost buried him and the company."

So on the one hand, a transition in the distribution situation hastened Horizon's demise. But there was more to it than that. "To be candid," says Tommy, "I thought too big too soon. I shouldn't have had more than an office and a secretary, but instead I hired Al Schmitt; I hired Bobby Dale; I had an assistant, Noel; and I had Freddy Mancuso doing promotion. So I had a big overhead, and of course I was doing what I always did, taking people out to dinner and taking trips. A lot of money was going out the door and nothing was coming in. And in the end, I didn't deliver a hit record. It's that simple. I spent about two million dollars with no hits to show for it."

And there was something else. "I have to be completely honest about this," Tommy says. "The failure of Horizon had something to do with the whole drug culture. I can remember one day walking into Freddy's office and he was talking to this disc jockey on the phone, and as he was talking he casually opened up his desk drawer and there was a china plate just piled with blow. He was taking hits like it was nothing, and pitching this guy, and I knew the whole thing was out of hand."

Maybe they called it blow because it blew so many people away. But by the end of the seventies, everybody on the A&M lot was referring to Horizon Records as NASA because they thought everybody up there was so spaced out. The whole experience was a wakeup call for Tommy. Although he continued to enjoy his smoke and a great bottle of wine, "when I left Horizon," he says, "I just stopped using drugs."

Track Seven:

Makin' Whoopee

In 1980, after Horizon's demise, Tommy went back to Warner Bros. with the title of vice president in charge of jazz. "I was very fortunate," he remembers, "that they were interested in having me come back with no recriminations or hard feelings about my having taken the year off to take a shot at A&M." At one time, the record business was like a big family where a person had a history, not just a bunch of numbers attached to his name.

The first thing he did when he got back to Warners was make a record for the singer Randy Crawford. The album turned out great but sold only a few hundred thousand copies in the States, not the big hit her previous single, "Street Life," had been for The Crusaders on Universal. Next he did a project with the group Yellow Jackets and also an album with the singer Brenda Russell, both really nice records but nothing much saleswise.

Once again, Tommy was starting to feel a little stale, like he was falling back into a rut. What he needed was a new challenge in his life. "I started to get the sensation that maybe my life was too easy for me," Tommy remembers. Maybe too much sunshine, not enough weather; he started to think seriously about moving back to New York.

In the summer of 1981, Tommy went to Montreux, Switzerland, to record Al Jarreau, Randy Crawford, David Sanborn, and the Yellow Jackets at the Montreux Jazz Festival. He arranged with his brothers Joe and Henry to meet him there. The plan was that after the festival, they would all take a train to Rome and then fly to Sicily to visit the town of Alimena, a family pilgrimage to the town of their father's birth.

The recording went well and the next day they jumped on the train from Montreux to Rome. When they got to Rome they bunked with some distant cousins, getting into the spirit of the adventure, ate a big reunion dinner, and got a good night's sleep. The next day, they flew to Palermo and met another distant cousin, Anthony Gerraci, and the four of them got in a rented Mercedes and left for Alimena.

This was a key moment for them all, a return to the scene of the crime, literally: the place where their grandfather had been murdered on the side of the path and where their family had lived in dire straits before their escape to America. It figured deeply in their personal histories, and there was a lot of anticipation in the car as they set off to drive the forty or so miles to the little town on the hill.

Joe was driving, Anthony was sitting in the front seat next to him, and Henry and Tommy were in the back. As they got closer, Anthony pointed up the hill to show Joe where Alimena was, and, Tommy remembers, "The next thing you know, I heard Joe say, 'Oh shit!' and then there was the most sickening crash." And then everything went quiet. Joe had run head-on into another car—driven, it turned out, by yet another distant cousin of theirs. They all wound up in an artichoke field, steam coming out of the rented Mercedes.

Tommy had hit his head on the roof of the car and slammed his bad hip on the armrest and found himself wandering around the field in a daze. His cousin Anthony walked up to him with blood running down his face and asked him, in Italian, "Excuse me, can you tell me what's going on here?" Henry, who had also hit his head on the roof, was standing in the field, probably concussed, looking into the distance. All of them were in shock. But Joe was in serious trouble.

Joe was pinned in the front seat of the crumpled Mercedes, moaning in pain. A passing car had stopped and some people were working frantically to pull him out of the wreck. They finally freed Joe from the car, and without any discussion this group of strangers piled him into their car and sped away with him. Not a word to the rest of the party. Five minutes later, another car pulled up and volunteered to take Henry, Anthony, and Tommy to the hospital. It was pandemonium. According to Tommy, they drove to a small town, where "The doctor looked like Zorba the Greek, an unshaven guy with a cigarette hanging out of his mouth. The first thing he wanted to do was give me an injection of some kind, but when he pulled out what looked like a used needle and a bloody cotton ball, I said 'No thanks' and walked out. But I was still in a daze."

Turns out Joe wasn't there. It took a while, but when they finally discovered where Joe had been taken, they all piled into an ambulance and drove to Palermo with lights flashing. The hospital in Palermo wasn't much better then the rural one; it was just bigger.

"The whole thing was turning into a Fellini movie," says Tommy. "In Palermo they wanted to take an X-ray of me with this machine that looked like it came out of Mel Brooks's *Young Frankenstein*. I refused. I went into the hallway and there was some guy laying on a gurney; he looked like he'd just had brain surgery, with a scar running down his whole head. Sitting on a bench opposite him was an old couple eating bread and cheese and drinking wine from a pint bottle. They were just kind of taking the whole scene in.

"At one point, I was standing by the entrance to the building watching a guy who I can only describe as the village idiot talking to himself, when an ambulance sped up. Two guys got out and started arguing about who was going to open the rear door. It was like a circus act."

They finally opened the door and there was Joe. The people who had driven off with him had gotten two kilometers down the road and then they had run out of gas and had to be rescued themselves. Tommy says he looked around him and thought, "That's why they lost the war."

The next day, Joe, who had a fractured hip, was released from the hospital and transferred to a suite in the Villa Igia Hotel, an old luxury residence where, by coincidence, Joe's hero Lucky Luciano had spent his final days after being deported from America. The circle was closing. For a few days, Joe was laid up in bed, giving orders to everyone. Tommy was making phone calls back to the States, trying to arrange for relief and release. In the midst of this angst, several cousins from Alimena arrived with the one who had been driving the car that Joe ran into. He was badly banged up and he wanted to know who was going to take care of *his* expenses.

Next an argument broke out, which veered into a discussion about some unfinished family business wherein Tommy's father's aunt had left some money in a hidden bank account and the cousins suspected that maybe Tommy, Henry, and Joe knew something about the missing account. It made no sense, but since Joe was the only one who could understand the cousins (only he spoke the local dialect), it was literally two days of miscommunication.

In the midst of this chaos, it was revealed that cousin Anthony, the passenger in Joe's rented car, had been transporting $25,000 in cash when the crash occurred and in his dazed condition he had forgotten that he had stashed the money in the glove compartment of the Mercedes. The money was never seen again.

The following day, Tommy got on the first plane back to the

United States. Henry stayed behind to look after Joe. "My brothers are totally opposite," says Tommy. "One measured his socks in the drawer to make sure they were lined up nice and even, and the other one was like a Damon Runyon version of Al Capone. When they finally returned to Cleveland, Henry said to me, 'I don't ever want to see him again . . . for a while.'"

In the end, the prodigal sons never did get to visit their ancestral home in Alimena. They got close—they could see it on a distant hill—but they were unable to walk the ancestral donkey path to the family mine.

On the other hand, when the album Tommy recorded at Montreux, *Casino Lights,* came out, it did very good business in the US and Europe.

New York was the center of both the world of jazz and the world of art, and by 1984, Tommy was using a lot of New York musicians on his records and getting very deep into the New York art scene. By this time, he had purchased so many paintings that he didn't have room on the walls to hang them; art works were now stacked up on the floor of his house in Westwood, beautiful paintings that you couldn't even see. Every time he went to New York, he would take a morning to check out paintings and he never came back empty-handed.

"I had developed such a passion for collecting that it was taking up a lot of my time," says Tommy. "The music was always there for me, but the art was like meeting a great new chick when you're a young man; it was seductive and all-consuming. I was being pulled into this fantastic world of American modernism. One day I woke up and turned to Gill and said, 'I think we should move to New York.' I certainly didn't have to convince her: she's a dyed-in-the wool New Yorker and her bags were already packed."

"I went to Mo Ostin and told him I thought I would be happier on the East Coast and he said, 'Go ahead, we have a New York office.' Two of our key guys, Bob Regehr and Russ Titelman, had already moved to New York, so there was no opposition at all." In June of that year, he sold his home in LA and moved to New York City.

For the next six months Tommy became totally absorbed in the world of art. He'd start every morning at the Salander-O'Reilly gallery, where he would hang with the owner, Larry Salander, and talk paintings and painters. "I'd get there about ten-thirty or eleven and stay until one or two; it was an education that money couldn't buy," says Tommy.

At the same time, however, even though he did a couple of okay recordings, one with Patti Austin and one with the group Aztec Camera, he was basically "just dilly-dallying" around in the studio (his phrase).

"One morning, I was on the phone with Mo Ostin," recalls Tommy, "and we were talking about someone who I thought wasn't doing that much, and out of the blue Mo said, 'Well, I haven't gotten that much from you either.' And that got my attention because he was right. I wasn't really doing much of anything. Was I a record producer or did I want to go deeper into the world of art? I started to really focus on this question, and then, not long after that phone call, I got the idea to do an album with Bob James and David Sanborn. Musically, it was a natural, and it was before all those duet concept albums hit the market, so it had a good story."

The term "smooth jazz" hadn't come into fashion yet, but the pianist Bob James was already getting the reputation for being kind of "soft"; he had had some big hits with Creed Taylor and several other poppy, radio-friendly things on Columbia that were definitely working against his credibility as a jazz player. But they were making him very popular, and he was still a lovely piano player and a creative arranger. So Tommy suggested to David that he do a duet album with Bob.

David didn't like the idea at all. "He was afraid he would be tagged as a 'smooth jazz' musician," Tommy says. Like a lot of guys who grew up wanting to be beboppers, David suffered from an internal conflict. On the one hand, he wanted to be a straight-up jazz player, but on the other hand, he liked the money and everything else that went along with making pop records. He liked being a star and all the trimmings, but he also wanted to be looked on by musicians as an artist. So he was more or less against the idea of a duet album with Bob James, on principle.

"I don't know how, but I convinced him to do the project. But all through the process he let me know he wasn't happy with it, like he was doing it against his better judgment. So the weight of getting this record done was entirely on me."

Tommy wanted to include one vocal, and his idea was to have Al Jarreau sing the classic "Since I Fell for You." "I could hear him sing it," says Tommy, "and David could kill the solo and Bob could do some beautiful orchestrations on synth. Both David and Al were managed by Pat Rains, which made my job easier. But when Bob James's manager, a guy named Peter Paul—never trust a guy with two first names—heard that two of Pat's artists were involved, he led Bob to believe that the project was turning into a Pat Rains production and that Bob was getting pushed to the side." Bob started pushing back. "I could tell," says Tommy, "because the afternoon we started running the song down, Bob said to me, 'Well, this is not my thing,' and he made it clear that he felt the whole thing was beneath him."

With David and Bob at odds, Tommy pressed ahead with the ballad. Eventually they got a great take of the song and it was obvious to everybody that it could be something big. "Gradually," says Tommy,

"Bob started coming around, but there was still some residual weirdness there."

"When it came time to mix the record," Tommy says, "both David and Bob were in the control room. Basically they each wanted to hear more of himself. Bob was saying, 'I wanna hear more piano,' David was saying, 'I need to hear more saxophone,' and the mix was sounding awful, no coherence, all performance. Finally I said to both of them, 'Look, guys. You have to do me a favor here. You have to leave the room and let us come up with a balance. There's too much input here. It's all piano and saxophone.' They left for an hour and we got it together. It sounded great. I called them back in the room and they got it. But they were both still wary."

The record came out on a Tuesday, and the following Saturday, Tommy got a call from Sanborn. He was calling from an airport and he was furious. He said, "Man, I fucking told you this was gonna happen. I just picked up a copy of *People* magazine and the record got a horrible review." Tommy heard him out and then gave him Krasnow's line: "David. Calm down. Tomorrow they're going to wrap fish in it."

The record wound up selling two and a half million copies, and that was the last time he heard from either David or Bob about *Double Vision*.

The first time Tommy met Miles Davis was at the jazz festival in Montreux, Switzerland, in July 1986.

Tommy had flown over to see him because Lenny Waronker had received a phone call from Miles's lawyer saying Miles was thinking of leaving Columbia. He was tired of playing second chair to the new trumpet star on the label, Wynton Marsalis.

"I had never heard anything but horrible stories about how hard it was to work with Miles," says Tommy. "My first thought was that I wasn't sure I wanted to do it. But how can you turn down Miles Davis? And when I walked into Miles's dressing room in Montreux he was very cordial and after we had a nice chat I told him, 'Hey, man, I'm going to split after the show, but when you're back in New York let's get together.' I relied on the business affairs people to deal with the details and I went about planning how to make a Miles Davis record that could bring him back into the greater popular consciousness. He had more or less been missing since his so-called hiatus in the late 1970s."

This was around the time that Miles had begun sketching, seriously, not just to amuse himself but with an eye on the extension of his own artistic expression. Everywhere he went he carried a pad and pens with him. When he walked into Tommy's apartment a few weeks later and saw all the art on the walls, even though he was wearing dark shades, he went straight to a painting by Maurer and said, "Man, who is this cat?" Art was the icebreaker.

Then they sat down and started listening to music. Says Tommy, "I played him a Scritti Politti thing and he liked where I was going. We talked about how the recording might go down and I mentioned that I had been working with Marcus Miller and I was thinking of having him involved and his response was, 'Yeah I love Marcus.' This was when drum machines were just starting to arrive on the scene and Marcus was one of the few cats who really knew how to program them so they didn't sound mechanical.

"Miles kept looking at all this art and listening to this music I was playing him, and just as we were leaving, he finally took his glasses off and put them up on his forehead. He had the blackest eyes you can imagine: pitch black. When he looked at you, it felt like he was staring straight through you. He grabbed me by both shoulders and he looked me right in the eye. He didn't say a thing but I understood: he was saying, 'Yeah. Alright. Let's do this.' I passed his test." It was the first day of a friendship that lasted until the day Miles died.

A few weeks later Tommy took a trip to LA and went to Miles's house in Malibu. "He was making chicken when I got there," Tommy remembers. "He was a good cook. In fact, he was a great cook. After lunch he said, 'Let's take a ride.' At the time, he was really into horses, and he said he wanted to go see this horse at a stable somewhere down the road.

"He had this great yellow Maserati in the garage so we got in his car and started driving. All I can say is I never laughed so much as I did with this cat that day. He really was one of the funniest guys I ever met in my life. There were times, later on, when I was on the phone with him where tears would be running down my cheeks. And maybe that's the reason we became really tight. I got his humor and he knew I got his humor.

"When we got to the stables we were talking to some woman there and some way or other Miles mentioned that he had stopped using drugs and alcohol recently, and when she said, 'Oh, my daughter was going through a problem like that, and since I'm a nurse I was able to get her all these drugs,' without missing a beat Miles said, 'Well, can you still cop?' The man was funny."

A little later, Tommy went to a rehearsal with Miles and his band. When he walked into the room, the guitarist Mike Stern was playing a solo. "He was playing about two hundred notes a minute," says Tommy. "Personally, I hate that kind of playing. To me, it's got to be melodic. When they finished the tune, Miles just walked up to Mike, put his hand on his shoulder, and said, 'Man, I'm gonna send you to Notes Anonymous.'

"Over the years, I tried to record some of my phone calls with Miles," Tommy remembers, "just to have a record of his humor, but it didn't work out. I had this suction cup device that you're supposed to put on the phone, and I tried to use it a couple of times, but it kept falling off and I never did get anything."

The morning of the first recording session for Miles's album, Marcus walked in with a drum machine, set it on the desk, connected it to the console, and played down this thing he had programmed. "I don't know how he did it," says Tommy, "but somehow he made this drum machine feel like it was swinging." Normally drum machines felt like what they were, machines—too perfect in their subdivision of time—but this program had a kind of triplet feel that made it feel more human. First they put the drum pattern down on tape and then Marcus went in and did his bass part. After that he did a couple of keyboard parts. And what emerged was the track for "Tutu."

The next day, Miles came in and played on top of it. After three or four takes Miles said that was it and packed up his horn. "I didn't realize how ill he was at the time," says Tommy. "He was exhausted after an hour. I said, 'That's cool, Miles,' and he split. We listened to all the different takes we had and started to build a complete melody and solo. When we finished I had a cassette made and went for a ride in my car. I drove from Vine Street all the way to the beach and back to my hotel in Hollywood just listening to this one performance over and over because I couldn't believe how great it was. He was all over the horn with total confidence."

Tommy called Miles the next morning and said, "Man do you have any idea what we got here?" Miles said, "Man, I'm so tired," and he canceled the session for later that day. But before he hung up he told Tommy something Tommy would never forget. Talking about what he had played, Miles told Tommy, "Man, it's just the blues. Everything emanates from the blues." From that point on, Tommy just kept saying to himself, "I can't believe this is happening." He was hearing Miles, one of his heroes, playing like he hadn't played in years, deep into the blues.

Tutu is the only record Tommy produced that relied on a drum machine. "My feeling," says Tommy, "is that when these new toys come out, everybody starts using them on everything, and it becomes a fashion statement instead of a tool; knowing *when* to use it and more importantly when *not* to use it is the key. At the time, a lot of hit songs were based on rhythm patterns coming out of the way these machines could be programmed. I like things to breathe, and drum machines don't usually sound like they're breathing."

But Miles didn't mind playing to the drum machine. He was able to groove with it. "With Miles," says Tommy, "there was no gray area. He either felt comfortable or he didn't. He didn't grow into things. Everything with this guy was right at the moment. His heart was on his sleeve. Nothing about him was premeditated. This was one of the things about being around him that I loved; he *was* the way he played."

Stories about Miles being in the present tense and without pretense are manifold. Tommy remembers one night when Benny Medina joined him and Miles for dinner—Benny was a young black kid who grew up in Beverly Hills (in fact the television series *The Fresh Prince of Bel-Air,* was based on his personal story)—and when Benny graduated from high school, Mo Ostin gave him a job at Warners as a favor to his father. When Tommy was doing *Tutu,* Benny wanted to meet Miles, so Tommy invited him along.

"The first mistake Benny made," remembers Tommy, "was getting too familiar. And then a couple of times he interrupted Miles while he was talking. Miles would stop and not say anything. But finally, Miles was in the middle of saying something and Benny jumped in and Miles just stopped and looked at him with those deep black eyes. The whole table just went quiet. He looked at Benny and said very calmly, 'Man. Shut. The. Fuck. Up.' I just cracked up."

The last time Tommy saw Miles was when Miles was in the hospital, not long before he died. "He called me up and said, 'Tommy, I got something I want to play for you.' I went to see him and he was in this bed with all kinds of stuff around him, tapes and drawing materials. He put in this cassette of something he had been working on. When it was over, I said, 'Yeah, Miles, that's nice. I think maybe you could—' and he interrupted me right there. He said, 'I don't want to know what you think about it. I just wanted to play it for you.'"

"I really miss the man," says Tommy. "There was absolutely nobody like him."

One day, Tommy discovered a record by Dr. John called *Dr. John Plays Mac Rebennack* and it was simply Mac playing solo piano. "Now as long as I had known him," says Tommy, "since '66, I never knew he was into jazz standards. But this album included a Duke Ellington tune, and when I heard it, I got the idea to do a whole album of standards with Dr. John." He pitched Mac the idea to do something "with that old Quincy Jones, Ray Charles, *Genius + Soul* feeling." Maybe even get Ralph Burns to do the arrangements. Mac loved it.

Shortly thereafter, Tommy was in a meeting in LA. "At Warner Bros., there was always a lunch meeting on Monday in the conference room. All the VPs would get together around a full deli from some place in Burbank, and Mo would go around the table and say to whoever was there, 'What's going on?' And depending on whether they were in sales or promo, he'd get their spiel. This time, when he got to me, I was excited about this project with Mac, so I said, 'Well, I'm going make this standards album with Dr. John.' Now all the time that I had been with Mo, I had never seen him second-guess anybody in his A&R department. Except once, and this was it. He said, 'Oh yeah? What label is it gonna be on?'"

But Tommy just laughed it off and went ahead and made the

record, called *In a Sentimental Mood*, with Mac. It was one of the first "standards albums," before a lot of pop artists (like Rod Stewart and Linda Ronstadt) went down that road, and Mac's record turned out to be very successful, in large part thanks to a duet Tommy arranged with Mac and Rickie Lee Jones.

"I knew that there was something special about Mac and Rickie together," says Tommy, "which must have been why I thought of introducing them in the first place. But I didn't think to put them together on tape until years later." So finally, after all the hassles of trying to sign Rickie to Horizon, of losing the label, it all came home for him. Tommy had Mac and Rickie record "Makin' Whoopee," and it turned out to be a huge hit. It was done in one take, with a lot of it improvised talk between the two of them. It was a natural. And it won a Grammy.

"Mac is similar to Miles," says Tommy, "in that they are both totally unique, spontaneous cats. Mac even has his own vocabulary, kind of like malapropisms, but more organic. Like when you had to get your parking ticket validated, he would say, "Where do I get this thing violated?" Or talking about a car accident he once got into, he called it 'an unavoidable collusion.'" Mac always had a little magic going on, some mystery that Tommy liked to leave alone.

Once, in New York, he had Mac staying in a suite at the Sherry-Netherland, and when he went to pick him up, he found candles and incense burning on every surface in the suite. "It might have been a voodoo thing, or maybe he just liked a lot candles and smoke. I don't know. Either way, I never asked him."

Making the records with Mac, Tommy discovered that there wasn't an area or a genre of R&B, bebop, or pop music that Mac Rebennack didn't know. It reaffirmed the belief that, like Miles said, the blues is the mother tongue—all the rest is commentary.

Track Eight:

Mourning Becomes Elektra

"I'm still friends with Mo Ostin," says Tommy, "but there was a moment when our friendship was really tested."

It was in May 1990, and Tommy's contract with Warners was up for renewal; he had been there seventeen years, minus the brief period at Horizon, and he felt that Mo needed to show him a sign of good faith, and show it to him with money.

"When it comes to business," says Tommy, "Mo Ostin is one of the toughest guys around. So I thought long and hard about the best way to approach the subject. I went to the girl who was the controller at Warners—she and I went back a long way, back to when we both worked at Liberty Records—and I asked her, 'Do me a favor. I'm having a meeting with Mo. Could you go back to 1974 and tell me how many records I've sold since I've been here?'"

A week later, there was a stack of computer printouts on his desk. The bottom line: Up to that point, Tommy's productions had sold more than 35 million records. He took the stack of papers into Mo's office, put it down on Mo's desk, and said, "Mo, I'm not here to negotiate; I've got my lawyer to do that. I'm just coming to you one-on-one and I want you to keep this in mind when you get down to the hardcore end of making the deal. Bottom line is thirty-five million records. Here it is in black and white. Put that in your mind." And he left.

The following evening, Tommy was back in New York having dinner with Bob Krasnow. Bob had also moved back to the city and was now the president of Elektra Records. Just before dinner, Tommy got a call from his lawyer, who said, "Are you sitting down? I just got off the phone with Mo and he's offered to give you a ten-thousand-dollar raise." Tommy says he hung up the phone, furious. "I thought, 'You got to be kidding me.' A ten-thousand-dollar raise! So I called Lenny and read him the riot act."

After he hung up the phone, Krasnow called to find out where they were having dinner. All Tommy said was "Hello," and Bob said, "Man, you sound terrible," and Tommy said, "Bob, I'm so pissed off at Mo right now if I had a place to go, I'd be gone." Bob said, "You got a place to go."

Right then and there, Krasnow offered to pay Tommy's lawyer's plane fare to come to New York and negotiate a contract. In the end, Tommy received twice the salary and an additional point to his royalties. For Tommy, this was a no-brainer; that single point would be worth a lot of money on any hit record.

Tommy called Lenny and told him he was leaving Warners. Lenny flipped out and phone calls started flying coast to coast. Finally Mo called. Mo was very close to Steve Ross, who owned both Warners and Elektra, and Tommy had the feeling that Mo was using this relationship with Steve as a lever. Mo said, "I can't allow this to happen," like he was going to call Steve and stop the deal. So Tommy said, "You can't allow this? Is this the plantation? Lincoln freed the slaves. My deal is up in May." Mo said, "Well, you can't do this." Tommy said, "Mo, if you screw this up for me you're going to have one mighty unhappy chappie on your hands."

A few hours after he hung up the phone he decided perhaps he had been disrespectful and booked a flight to LA for the next day. When he landed he went straight to Mo's house. Tommy started by saying, "Look, this is an emotional thing," but it turned out that Mo's wife, Evelyn, had already talked Mo through it and he and Tommy ended up hugging. The following week he started working at Elektra.

The record industry took a nasty turn at the end of the twentieth century. The decline started in the late 1980s with video games and gangsta rap and unwound in the 1990s with Napster and the big corporate fish finally swallowing most of the smaller corporate fish. Lots of these fish weren't even swimming in the same ocean: Instead of record men running the business, many record companies were now being run by men from businesses that had nothing to do with music, like waste management. By the end of the century, virtually all the old familiar record industry faces were either gone or emeritus, and few were in charge.

Even Steve Ross, whose Kinney Corporation owned Warners, was having financial problems—Warners had purchased Atari, the video game company that turned into a total disaster and brought Warners' stock down from $70 to $12. So in 1985, Ross asked his friend Hugh Carey, the governor of New York, if he knew somebody with the financial expertise to help him sort it all out. Carey recommended Bob Morgado. Ross brought in Morgado, and after Morgado helped straighten out the Atari mess, as payback, Ross gave him the position of running the entire entertainment division of Warner Bros. The man had absolutely no prior experience in the entertainment business, a sign that from now on, it was all about numbers and money, not music.

Before Morgado took over, David Horowitz, had been the president of Warners Entertainment, and he was the one who had made Bob Krasnow the head of Elektra Records. It was probably the best thing he could have done for the label: Bob was a record man from his head down to his socks. Over the next few years, as president of Elektra, Krasnow's signings contributed many millions of dollars to the company's bottom line.

When Tommy arrived at the company in June 1990, he had one brief conversation with Morgado. Morgado asked him, "Hey, what happened between you and Mo?" Tommy told him the story, and Morgado said, "Well, Mo wants you to come back to Warners, at the salary that you're getting now at Elektra, but he wants Krasnow to pay for it." Tommy said to him, "Look, I don't know you that well, but one, Krasnow is not gonna pay for it, and two, it's done. I'm one of those guys, when I make my mind up, that's it. Next case."

In 1991, when Tommy delivered the Natalie Cole record *Unforgettable,* it was a smash hit, and Mo finally said to Tommy, "I have to admit you guys really did something great here." "He's not afraid to admit when he's wrong," says Tommy, "and he understands the human aspect of this business. It's not all about the numbers. There's a chemistry to it. And one of the things that made the Natalie Cole record possible was the camaraderie between myself and Bob Krasnow. We had that chemistry. And I never heard from Morgado again."

"All I knew about Natalie Cole," says Tommy, "was that she had a couple of hits on Capitol. I was a huge fan of her father, but there was nothing that said I should listen to her. But then one day, back when MTV was in full force, I saw a video she had done of the Bruce Springsteen song 'Pink Cadillac' and I liked the whole vibe; she sang the song like she owned it, and she looked great in the video. A couple of weeks later, by coincidence, Krasnow called me and said, 'I just got a call from Natalie Cole's manager; what do you think, should we take a meeting?'" They set up the meeting for two weeks later.

"I always like to come into these meetings with a point of view," Tommy says, "and this time, I was thinking that Natalie couldn't have grown up in that house without knowing how to sing standards. I got the idea that it would be great if she did an album of her father's songs. I told Krasnow the idea and he said, 'That sounds great.'"

The day of the meeting, Krasnow was in the hospital—he was in a recovery suite after a hip operation—so they ended up having the meeting there; Bob was in a wheelchair with his leg up, but everybody just took it in stride, so to speak. Natalie showed up with her manager and Bob opened by saying, "Tommy has this idea of doing your father's songs and I think it's really a great idea," and she said, "I've been wanting to do something like this for a long time and Capitol thought it was a bad idea. But you know, I don't want to do it for the first album. I'd rather do something else first and then maybe do it for the second album."

Tommy jumped in. "Natalie, I just want to leave you with this. An idea is like a virus. And once it's in the air, somebody's going to do it, and the last thing you want is somebody like Johnny Mathis to have the same idea and do a Nat Cole album. Whether it's your father or not, after somebody does it, then it's old." By the end of the meeting, he had convinced her.

They went through the Nat King Cole songbook and picked out their favorite things and came up with two dozen songs, so Tommy decided to do a double album. He couldn't produce the whole thing himself, so he started thinking about other producers to pick up the slack. Natalie had done some work with David Foster, and at the time, her husband, André Fischer, wanted to be a producer, so they split it three ways, each doing eight songs.

Natalie happened to mention that she had been ending her live shows with a duet with her father. She had gone to Capitol Records and found the master of the song "Unforgettable," which Nat had recorded on a three-track machine; they had the rhythm section on one track, the orchestra on another, and Nat's vocal on the third. Natalie had Capitol remove the parts of her father's voice she wanted to sing herself and ended her show trading verses and singing harmony with her father. It was such a natural idea that Tommy decided to end the album that way too.

When it came time to do the song, he transferred the three-track master to a fresh multitrack tape and had the drummer play a crossstick click, just to nail down the rhythm. "We started our version with just Nat's voice and this click track," says Tommy. "Al Schmitt managed to equalize Nat's voice so it didn't sound so old-timey. Then we removed his voice from the spots where he wasn't going to sing, brought in a new rhythm section and orchestra, and recut the whole song on top of the old voice."

The record ended up selling fifteen million copies—it was number one for several weeks and won five Grammys. It was a phenomenon that no one could have predicted, but it just goes to show that a good idea is indeed like a virus, and when its time has come, look out!

Over the years, Tommy produced many albums because he felt they needed to be made, regardless of whether he thought they had a big sales potential. Of course he never wanted to lose money, but money was not the driving factor in a lot of the projects he took on. He always believed that if the music was right, the money would follow.

After the huge success of Natalie Cole's album, he had the leisure to make one of these projects. He decided to record Little Jimmy Scott, a jazz singer who had never sold more than a few thousand records but was a soulful guy who influenced a lot of other singers and moved a lot of hearts. "I loved his music back in the day," says Tommy. "His style reminded me of Dinah Washington—and later on I discovered that he also came from Cleveland. In fact, we had grown up a few blocks of each other, but because he was ten years older, I never knew him there, though I certainly knew *of* him."

Jimmy had had a particularly hard life. He was born with a rare hormonal disorder that affected not only his voice—he sounded like a woman when he sang, which is why he influenced so many female singers, especially Nancy Wilson—but his physical appearance as well; he had no facial hair and seemed a little soft, but there was no doubt he loved women. "He was a man through and through," says Tommy.

"I had a meeting with Jimmy and he turned out to be such a sweet guy. From the moment I met him, we were in total harmony. We talked about music and he was so relaxed and open to my ideas. This is so rare, to find a stylist who is so down with themselves that they're totally comfortable letting you do what you do."

With Jimmy, the production was simple: Bring in a first-rate jazz trio and then dress the lady up in strings. "We approached the recording like an old-school jazz date," says Tommy. "The pianist, Kenny Barron, wrote out the chord charts and we just came up with the arrangements in the studio. I had Ron Carter on bass and Grady Tate on drums. I knew that I was going to surround Jimmy with an orchestra, so I really wanted the basic tracks to be pretty simple."

Sometimes simple is the hardest thing. "At one point," Tommy says, "Grady copped a bit of an attitude. I said something to him about keeping it simple, and he said, 'Hey, you got all these great players here, man, why you wanna tell us not to play?' So I took him aside and said, 'Look, man, maybe I should have explained this in front, but I have an idea of where I'm going here and I need you to be sparse." He understood and they went on.

The only other glitch was trying to cut the Burt Bacharach song

"A House Is Not a Home," which had an odd 5/4 bar inserted. "Jimmy was one of those old-time cats," says Tommy, "who does what he does and knows what he knows, but the minute you put something odd in front of him, if it doesn't make sense to him it will cause him to shut down. As soon as we started trying the song it was obvious the 5/4 passage didn't lay right for him." In the end, they decided to cut a backing track of the song and send Jimmy home with a tape to rehearse in private. A week later they came back to the studio and tried it again and it still wasn't working.

Tommy knew it was round peg in a square hole for Jimmy, and at one point he turned to Al Schmitt and said, "I'm gonna give this cat one more time and then we'll just move on," and just as he looked up, there was Jimmy shaking his head and saying, "You know man, this song and me just can't get a relationship going."

A lot of times when an artist is having trouble with something in the studio, they will take their frustration out on something or somebody else in the room to cover up their insecurity. Anything to deflect attention from the situation at hand. But Jimmy just got right down to the nub of it. "I thought that was beautiful," says Tommy. "I just walked out to the studio and gave him a big hug and said, 'Jimmy. I got it. No sweat. Don't worry about it, man. Next case.'"

When Steve Ross died in 1994 there was huge political upheaval at WEA—the parent company of the Warner Bros., Elektra, and Atlantic record labels. The big question was who was going to take over, and in the end, Bob Morgado won. He had been trying to out-maneuver Mo Ostin since he first arrived ten years earlier, but Mo had put his foot down; he went to Steve and said "I'm not reporting to this guy," and Steve told him, "Don't worry, you report to me." Morgado never forgot that.

So with Steve gone, suddenly all these stories started appearing in the press—planted by Morgado's publicity guy—saying things like Mo was thinking of leaving, and within the year, all of Tommy's old friends and associates had left WEA—not just Mo Ostin but Bob Krasnow and Lenny Waronker as well. Tommy had a "key man" clause in his contract, which stated that if Krasnow ever left Elektra, for whatever reason, Tommy could leave too. At the time, he still had two and a half years to go on his contract, and without this clause he would have been locked in a hostile environment. But when Sylvia Rhone took over Bob Krasnow's job (she is the woman credited with championing "gangsta rap," Tommy's least favorite kind of music), he had one meeting with her, then walked the fifty feet to his office, called his lawyer, and said, "Get me out of here."

The Breezin' team in the studio.

With George and Barbra at the Grammy ceremony.

Tom and Miles.

Horizon recording session with (l to r) Abe Laboriel, Al Schmitt, Linda Tyler, Lee Ritenour, Ben Sidran, Mike Mainieri, Tommy, Steve Gadd, Buzzy Feiten.

With Diana and Mac.

The road to Alimena, Sicily, where the brothers went to find their roots.

With Al Schmitt in the studio, their natural habitat.

With Barbra and Diana.

With Diana.

With Paul McCartney.

With Willie Nelson.

Ben and Tom at his 80th birthday tribute in Cleveland.

Tommy in his wine cellar before he got the bad news from his doctor.

Tommy and Gill.

Track Nine:

The House That Diana Built

Tommy had been remarkably lucky in finding new opportunities when the inevitable downturns and political squabbles in the record industry happened. In 1994, just as he was leaving Elektra, he was offered the presidency of Universal's jazz label, GRP Records. His first reaction was somewhat mixed: He was happy to get the call, but GRP was a "smooth jazz" label and he did not see himself as a smooth jazz kind of guy. He never listened to the stuff; he would have preferred the opportunity to run a hardcore jazz label like Verve.

But his choices were limited: to go independent or take the offer at GRP. Being president of a company was problematic for him; his tenure at Horizon had not gone well. "I have never been fond of administration," he says. "My world is in the recording studio. But challenges never scared me off either. And I had always worked for somebody. In 1994 I was fifty-eight years old and I didn't want to get into the hustle of independent production."

He had a meeting with Dave Grusin and Larry Rosen, the G and the R in GRP. The three of them had known one another since the sixties, when Dave was the piano player with Andy Williams and

Larry was Andy's drummer. Dave and Larry said they were "over the moon" about the possibility of Tommy running the company. It was a legacy issue for them, and Tommy knew where they were coming from. They told him, "You can do whatever you want with the label," and in the end, he took the job.

Zach Horowitz, the head of business affairs for Universal, made it happen. Years before, the great record producer Jerry Wexler gave Tommy some advice. He said, "Tommy, the most important thing in this business is that you always have a rabbi at the company, somebody who is going to be your champion." "Thinking back," says Tommy, "I realized that I always did have a rabbi: Phil and Bob Skaff at Liberty, Herb and Jerry at A&M, Bob Krasnow at Blue Thumb and Elektra, Mo Ostin and Lenny Waronker at Warners, and then Zach Horowitz at Universal. No matter how styles changed or how people went from one fashion to another, I just basically did what I did, and some way or other I always ended up with records that were profitable and people left me alone."

He was scheduled to start at GRP in September, and in August he went in to meet with Larry and talk about the catalog. Larry said, "There's this girl we're thinking about signing, I want you to hear her." She had made a previous record for a small company. "They played me that record," says Tommy, "and I didn't like it—it sounded like cocktail music from a hotel lounge. Not wanting to shut the thing down totally, I said to Larry, 'Do you have anything else by her?' Larry played me a video she had done for BET, just her at the piano singing 'Body and Soul,' and that just knocked me out. I immediately got a sense of how great she was. Of course, later, as things got bigger and bigger, I thought 'Thank God they played that second thing for me' or I could have passed on Diana Krall."

Starting out, Diana was strictly a jazz act, so the first album they did together was recorded direct to two-track to save money. Al Schmitt is a master of live recording—when he first started making records he was going direct to two-track all the time and before that, he was going direct to mono—so he knew how to balance sounds on the fly. They did the album *Only Trust Your Heart* in two days. It cost ten grand and sold about eighteen thousand copies, a very nice profit for a jazz record.

Next they did a tribute to the Nat King Cole Trio, just piano, bass and guitar, called *All for You*. It sold about thirty thousand copies. Then, for the thirtieth anniversary of the Beatles, the general manager at GRP had the idea to get each of the acts on GRP to do a Beatles cover, so Diana did a version of "And I Love Her" that was, says Tommy, "a revelation." They used Christian McBride on bass and Lewis Nash on drums. "It was the first time that we were able to go into the studio with a great rhythm section," says Tommy, "and take our time to pick a tune apart and put it back together.

"Because basically, this was how I usually made records, carefully, with a lot of consideration as to the structure and the tempo of the songs; we would deconstruct and reconstruct the song before we recorded it. We might only do one or two takes, because we had done our homework. I don't think Diana had ever experienced this process of tearing a song apart, figuring out the best way to structure it, then go back and recut it, listen to it again, and maybe making a few more changes. It's a process. We spent a little more than an hour on that one song, and in the end, she dropped this unbelievable performance.

"I was sitting in the room with her and I heard this fantastic take come down and when it was done I looked right over at her and said, 'Baby, that is a great take. We should listen to that.' She said, 'Really?' I said, 'Yeah. Let's check this out.'" When she heard it, he could see in the look on her face that she understood: "'Oh, *this* is how you get the magic to happen.' She understood how great records were made."

The next record they made was called *Love Scenes*, and it included a Dave Frishberg song Diana found called "Peel Me a Grape," which set the tone for the whole project. Again they had Christian play bass, and since they didn't use a drummer on the Nat Cole record, they kept the same setup. But, like doing the Beatles song, they took their time coming up with the right format for each tune. They did the album in four days; it sold ninety thousand copies, and that blew everybody away because jazz acts weren't supposed to do those kinds of numbers. Something was really starting to happen here.

Next, Tommy got Johnny Mandel involved. When they were going through potential songs, Diana said, "You know, I got this idea, to do 'I've Got You Under My Skin.'" Tommy said, "I don't want to discourage you, but Frank Sinatra put his stamp on that one." She said, "No, I think I have something different on it." They wound up doing it, and that album, called *When I Look in Your Eyes*, sold two million copies and was nominated for the Grammy for Album of the Year. It was only the second time that a jazz album was nominated for Album of the Year—the first time had been George Benson's *Breezin'.*

The Grammy Awards had become a major television production, and the ceremony was being presented at the Staples Center, an enormous venue. The year before, they had done it at a smaller venue, the Shrine Auditorium, and it still felt somewhat personal. But this year, it was going to be like going to see the Lakers play ball.

Because of the costs involved, the producers of the show were very concerned about ratings, and they didn't want Diana to perform the song the way she had recorded it, small and intimate. They wanted her to perform with the rock guitarist Richie Sambora, from Bon Jovi, on guitar. Tommy flipped out. "With all due respect to Richie Sambora," says Tommy, "the man knew nothing about Diana Krall. Diana was nominated for one of the biggest awards of the evening, and you would think that would have given her the ability to do whatever she wanted in the way of performing the song. But no. They were firm on this Sambora thing."

Tommy called Pierre Cossette, the lead producer of the Grammy show, and was told "No no no, we gotta think about television here." "The only thing I was able to convince him of," says Tommy, "was to use George Benson on guitar instead of Richie Sambora. That was something. But then, for some weird reason, they had Diana sing "Up a Lazy River" and they put the singer Erykah Badu on the stage—simply because she was hot at the time—and she just sat in a chair swinging a beaded purse. Like she was back in the twenties or something. It was a disaster. It was demeaning, it was stupid, and it was disrespectful.

"I will never forgive the Academy for that. The fact that they didn't let this girl go out there and do what she did, what she had been nominated for. She sold two million albums to get to that point; you'd think that that would be enough. That was the moment I hung up my game shoes as far as the Grammys were concerned." But it wasn't the last Grammy he would win.

For the next album, Tommy wanted to get Claus Ogerman involved. Diana loved a couple of the albums Tommy and Claus had done together, particularly one called *Gate of Dreams*, but at the time Claus had stopped doing any pop things; he was writing a series of classical pieces and he was afraid that if he continued to arrange pop music, the classical world would write him off. He told Tommy, "I can't do it."

Later that year, Tommy was visiting Claus in Munich and Claus happened to mention that he had just written a piano concerto. He gave Tommy the recording of it and said, "Gee, it would be great to get this released on Polygram." Polygram, like GRP, was owned by Universal, and it occurred to Tommy that perhaps there was a symbiotic opportunity here.

The guy in charge of classical projects for Polygram, Chris Roberts, was an acquaintance and so they had lunch together the next week when Tommy was in London. Tommy suggested that perhaps if Chris was willing to release Claus's piano concerto, Claus might be willing to consider the Diana project. Tommy even offered to pay. "I said to Chris, 'I'll give you the money to release this classical record and press up like three thousand copies. I'll pay for it, you just put it out. I got a feeling this will spur him on.'"

"It turned out," says Tommy, "that Chris was a fan, so it was not a hard sell." Tommy called Claus and said, "Hey, man, great news. I played your piano concerto for Chris Roberts and he loves it and he wants to release it." And by the end of that conversation, Claus said, "Hey, when do you want to do that Diana album?" Tommy didn't even have to ask.

The album they did together, called *The Look of Love*, sold four and a half million copies. And then every album Tommy and Diana did after that, worldwide, sold at least two million copies. There had never been a jazz act that sold those kinds of numbers. For Tommy, it was gratifying to be making beautiful, authentic music that spoke to so many people. In a way, it justified his whole musical path.

At one point, Tommy got a call from Danny Bennett, Tony Bennett's son and manager, about doing a duets album with his father and Diana Krall. They were traveling together and it seemed like a natural. "As we were talking about putting a rhythm section together and potential dates, I said, 'We got to get Christian McBride to play bass.' I called and he was booked for a couple of months, so I called Danny back and said, 'Hey, man, we're gonna have to wait.' And he said, 'Hey, man, there are other good bass players, you know.'"

Tommy said, 'Of course there are other good bass players. But there's only one Christian McBride.'" This is how strongly Tommy had come to believe in the "casting" of the albums he made.

To Tommy, recording the music is literally a form of magic. Of transcending the mundane. It's like the iceberg; what you see is only the tip of what's going on under the surface. The same with music: a lot of the human stuff is happening below the surface, and without it, in Tommy's expression, "there wouldn't be anything to talk about." Tommy was very specific and precise about how he made records. When he went into the studio, to court that magic, if he had something he knew that worked, he didn't treat the synergy as something convenient or trivial.

"I knew that Christian made Diana's blood move," says Tommy. "And once that chemistry is right, nothing can be worse than disrupting it by miscasting the session, getting a player—and they may be a great player—whose chemistry isn't exactly right. The point is, making an album, particularly a jazz album, is a kind of dance; everybody has to be in tune and in step with everybody else."

This was an element of production that Tommy faced more than once and something he became more adept at handling. Once, when he was doing a Randy Crawford date with Joe Sample on piano, they had a great guitar player, but, says Tommy, "he was playing things that I could see were bugging Joe. Joe was getting irritated and it was distracting him. At one point, Joe just stopped—he doesn't mince words—and he said, 'Man, you're fucking with my groove.'" They bagged the guitar player, great as he was.

This idea of the groove as being something magical is no mystery to studio musicians. You can't say exactly what it is, but you can often point to where it comes from. With Joe, he always came up with some little musical hook that suggested an internal rhythm or a snippet that would support the whole song. Almost like a musical meme. "Great players always think about this," says Tommy. "What is the first thing I can play that's going to get people's attention. And Joe would always come up with a melodic line or some little rhythm thing and then the drummer could pick it up and run with it." That back-and-forth is where the groove comes from; the groove is all about interaction between sympathetic souls.

Every producer has his own style and his own way of inspiring or capturing it. Tommy says, "You can go and see an act in a club six days in a row and maybe out of the six days, three will be good, one is exceptional, and the other two are just okay. It's no different in the studio, except the odds are even worse, because at the club you have an audience there to inspire the performance. In the studio, there's nothing to take you out of yourself, and there is always the tendency to feel self-conscious during playbacks. So the producer has to create an atmosphere where the artist can forget about the surroundings and make room for the inspiration to happen; you set up the conditions that are conducive to the magic happening.

"Sometimes," says Tommy, "it's as easy as getting the right tempo. Maybe the tempo isn't quite settled. There's a sweet spot. You've got to find that tempo that just *feels* right. And a lot of times when you do have that tempo, somebody makes a mistake or stops in the middle of a take that's feeling pretty good, and before you start again, you have to go back and listen to the take that broke down so that the drummer can get a sense of where it was. The drummer is very important. The only instrument that you can't redo is the drums. If the drums aren't right it's never going to be right. But if the drums are solid, you can redo the bass, you can redo the guitar, you can redo anything, and it can still feel great."

There are physical things that affect the groove as well. Obviously, the earphone mix is critical. "There are certain things that the engineer has to provide so that there's this moment when everybody can hear themselves and the band at the same time," says Tommy, "Also,

I have a rule about clocks in the studio. No clocks. To me, the musicians get there when they get there, and when everybody starts getting fatigued, that's when we finish. The time in between, we stop and have lunch, we bullshit, you know, we have some fun. And we make music. It's very important to me to make everybody feel as relaxed as possible and to forget about the surroundings." A lot of times the groove can be a matter of what you don't do as much as what you do. And clocks are the kind of timekeeping that has no place in the groove.

But the most important elements in any Tommy LiPuma production are the artist and the song. They have to inspire the musicians to create that magical space. That's why Tommy doesn't like recording without the main artist performing at the same time, making what are essentially backing tracks. "I always want the artist in the room on the date," he says, "singing or playing as the track goes down. If you want to change something later, re-sing it, or just fix it, fine. But if the musicians don't have a sense of what the artist is doing with the material, they're just playing to a chord chart."

With a great artist, a great song, and great musicians, it's just a matter of time before the good stuff arrives. "There's always that one point," says Tommy, "whether it takes five minutes or fifty minutes to get there, where you start feeling a presence in the room, like, 'Okay, this is sounding awfully good, let's not waste it on the air; let's take it.' Musicians can get hung up on the details and it's my job to start *feeling* it, to hear the overall sound and recognize when that moment is about to arrive, when you're one take away from getting it.

"It's not an intellectual thing. It's in the body. It's all about 'Are you moved'? I mean, when you're listening to a great performance on a record, it's like you're put on this magic carpet and it just takes you away. You lose a sense of time, you lose a sense of everything. You're just being held in the grasp of this great performance. It really is all about capturing a moment in time, and every moment only happens once. I pride myself on recognizing when that moment arrives and getting it on tape." Transcendent moments are a recurring theme in Tommy's life.

When Tommy signed Horace Silver it was a dream come true: Horace had been one of the first jazz musicians he listened to back in Cleveland. The albums they ultimately did together, like *Jazz Has a Sense of Humor* and *Hardbop Grandpop*, were Tommy's attempt to keep Horace's brand alive and to pay back a little of what Horace had given him as a young man. It couldn't have happened as a GRP release, but by then Tommy had inherited the presidency of Verve, and it was a good marriage of artist and label.

"Horace was the sweetest dude," says Tommy, "very soft-spoken, very old-school. Over the years he had written all these loose, funky things like 'Sister Sadie' and 'Filthy McNasty,' but when you got to know him, he was just the opposite of this good-time image. He was very conservative and he lived a very modest, even sparse life. When we did recording dates in New York, for example, he would always stay at this two-star hotel where you'd have to share the bathroom, to save money. I told him this was really unnecessary, but he had found this place where he got cheap rates and that's where he always stayed when he came to New York."

At one point Horace actually looked at the budget for his record and said, "Tommy, what's this three hundred dollars for lunch?" Tommy said, "You know, when we take a break we'll have lunch . . . ," and Horace said, "Can't the musicians buy their own lunch?" Tommy said, "Well, Horace, if you want to go around with a coin changer like a conductor and get ten bucks from this guy and eight bucks from that guy, it's fine, but look, man, I'll take care of it." So from then on, he never charged the food back to Horace's project. Horace came up in an era where being a jazz musician was literally a matter of survival.

In some ways, Horace was one of the smartest cats going. He had held on to his own publishing and owned the copyrights to all his great songs. But in other ways, his cautious nature was not always in his best interest. For example, he was getting ripped off by rap groups who essentially stole snippets of his older Blue Note material, but because he refused to hire a subpublisher and pay them 15 percent to run down the guys who were stealing his music, he was losing a lot of money. Penny wise and pound foolish. This is where "old school" becomes "no school," like burying your money in the backyard to keep it safe from the banks. If you're going to make and spend some money, you're already playing the game.

But Horace's way of doing things reflected the way it was for him coming up. "He had undoubtedly seen a lot of guys getting ripped off and pushed around," says Tommy, "so, like. any songs or tracks that we didn't use for an album he insisted that we get rid of immediately. At the end of every recording date, he would sit with me and Al Schmitt and we'd have to literally erase all of the takes except for the masters. Nobody was going to second-guess him later or put out something he had rejected."

"I don't blame him," says Tommy. "A man has a right to shape his own legacy."

One unexpected bonus of Tommy's situation at GRP/Universal was that he was eventually reunited with the Blue Thumb label. ABC Paramount had bought Blue Thumb initially, and then some years later, Universal bought ABC, so Tommy, as president of Universal's jazz division, inherited Blue Thumb. Something similar happened with Impulse, which was one of the most prestigious jazz imprimaturs. Tommy found himself in the enviable position of being in charge of more than 50 percent of the great recorded jazz music on the planet.

This also gave him the advantage of using Blue Thumb and Impulse for some of the side projects he wanted to do that were too left-of-center for GRP, to sign artists that had more of an edge to them. So when he signed Jonatha Brooke, he could put her on Blue Thumb, or when he signed straight-ahead jazz artists like Shirley Horn or Danilo Pérez, he could put them on Verve or Impulse.

As the Universal jazz portfolio continued to grow, Tommy found himself being pulled in several directions. "My biggest asset as the head of the company," he says, "was that, for the most part, everybody liked working for me and I liked building the team. People went that extra step for me because we had a personal relationship. But my biggest liability was that my eyes would cloud over when I went into financial meetings and started to hear about EBITA (earnings before interest, taxes, and amortization). It wasn't that I wasn't bottom-line-conscious, but I was primarily interested in the music. And the more time that went by, the more I realized how much of it I was spending in the office instead of in the studio.

"The studio made sense to me; the business side often did not. For example, I was once in a meeting and I asked this person why something that was supposed to happen didn't happen, and he said, 'Well, I emailed the guy and I never heard back.' I said, 'You emailed him? Your office is right next door. You couldn't get up and walk in and ask him a question?'"

Technology in general was making the industry more complicated than it had been, and the people at the top really didn't have a good map of the territory. They did not know how to respond to it, which was clear in 1999, when Napster came on the scene and record companies immediately shot themselves in the foot. "We should have bought the service," Tommy says, "instead of suing Napster and our customers. What kind of business model has you suing your customers? It made no sense at all. There was a revolution going on, but it was not being taken seriously by the people in charge of the record business."

Also, the mechanics of the business were changing, not just rapidly but in a way that Tommy admits he didn't understand. He didn't understand why companies promoted a particular project for a few weeks and then decided to let an artist go. When he was at Warners, the promotion and marketing people would work for a year to break the record. Now it was "six weeks and out." "There was an assembly line, a conveyer belt with an endless amount of dreck coming down," says Tommy, "most of it nameless music that would disappear as soon as it was played." It was actually designed to disappear so that the next piece of dreck could show up.

By the late nineties there was another situation making life miserable in the record business: it was called "independent promotion." All the big companies were vying for space at radio and retail, and to muscle their way in, they were spending unbelievable amounts of money on so-called "independent promotion." "So-called" because there was nothing independent about it. Record companies hired guys who were not officially on their payroll but who took their marketing money and spent it however they saw fit. This kept the record companies at arm's length from any accusation of "payola" or improper expenditures. Of course, eventually some people got caught and went to jail for it.

"There were maybe five or six of these so-called independent promoters, the big guys, who had the whole thing locked up," says

Tommy. "Eighty percent of the marketing money in the record business, millions of dollars, was going directly to these guys. You couldn't get a record played on the radio if you didn't hire them. You might spend a quarter of a million dollars to make a record, and then you would have to spend another quarter of a million to hire one of these so-called independents to have a chance of getting any airplay.

"You have to go back to the mid-seventies to find a time when somebody at radio would actually say, 'This is a good record, I think I'll play it.' Back then, a record would start getting airplay, and *then* the company would start getting orders, and *then* it was wake-up time for the record company; once a record started selling, *then* they started spending money. They rarely if ever spent money before there were sales."

But by the nineties, it was the other way around. To compete with the other majors, you had to do what they were all doing. And the majors all had their "priority acts," big acts that they committed money to in front, often before the record was even made, and these were the records that would get independent promotion. "If it wasn't a priority, you were on your own. This wasn't just the way it was at MCA/Universal. It was prevalent throughout the industry, at Sony and RCA and Warners: What were the priorities this week? And then, maybe two weeks later, the minute it was felt that the record no longer had 'legs,' suddenly it was no longer a priority and it was dropped like a hot potato." Nobody in the business ever wanted to be associated with a perceived failure. It was all a game of hypesters hyping the hypesters.

"I guess," says Tommy, "I came along right at the end of the time when promotion and promotion men really meant something to the success of a record. When it was still about people and not just about money."

In 2000, Tommy handed off the presidency of the Verve Music Group to an associate and took the title of chairman. A bit later, he took the title of chairman emeritus. It was more or less an honorary title; he really just wanted to be free to continue making the records he wanted to make—even if it was for other labels—and it kept him on the Universal payroll in a minimal fashion. Many of the records he produced during this period were great musical adventures and fun projects to do, but not big sellers. To name a few: Danilo Pérez's *Panamonk* and *Central Avenue*, Claus Ogerman's *Across the Crystal Sea*, and Shirley Horn's *You're My Thrill*. Tommy was passively effecting his departure from the record business.

Things had changed; there had been too much water under the bridge. For example, while working with Gladys Knight, he became aware that "even though she was one of the greatest singers of our day, I wasn't catching her when she had a fire in her belly. By the time we got together, she was playing Las Vegas year-round. She owned two houses there and she would do one show a night—they would stuff the people in at nine o'clock, she would do one set, and she was home by eleven. She sang her ass off, but it just wasn't what it *was*. Same thing with Queen Latifah. She was terrific, really talented. But the whole thing was starting to lose its meaning. People didn't have that hunger anymore. And again I was getting bored.

"I was becoming more and more focused on the art world. I was still listening to music, but mostly it was music from the past, like Duke Ellington and Johnny Hodges and Ben Webster. I started to really miss that golden period, and I was acutely aware that it was being lost. I was becoming nostalgic; I guess it comes with the territory as you get older. And at the same time, I had built up an immense collection of paintings: Maurer, Hartley, Marin, Friedman, all of these great American artists. So in 2006, I started to actively plan my exodus from the corporate world.

"The only way I was going to get my ultimate freedom was to

sell some of my paintings. In the end, I decided I was going to have to sell some of the best ones. I sat down with some financial people, figured out what I would need to maintain my lifestyle, and then put a lot of the gems I had collected up for auction. And it was like a fire sale. They went in a heartbeat. I only had to sell about ten pictures but those pictures assured my future. It hurt to sell them, the Hartley, the Baziotes. These guys didn't paint that many pictures and the next thing you know, they were gone."

Nostalgia is a funny thing. It not only colors the past, it also colors the future. Tommy was really starting to feel at a loss about the prospects for the business he was in and for the music he loved.

"There used to be so much great music being played," says Tommy. "And it wasn't just that there was so much of it but that everyone was *interested* in music. Music was the *thing*. Music was the Internet. It was social media. It was whatever there was. It was what was happening and you had to go get it on a record, a piece of vinyl, from a store. Or you had to go out and turn on your car radio. But you had to be somewhere in the world, you weren't always just sitting alone in a room.

"And the way I made records when I started producing was always with this in mind. Every album was a kind of experience, a journey, and it had a flow to it. But when the business became completely hit-driven, what started happening was A&R guys would say, 'Let's just have a bunch of producers trying to cut hits and then we'll make an album out of that.' The idea of musical flow went out the window."

It's a small part of a bigger problem. Today nothing is sacred; as the saying goes, we know the price of everything and the value of nothing. "A song comes out," says Tommy, "and as soon as it becomes a hit, it's immediately used in a commercial. Everything's for sale, and that kind of establishes how people feel about music today." Music just becomes more product and the people who listen to it just become consumers. "We've lost that sense of music and the people who love it as being special. And truth be told, record companies don't even think about records in the same way. Now they really only think about 'market share,' because they're not really selling records. The actual sales of CDs have been declining around ten percent a year for a long time. Today, if you're Universal Music, which currently has the biggest market share, you have the ability to go to a streaming service like Spotify and say, 'Look, we have a forty percent market share, so you have to give us forty percent of the revenue available.' Today this is what the business is about: market share.

"And then on top of it, record companies want '360 deals,' which means they are entitled to a piece of every aspect of the artist's work—ticket sales, merchandise, publishing, everything. Talk about slavery. If you come up with a cure for cancer, the record company owns part of it.

"This is a business that was started by small entrepreneurs where talent was developed. It is no longer a question of talent or development. It's a question of hitting the numbers. Today, you can go from selling fifteen million to three hundred thousand on the follow-up and the next thing you know you don't have a deal any more. Not to sound too dire, but it is pretty widely recognized that the record business as we used to know it is over."

Track Ten:

American Classics

In 2009, Diana Krall asked Tommy to help her produce an album of jazz standards with Barbra Streisand for Columbia. The most memorable moment for Tommy came during a break in the action.

"Over the years," says Tommy, "I've used hundreds of orchestras, and you get certain people, a few concertmasters and such, that you always ask for on dates. And I would always ask for this one harpist who was great. Her name is Gail Levant, and over a period of twenty-five, thirty years, I must have had her on dozens of dates.

"So when we were doing these Streisand sessions, at one point, Gail comes up to me and says, 'Tommy, I want you to see this book. They just did this book on harpists and they do a whole chapter on me.' The next thing I know, I'm looking at a picture of her on a swan. I said, 'Gail, please tell me that picture was taken at the Aegean of the Sea at the Desert Inn.' She said, 'How did you know?'"

Another day, while on a lunch break at a recording session, Tommy got a call from Sam Feldman, an artists' manager, asking if he had any interest in producing Rod Stewart. Sam was calling on behalf of a third party.

At that point, Rod had done three very successful albums of the Great American Songbook. Not that Tommy would ever turn down a good paycheck, but his instinct told him that his "taste and style didn't jibe with what he had heard of Rod's venture into this genre." He told Feldman he didn't think so, but to give him a few days to think about it.

He went back to the control room where they were still having lunch and told Al Schmitt about the call. Ten minutes later he got a call back from Feldman saying he had just gotten off the phone with Rod's manager, Arnold Stiefel, saying that the producer of Rod's last two albums, Richard Perry, had just called him and asked if it was true that Tommy LiPuma was going to do the next album. The guitar player having lunch with Tommy overheard his conversation with Schmitt and because he was friends with Perry, he called him, who in turn called Stiefel, who in turn called Sam Feldman. "Not only does it teach you how small the record business is," says Tommy, "but it teaches you to keep your mouth shut." Tommy passed on Rod Stewart.

A few years later Clive Davis, president of Arista Records, called to ask him about producing Rod. "Aside from everything, I've got respect for the guy," says Tommy. "He's been very successful. But, with the exception of Whitney Houston, I'm not that inclined toward what he's done musically. But I figured that out of respect, I should take the meeting."

Tommy had known Clive peripherally since the '60s but never personally. "I had never gone to one of his parties," says Tommy. "But when I walked into his office he was very cordial. There was an A&R guy there and I had done my homework. As difficult as it was to do, I sat through the last three albums Rod Stewart had done, which I hated, and when I got there, Clive was playing one of them. And then at one point he turns the sound down and says, 'Basically, this is what we're looking to do. But it's got to have that 'Fred and Ginger' thing.'"

Tommy said, "Look, I got it. I know what you're looking for here. I'll be frank with you. I'm not sure if I'm the right person. But I've got a lot of respect for you and what you've done, which is one of the reasons I took the meeting, so give me the weekend and I'll give some thought to it." Clive said, "Fine, absolutely."

He called Tommy over the weekend—three times—and continued to pitch him. "Coincidentally, he lives about five minutes from me, so before we hung up I said, 'I'll call you and we can set up a dinner.' He said 'Fine.' By Monday morning, I had decided that I better not do this, so I called him back and said, 'Look, I really appreciate you thinking of me but I honestly don't think I'm the right person for this,' without getting into the fact that I felt his taste and my taste were not the same."

"A month later, I called Clive about that dinner. And I never got a call back. So I guess basically the deal is you don't say no to Clive Davis."

As a sidebar, pianist Rob Mounsey tells the following story about the time he was working on the first Rod Stewart "standards" album. The arranger, George Calandrelli, who lived in LA, had done the charts and sent them on to New York. But he couldn't come in. Nobody knew what to make of them, so Rob, was simply playing the piano—sight-reading the scores—to help the guys get through the charts. In the midst of this rather tedious process, Clive Davis walks into the control room, hears what's going on, gets on the talkback, and says, "Piano player! Piano player!"—the first indication that the person speaking doesn't know how to talk to musicians—"Piano player! I don't want it to sound like that. It's got to be more Fred and Ginger."

Bruce Lundvall, the president of Blue Note Records, asked Tommy if he was interested in doing an album with Willie Nelson. "I loved Willie's standards album," says Tommy, "and my first thought was to use Joe Sample—like Willie, Joe is from Texas—so Joe and I went to Austin to spend a day at Willie's ranch. How shall I put this? It's a place of ultimate highness. It's not like it's over the top, but every so often, Willie's got this smoking contraption that's on a stand and he fires it up. Willie is high most of the day and into the night.

"We spent a whole day going through tunes. He was right there with us, and he was just great. He has a real 'standards' aesthetic. He really knows this stuff upside down, backwards and forwards.

"And at one point, when we had gone through all the tunes, he said, 'Come on, lemme show you around the ranch.' Willie's got several hundred acres; there's what looks like a Hollywood set on the property. We got into his truck and the first stop we made was this little church that looked like it was right out of the 1880s, pews and all. Then we got back in the truck and we ended up at what looked like a Western town, with a saloon with swinging doors, the whole thing. We went in and there were all his pals sitting around drinking beer.

"He's got a lot of very interesting buddies. Not just the guys who were there drinking beer. At one point, I got thirsty and I said, 'You got any water back there?' He said, 'Right over there,' so I took a glass, and man the water tasted great! I made a remark, because there was no bottle on top of it, like at a water cooler, it was just coming from a pipe straight out of the wall. I said, 'Is this your tap water?'

and he said a friend of his invented this thing that grabs the moisture out of the atmosphere and turns it into pure drinking water. Willie's got some hip friends."

A few months later, Willie, Tommy, and Joe all met up in New York at Right Track Studios, where they had a big studio for the band and a nice little isolation booth for Willie. Willie's booth was connected directly to the control room, and of course wherever Willie goes, his pipe goes with him. You couldn't enter the vocal booth unless you were willing to have an attitude adjustment.

Willie had parked his tour bus in front of the studio on Forty-eighth Street, and when he wasn't recording, he would hang out there. He also slept on the bus. After a couple of days, somebody called Tommy and said, "Check out page six." Tommy opened the *Daily News* and read, 'Willie Nelson is apparently in town recording an album at a studio on 48th Street. You can tell from the wafts of smoke coming out of this bus as you walk down the street.'" Pretty soon, Tommy was hanging out on the bus too, using Willie's sound system to check out the recordings. By the recording's conclusion, Tommy and Willie were like two old shoes.

In 2010 Tommy got a call from Paul McCartney's office, MPL. Nancy Jeffries, the woman on the phone, said, "Paul's been thinking of doing a standards album for a long time and if he doesn't do it now he'll never do it. So they asked me to come up with a list of names for producers and I only came up with one name and that was yours." A few days later, he took the meeting with Paul and they tossed ideas around: "It was really just a chemistry lesson at that point, seeing if he felt comfortable with me," says Tommy. "Nancy called back to say, Yeah. He liked you."

Several months went by without hearing anything, and then he got another call from Nancy, this time saying, "Paul wondered if you could go over to England and spend some time going through song ideas." Tommy flew over with forty or fifty song ideas and a piano player, Tamir Hendelman, "one of these guys who can read music like you would read *The New York Times*," says Tommy. "Not only can he play anything, but if suddenly you have to transpose the key from E-flat to G-sharp, he can do it in a flash."

They met at Paul's studio, Hog Mill Farms, and "at first," says Tommy, "I must admit it felt a little shaky. I wasn't sure whether or not this whole project was going to work for Paul. But then we turned to this song from *Guys and Dolls* called 'More I Cannot Wish You.' In the show the father sings it to his daughter. It was probably a combination of Paul having an eight-year-old daughter of his own and this being a great song, but when he sang it, everything just clicked. Paul's the kind of singer who has to have a personal connection to deliver a lyric, and when he does, look out. When I heard him sing this song, I thought, 'Yeah. He's got this.'"

They spent more than a year on the preproduction of the album, going back and forth about songs. They ended up with twenty things. At that point Tommy brought up the idea of having Diana Krall play piano. At first, Paul thought that he was suggesting doing a duets album, and he was obviously leery of that, but Tommy told him, "No, Paul, I'm talking about just using her as a piano player. She's a fantastic accompanist aside from being a great singer in her own right.'" They went with it. And in the end, it made all the difference.

"It's all part of that casting thing again, finding the right people for the part," says Tommy. "This is so important because a lot of the record happens before you even get into the studio. And if you make the right decisions before you go in, get out of the way. The rest of it can happen on its own."

Another important aspect to the success of a recording session is deciding what song to start with. "I would always think very seriously about that," he says, "because you can make or break a date based on how the first thing comes out. For the first date, Paul was really hot on starting with the song 'Cheek to Cheek.' At one point, we got a decent take, but *he* wasn't really happening. And I remember saying, 'Look, why don't we put this aside for a minute,' and I suggested we do 'More I Cannot Wish You.'

"You go in with songs, you go in with players, but it's all still just an idea until you physically get something down on tape, something that you can listen back to; then it's the real thing. You've captured it. When that comes out great it puts a positive feeling in the room and gives everybody some confidence that, hey this is really happening. If I had done one or two more takes of 'Cheek to Cheek,' I probably would have gotten a call the next day from Paul saying, 'Hey, man, see you later.'" But after they did "More I Cannot Wish You," everybody started to relax.

After the album was technically finished, they went back in to do one more thing, a version of "The Christmas Song." "To me," says Tommy, "his performance on this one was better than anything he had done on the rest of the album. And it occurred to me that maybe it was because he'd had time to reflect and listen to himself as *that guy* who sang standards. It was like he had gotten comfortable with *being* that guy, and so when he approached 'The Christmas Song,' he just totally relaxed and owned the performance.

"Some singers can pretty much sing the phone book and make it sound believable," Tommy says, "but Paul has to understand and believe in the song before he can deliver a great performance. For example, the original lyrics to 'The Christmas Song' are 'Everybody knows a turkey and some mistletoe / Help to make the season bright.' But Paul is a strict vegetarian so he changed those lyrics to 'Everybody knows *some holly* and some mistletoe / Help to make the season bright.' It was a small thing, but it made a big difference to Paul: that's who he is and that's how he's going to sing it if he's going to sing it at all."

Helping the artist find a way to *be* the guy who's singing the song can be a big part of the job. In the end, that record won two Grammys.

In 2011, Claude Nobs, who ran the Montreux Jazz Festival, wanted to celebrate Tommy's seventy-fifth birthday, and when they were putting together the list of who should be involved, Tommy said, "You know, Leon Russell was a really big part of my life in the beginning. It would be great if we could get Leon to come." Leon accepted and the next thing you know, they were at Montreux together, talking about old times. Leon said, "Hey, man, why don't we do an album together?"

Not long thereafter Tommy went down to Nashville to meet with Leon. He had told him, "Look, man, just think of things that you loved as you were coming up." Tommy brought in a bunch of possible tunes too. At first Leon didn't say much. At one point, Leon asked Tommy, "Do you like hillbilly music?" Tommy said, "Do I like hillbilly music!" and pulled out his computer and played George Jones's "When the Last Curtain Falls." "Suddenly Leon realized that I love all kinds of music," says Tommy. "He told me later that the one thing he had been worried about was that I was a jazz snob, or as he put it, that 'I was bitten by the jazz bug.' Once he discovered that I was wide open as far as music was concerned, he relaxed." But Leon still didn't want to sit down at the piano and play for Tommy.

Leon was recovering from a serious surgery and was physically challenged at the time, and he had told Tommy, "Man, I have a hard time playing those wooden pianos." But an hour before Tommy was scheduled to leave for the airport, the engineer reminded Leon, "Hey, man, they're coming to pick up this electric piano today," referring to a Yamaha that was sitting in the studio. Tommy tuned in and said, 'Well, hey, man, before they pick it up, would you mind playing me a few things on it?'"

Leon got up and hobbled over to the Yamaha piano with his cane. But the minute he sat down and started playing, Tommy saw "this aging seventy-year-old man turn into this roaring twenty-five-year-old monster." The first thing he played was "Come On In My Kitchen," the old Robert Johnson blues, and Tommy said, "Fucking great!" It became the opening cut on the album. "I kept saying to him, 'That's the shit man. That is the shit.'" Then the engineer said, "Play him 'Georgia.'"

"Now, everybody knows the Ray Charles version of that song," says Tommy, "and you can't help but think of Ray's version. But Leon played it and it was just great and I knew we would have to do something different, and that's when I got the idea to do it with a big band. I said, 'You like big bands?' He said, 'Man, I love Basie.' So when we recorded it, I got John Clayton to do the arrangement. Leon was just blown away."

The album, called *Life Journey*, wound up selling very few copies, but meant a great deal to Tommy. Leon was the first musician he had heard in LA and had been very helpful to Tommy on the first few sessions he produced. Tommy remembers one time, when he was really nervous and Leon was on the date; he called Leon into the control room and said, "Look, man, I do not have a clue as to what my next move is here." And Leon told him, "Well, do this and do this and do this and don't worry about that and it'll be okay." And it was.

In 2013, after fifty years in the recording studio, almost a hundred fifty albums made and approaching eighty million records sold, Tommy officially retired from Universal. It was the first time in half a century that he didn't work for somebody. That he no longer had a rabbi.

Track Eleven:

Camp Cheerful

In July 2014, Tommy went back to Cleveland. A car and driver picked him up at the airport and, on the way to the hotel, took him on a little tour of the old streets. There was Volsky's candy store; there was the porch where Eddie had worn grooves into the floor swinging for hours on end. The grooves were still there.

Tommy was back in town to do a fundraiser for his next project. He had decided to produce a record with a Cleveland trumpet player named Dominick Farinacci and to record it at the new Gill & Tommy LiPuma Center for Creative Arts, which was connected to the Rock and Roll Hall of Fame Archives at the Cuyahoga Community College (Tri-C) in Cleveland. The school came up with half the money for the recording, and they were hoping to raise the other half at a private party being thrown at the home of a local Italian community leader.

The day of the fundraiser, a big lunch was served; Dominick gave a short speech and then introduced Tommy. They talked about their hopes for the project, for the school, and for the community. Pledges starting coming in, and it was interesting, says Tommy, that the first pledge of the day, and one of the largest gifts of the event, came from Jules Belkin, a Jewish concert promoter and the only non-Italian in the room.

Dominick had attended school at the Tri-C Center when he was thirteen, long before Tommy was associated with the Center for Creative Arts. At the time, they had a young students program, and kids were able to go to Tri-C instead of attending a regular city junior high; students would do several hours of music in the morning and then several hours of regular schoolwork in the afternoon. Tri-C had dropped the program, which was another thing Tommy was hoping to correct by lending his name and resources to the college. He told them, "You got to get these kids when they're twelve, thirteen, even ten years old. Otherwise, you can forget it. By the time they're fifteen or sixteen, it's too late."

Tri-C is located at Twenty-second and Woodland, almost the exact corner where Tommy's father had lived when he first got to town. "I remember that corner back in the 1950s," says Tommy, "when all the downtown property that is now part of the Tri-C campus was a vibrant neighborhood with lots of single-family houses and small shops." Today where there once were houses there are now housing projects. The projects went up in the sixties and the neighborhood went down from there.

"But I remember the area as a busy intersection of Italian and Jewish shops," he continues. "Clothing stores, dry cleaners, grocery markets, pharmacies, all jumping." When they put the freeway in, it basically wiped out the neighborhood. Now Woodland was a four-lane obstacle course and everywhere you looked was concrete. Then Tri-C came along and did triage.

Tommy first met Dominick when a team from Tri-C came to New York to pitch him about making a major gift to the school. "I could tell that he was a serious musician and a dedicated teacher," says Tommy. Back in Cleveland, he witnessed a couple of classes

Dominick taught; in one, Dominick asked the kids to name a tune, and when they came up with a Clifford Brown song, he not only knew it, but he knew Clifford's whole solo. That got the kids' attention, and Tommy's too.

But what really got to Tommy was that this demonstration took place at the Shaker Heights school where, sixty years before, Tommy had been a young music student himself. "Once upon a time, that was me sitting there," says Tommy. And then when he discovered that Dominick's grandmother Clara had been a good friend of Tommy's sister and that Dominick's uncle Mario had actually been the drummer in the Sammy Dee band. "Well," says Tommy, "the whole thing was so Sicilian I could hardly believe it."

Perhaps Tommy felt that Dominick was like the musician he might have become if he had stuck with it. Like him, Dominick was open to all kinds of music. "Anything I played him," says Tommy, "he jumped right into it. It reminded me of me with Bobby Dale, but this time the roles were reversed." Now he was in a position to pass something on. The boy who couldn't take tests was teaching another grateful student.

And he was also thinking that here was a chance to create a legacy that was more than just a name on a building. He wanted to see more Dominick Farinaccis come out of Cleveland. He wanted to know it was possible to help make kids' lives better. "The whole thing for me," says Tommy, "was very personal."

That same trip, he went back to Camp Cheerful for the first time. When the limo pulled in to the circular gravel drive, everything seemed to go very quiet. The place was pretty much the way he remembered it from back when he was a camper a half century before. Kids were moving around the grounds, some having difficulty walking, one in a wheelchair, another just taking in the sun. He got out of the limo, and when he saw the Chippewa bunkhouse, the little log cabin where he had lived that summer so long ago, just being one of those kids, something inside of him seemed to crack. "I can't really describe it," he says. "It felt like I was falling."

Then he walked into the social hall, where a dozen kids of various ages were sitting around a long table doing art projects. Mounted on the wall behind them was an old television set on which *The Wizard of Oz* was playing. The story was just at the point when Dorothy and Toto take their first tentative steps down the yellow brick road; in front of the screen stood a little girl holding a small portable keyboard, obviously broken, who was crooning to herself. She was staring up at the screen watching Dorothy step into her golden future. It totally wiped Tommy out. "I don't think I ever really experienced anything like this before," he says. "I felt for the first time the truth of the saying 'There but for the grace of God go I.'" By the time he got back into the limo, he was an emotional wreck.

Seeing those children, each with their own cross to bear, was almost too much for him. His body may have been in 2014, but his mind was back in 1948. The limo ride from Camp Cheerful back to the Tri-C campus was only ten miles, but it took Tommy sixty-seven years to make the trip, and he remembered every one of them. Today, seventy thousand cars a day drive this section of highway 71, and their drivers can't help but notice a large sign on the side of a modern brick building that reads THE GILL AND TOMMY LIPUMA CENTER FOR CREATIVE ARTS. The old neighborhood is gone; the streets have been widened and repaved, and the interstate has leveled everything for miles around. But something was still very much alive here for Tommy.

They say you can't go home again, but no matter how far you travel, you can't ever really leave. Something inside of you is still there from when you were a child; you are still looking out of that same child's eyes. "And," Tommy says, "I realized then that there are still certain things that you don't want to let go of from your youth. Whether it's something you need to feel or there's some sort of comfort in just remembering those early moments and thoughts. The things that you remember as a kid, you want to hold on to. It's a big part of who you are."

The first week of February 2015, Tommy was back in Cleveland to make Dominick Farinacci's record. Musicians began arriving from all points east and west: the pianist Larry Goldings and the guitarist Dean Parks from California, the drummer Steve Gadd from Arizona, the bassist Christian McBride from New York. Tommy even had the vocalist Jacob Collier as a special guest come in from London.

A massive snowstorm was starting to build, but the weather was the least of Tommy's immediate problems. The stress of what he had proposed to do was starting to hit him. He was not simply going to make a record on a college campus, he had also agreed to provide master classes, workshops, interviews, and a live video feed so that students in other parts of the building could actually observe the musicians in real time, tracking a major recording production as it happened. A constant stream of VIP visitors and donors to the recording project would be passing through the studio; it was like attempting to paint a picture in the window of Macy's.

"My approach to production," says Tommy, "has always been about making people feel comfortable so that they can do what they came to do, and if I do my job right, it can appear I'm not doing anything at all. I generally operate under the radar. It's my comfort zone."

This time, when he entered the building, there were posters everywhere announcing DOMINICK FARINACCI / TOMMY LiPUMA—THE

RECORDING PROJECT! with bios and photos of Tommy and all the musicians. Down in the basement recording studio, there were cameras everywhere, and along the back wall of the control room were two rows of chairs for production people as well as students and interns. And off to the side of the control room there was a teaching room set up so students could look directly into the studio and watch the recording session, or they could watch a ten-screen video feed of all the players individually. It was a full-blown media circus.

Music is a delicate thing, and when it arrives in the room you have to give it your full attention; Tommy was determined not to let the winds blowing off the lake or the media storm inside Tri-C distract him if he could help it.

The next day was Monday and the snow kept falling. When he got to the studio he found that nothing had been set up, the recording system hadn't been calibrated, and general studio maintenance had been ignored. It was the first indication that Cleveland was much further away from either coast than the matter of a few thousand miles. Those things should have been taken care of on a daily basis.

Over the next ten hours, they managed to solve many of the technical problems and to record several interesting things, including Tom Waits's "Soldier's Things" and Horace Silver's "Señor Blues," newly updated with a great Steve Gadd swamp groove and Jacob Collier's haunting vocal harmony sounding like a lonesome train whistle.

The next morning, Tuesday, four more inches of snow fell—so far the storm had dumped well over a foot of snow and it was still coming down—and Jacob Collier was giving a master class on the art of arranging. Jacob was a nineteen-year-old musical savant from

London who had flown in to do vocals and arrangements, and at the conclusion of his presentation to the students, Tommy turned to Al Schmitt and said, "I guess the message here is that there still are no rules."

When they got back to the studio, the Hammond organ was no longer working, so instead of doing "Crazy," the Gnarls Barkley tune they were planning to record, they started to work on "Sunshine of Your Love." The change in plans meant more distractions, but Tommy stayed focused and the musicians continued to make it look easy; like the acrobats of *Cirque du Soleil* who casually climb a rope to the ceiling with one hand free and a smile on their face, studio musicians know how to court the magic. Eventually, three more things were recorded that day, and hundreds of students around the Tri-C campus witnessed what made Tommy LiPuma a five-time Grammy winner.

Wednesday, another eight inches of snow fell. It was coming down hard and blowing sideways—exactly the kind of weather that drove Tommy out of Cleveland in the first place—but Tommy was back in the control room, setting up for another full day of classes and recording. An older couple, former high school classmates of Tommy's, were sitting in the VIP section of the control room. Somebody asked them if back in the day they had any sense that Tommy would get out of town and make musical history, and the man said, "What we knew was that he was going to be a barber. His father was a barber. It's what you did. Maybe it was an Italian thing. But we did know he could really blow on that sax." No, they had no idea.

On Friday, Al Schmitt and the musicians left, so it was just Dom and Tommy in the control room listening to what had gone down during a difficult week. In Tommy's phrase, making the record had been "like landing on Normandy." But with the room finally devoid of emotional clutter, it was clear that they had managed to record some great music. Somehow, through the blizzard of snow and technical problems—and the constant flow of students and tourists—it still had that Tommy LiPuma stamp of perfection and authenticity.

In May 2015, Tommy went back to Cleveland to finish Dominick's record and also to receive an honorary degree from Tri-C. All the recording gear in the Tri-C studio was now in top shape, and on the morning of the third day, Tommy, who never graduated from high school, was awarded a Doctorate of Humane Letters in recognition of his life's work.

Sitting on the dais that morning, not far from where his father's barbershop had been, he couldn't stop smiling. Back then, there had been no plan; things just happened. But if his life was about anything, it was about the power of the human will. His being a record producer, even a successful one, was no accident. He had made it happen.

But clearly he hadn't done it alone. In the audience, his wife, Gill, whom Tommy called "a tough, funny, bright Jewish girl from Queens who doesn't let you get away with anything and doesn't care what you think about it," was smiling back at him. Tommy and Gill had been together for almost fifty years and she was still his rock.

And there had been so many others along the way, his teachers, his "rabbis," his gurus, his friends, and every one of them had played a part. As he wrote to a friend several days later, "I might have been *on* my own at times but I was never alone. When you're blessed with the love of music, you are never alone."

Coda:

March 13

It had been clear for more than a decade that the record business, and particularly the jazz business, was not doing well. Everybody saw it coming—the revenue streams and the creative juices had been running dry for some time—but nobody could have predicted how quickly it would all go south. And while there were still brilliant young musicians arriving every year, terrific singers and instrumentalists fresh out of jazz programs from around the world, there was not the kind of cultural infrastructure—steady work, dedicated bands, common repertoire—that helped musicians develop an original voice.

And so, while there were many great players, there were few great artists. In fact, it seemed the faster the education system cranked out new musicians, the quicker the underlying musical life was slipping away. Jazz, in Tommy's words, had become a "was" business. It seemed possible that in a few years it might become a luxury available only to those middle-class kids who could afford the tuition at jazz schools.

For Tommy and members of his generation, the music had been free, in the air, part of life itself, but to own it, you had to earn it. It cost you plenty. In his case, he came to it the old-fashioned way, through physical pain and suffering. After being injured playing America's favorite pastime, he found salvation listening to America's most original music.

Eventually, when the saxophone became an extension of his own voice, able to say things that he could not articulate in words, jazz provided his ticket out of the isolation of illness and hard times. It was his main means of transportation, physically, emotionally, spiritually. And when he finally became successful, his interest in early American modernist art might well have reflected a prophetic vision from the very time his father first arrived in America. Sometimes it seemed that his personal success was in part a cosmic payback for a murdered man on a distant path.

Over the past several years, he had been honored with retrospectives and tributes, and he felt it to be a double-edged sword. "It's like," he said, "are they trying to tell me something? Here's your hat, what's your hurry?" Nonetheless, when the Tri-C jazz festival proposed an all-star "Tommy LiPuma Birthday Bash" featuring Diana Krall, Dr. John, Al Jarreau, Leon Russell, and the Clayton-Hamilton Jazz Orchestra, Tommy agreed to do it.

Scheduled for June 23, 2016, it would be more than a homecoming; it was going to be a communion. It would be held at the Palace Theater in Playhouse Square, a beautiful two-thousand-seat hall built in the early 1920s by men exactly like Tommy's father, if not Sam himself, and it was located in the Keith Building, literally a hundred feet from where his barbershop had been sixty years before.

To make matters more interesting, the day before the "Birthday Bash," the day of rehearsals, was also the day that a million basketball fans gathered in Cleveland to blow horns and welcome LeBron James and the Cleveland Cavaliers back as NBA champions. It was a beautiful spring morning, sunny and 75 degrees, and up in a clear blue sky, high above the Keith Building, the Goodyear Blimp was frozen in space; Cleveland had turned into one gigantic picnic to honor its native sons, and one couldn't be blamed for thinking that today, Tommy was among the returnees being honored.

By noon the off-ramps of Interstate 90 were parking lots: people just pulled off the highway, left their cars by the side of the road and walked into town. It was turning into a massive civic party. Swarms of people were all heading downtown, a parade of happy moms and dads, young and old, white and black, a rainbow of humanity. Sitting in stalled traffic watching waves of people stream past, one heard the voice of Donald Trump on the car radio and was reminded that he, too, was on his way to Cleveland in a few days for his coronation at the Republican Convention. Cleveland felt like ground zero for a very strange version of the American Dream.

Inside the cavernous space of the Palace Theater, the past was alive and kicking. Eighteen of LA's best jazz musicians, the Clayton-Hamilton big band, rehearsed new arrangements for the next day's gig, and, sitting in an otherwise empty theater, Tommy seemed bemused and a little off balance. "It's really weird to be here," he says. "This is the theater where I first saw Harry James when I was nine. It blew my mind." He, too, was at ground zero, but his dream was personal: the ex-sandlot-ball-player, ex-barber, ex-bebop-tenor-player, ex-record-executive was deeply feeling the passage of time.

That night, at a dinner for musicians at a nearby restaurant, Tommy was back in his element. He had airlifted two cases of exquisite wine from his personal collection and was busy decanting it for friends. Filling glasses, laughing, telling jokes, he and his pals were clearly enjoying themselves. The conversation around the table was like the retelling of old war stories by grateful survivors, amazed to still be in the here and now. For working musicians, it wasn't ever about the notes; it was always about the spaces between the notes: it was about the hang.

Tommy is a man who did not have a lot of luck in school as a boy who now had a school named after him. There are some educations you just can't buy; you have to live them. And even though today it appeared he had traveled only a few hundred yards in the past fifty years—from the barbershop on the seventh floor to this theater in the basement—his journey was proof that if you can transform your mind, you can change your world. And in the process, you can change the world around you.

The next night, the twenty-third of June, 2016, the Palace Theater was filled with two thousand folks in formal wear. Every kind of everybody was there: the jazz fans, the Italian community, the Tri-C cohort, the family, the cousins, even the barber who'd worked in the chair next to him back in the day. Tommy and Gill and their two girls sat in the second row. The Clayton-Hamilton band played two swinging numbers and then Dr. John strolled out to the piano wearing a lime-green suit and draped in the usual array of beads, mojos, and feathers. He was using a walking stick and was helped onstage by a personal assistant; he sat down and sang the blues, called Tommy's name a few times, and, after three songs, strolled off, with help.

After a few video testimonials—one from Barbra Streisand (holding a bobblehead doll of Tommy, saying how much fun she had working with him), another from Paul McCartney (who shouted out his name, "Tommy! Tommy!" into the camera)—singer Al Jarreau took the stage; he, too, suffering from a long-standing bout with back problems, needed assistance getting on and off the stage.

After Al's set, more tributes. Then Leon Russell arrived to perform "This Masquerade," the song he had written that launched Tommy's string of platinum records and Grammy Awards. That night, Leon, too, appeared fragile, and was also using a cane to walk the few feet to the piano.

The evening had become a cavalcade of walking sticks, a deep irony both as a metaphor for an aging record business and a tip of the cosmic hat to Tommy, who had been using a walking stick his whole life.

Finally, Diana Krall, in a simple black dress, performed several elegant numbers, and then a five-foot birthday cake was rolled out onto the stage and Tommy cut the first piece. But words failed him. He had a paper in his hand with the speech he had written the night before, but he put it down on the lectern and said, simply, "I can't read what I wrote." He was choked. All he could say was "Thank you," and left the stage; later he would call each of the people he had intended to thank in his speech and tell them personally how much they meant to him.

At the afterparty, an open-bar celebration where Tommy was both the rabbi and the bar mitzvah boy, he was surrounded by friends and family and entertained by four tenor saxophone players who roamed the hall and created tuneful chaos playing variations on a jazz theme. Tommy worked the crowd, smiling but clearly ready to leave.

Turning eighty is enough to give anyone pause, but the fact that the music business was gone raised interesting questions: With the structure, the artifice, the ladder, the airfoil, the old folks, the old ways, all gone, pure gossamer, who was he now? What was he going to do? Was it all just one big afterparty?

By the end of the year, Dan Hicks had died. So had Leon Russell, Bob Krasnow, and Al Jarreau. Even Natalie Cole had passed away the year before. It was getting a little thin on the ground. Tommy, too, had health issues. Sometimes his heartbeat was all over the place, and his doctor, after a series of tests, told him to cut out the wine—so Tommy sold his vast collection—and to avoid having coffee after dinner. Plus a nagging cough was making smoking pot a problem; it wasn't the same. "What's the point?" he asked a friend.

But he and Al Schmitt were back in LA making a new album with Diana Krall, and it was coming out great. By late February 2017, he was home and talking about making an album with Dr. John—a tribute to Fats Waller—and about taking a trip to Sicily in the summer; a promoter there had reached out to him, offering to bring him back to the old country by naming a jazz festival in his honor and arranging for him to receive the key to the city of Palermo.

He would also be able to attempt another trip to Alimena, the town where his father was born, to the hill where his father, as a six-year-old boy, had led that donkey up and down until the life seemed ground out of him. It would complete a kind of circle for Tommy. The key to the city of Palermo! He was laughing about it, but there was this one last thing. He'd been feeling a little out of breath lately. So the last week of February he went in for another series of tests.

The tests were never conclusive. Tommy LiPuma died March 13, 2017, about 10:30 p.m. The weather service had predicted the biggest nor'easter of the century for that day, a snowstorm so furious that all public transportation systems had been shut down by midafternoon and the mayor pleaded with people to go home and stay there. Around 10:45 that night, it started to snow in New York. And it snowed and it snowed. A yawning white silence fell over Manhattan.

The only mitigating thought one had was that perhaps during his last hours—unconscious and on a morphine drip—Tommy was able to return to that magic place he had visited once as a kid, the space he was never really able to recreate throughout the rest of his life, no matter how hard he tried, no matter what he ate, drank or smoked, no matter how hard the band swung or how many copies the record sold, that place of freedom and cool, of no pain and pure groove, of transcendence.

Discography

HOLLIS KING

LIBERTY / IMPERIAL (1961–1965)

A&M (1965–1969)

BLUE THUMB (1969–1974)

WARNER BROS. (1974–1978)

A&M / HORIZON (1978–1979)

WARNER BROS. (1979–1990)

ELEKTRA (1990–1995)

GRP / VERVE (1995–2011)

LIBERTY / IMPERIAL

1965 *Our Day Will Come*, Tommy Tedesco
1965 *Comin' Through*, The O'Jays

A&M

1966 *Guantanamera*, The Sandpipers
1966 *The More I See You / Call Me*, Chris Montez
1966 *Time After Time*, Chris Montez
1967 *Misty Roses*, The Sandpipers
1967 *Claudine*, Claudine Longet
1967 *Look of Love*, Claudine Longet
1968 *Softly*, The Sandpipers
1968 *Colours*, Claudine Longet
1968 *Love Is Blue*, Claudine Longet
1968 *Roger Nichols & the Small Circle of Friends*, Roger Nichols
1969 *Rock Salt and Nails*, Steve Young
1968 *Randy Newman*, Randy Newman (Warner Bros.)

BLUE THUMB

1970 *A Bad Donato*, João Donato
1970 *Alone Together*, Dave Mason
1970 *High Contrast*, Gábor Szabó
1970 *Magical Connection*, Gábor Szabó
1971 *Where's the Money?* Dan Hicks
1972 *Darkness Darkness*, Phil Upchurch
1972 *Mark-Almond II*, Mark-Almond Band
1972 *Striking It Rich*, Dan Hicks
1972 *Headkeeper*, Dave Mason
1973 *America Wake Up*, Paul Humphrey
1973 *Last Train to Hicksville*, Dan Hicks

1973 *Lovin' Feeling*, Phil Upchurch
1973 *What a Place to Land*, Southwind
1973 *National Lampoon Lemmings*, National Lampoon
1974 *Italian Graffiti*, Nick De Caro
1974 *The Way We Were*, Barbra Streisand (Columbia)

WARNER BROS.

1975 *We Be Sailin'*, B.W. Stevenson
1976 *The Art of Tea*, Michael Franks
1976 *Breezin'*, George Benson
1976 *Glow*, Al Jarreau
1976 *Stuff*, Stuff
1976 *Urubu*, Antonio Carlos Jobim
1977 *In Flight*, George Benson
1977 *Look to the Rainbow*, Al Jarreau
1977 *Sleeping Gypsy*, Michael Franks
1977 *Weekend in LA*, George Benson
1977 *You Must Believe in Spring*, Bill Evans
1977 *Amoroso*, João Gilberto
1977 *Gate of Dreams*, Claus Ogerman
1978 *Burchfield Nines*, Michael Franks
1978 *It Happened One Bite*, Dan Hicks
1978 *Love Island*, Deodato

A&M / HORIZON

1978 *Jungle Fever*, Neil Larsen
1978 *City Lights*, Dr. John
1978 *Yellow Magic Orchestra*, Yellow Magic Orchestra
1979 *High Gear*, Neil Larsen
1979 *Light the Light*, Seawind
1979 *Tango Palace*, Dr. John

WARNER BROS.

1979 *Livin' Inside Your Love*, George Benson

1980 *One Bad Habit*, Michael Franks

1980 *Red Cab to Manhattan*, Stephen Bishop

1980 *Terra Brasilis*, Antonio Carlos Jobim

1981 *Secret Combination*, Randy Crawford

1981 *Yellowjackets*, Yellowjackets

1982 *Cityscape*, Michael Brecker

1982 *Full Moon*, Full Moon

1982 *Windsong*, Randy Crawford

1983 *Mirage à Trois*, Yellowjackets

1983 *Nightline*, Randy Crawford

1983 *Two Eyes*, Brenda Russell

1984 *Once in a Lifetime*, Michael Ruff

1985 *Samurai Samba*, Yellowjackets

1985 *Take No Prisoners*, Peabo Bryson

1985 *Gettin' Away with Murder*, Patti Austin

1986 *Double Vision*, Bob James & David Sanborn

1986 *Tutu*, Miles Davis

1986 *While the City Sleeps*, George Benson

1987 *Collaboration*, Earl Klugh

1987 *Get Close to My Love*, Jennifer Holliday

1987 *Love Songs*, Randy Crawford

1987 *Music from Siesta*, Marcus Miller

1987 *Love*, Aztec Camera

1988 *Land of Dreams*, Randy Newman

1988 *Nothing but the Truth*, Rubén Blades (Elektra)

1989 *Amandla*, Miles Davis

1989 *Spellbound*, Joe Sample

1989 *Tenderly*, George Benson
1989 *In a Sentimental Mood*, Dr. John
1990 *Nightwatch*, Ricky Peterson
1990 *Ashes to Ashes*, Joe Sample
1990 *Blue Pacific*, Michael Franks
1990 *Language of Life*, Everything but the Girl
1990 *Marksman*, Mark Whitfield

ELEKTRA

1991 *Affinity*, Thrashing Doves
1991 *Unforgettable . . . With Love*, Natalie Cole
1992 *All the Way*, Little Jimmy Scott (Sire)
1992 *Glengarry Glen Ross*, Original Soundtrack
1993 *Here It Is*, Jevetta Steele (Sony)
1993 *Invitation*, Joe Sample
1993 *Take a Look*, Natalie Cole
1994 *Hearsay*, David Sanborn
1994 *Rhythm of Love*, Anita Baker
1994 *Holly & Ivy*, Natalie Cole
1995 *Pearls*, David Sanborn

GRP / VERVE

1995 *Afterglow*, Dr. John
1995 *Only Trust Your Heart*, Diana Krall
1996 *All for You*, Diana Krall
1996 *Hardbop Grandpop*, Horace Silver
1996 *Panamonk*, Danilo Pérez
1996 *That's Right*, George Benson
1996 *Two for the Road*, Dave Grusin
1997 *Love Scenes*, Diana Krall

1997 *Prescription for the Blues*, Horace Silver

1997 *Salinas*, Luis Salinas

1997 *Nouveau Swing*, Donald Harrison

1997 *What the World Needs Now*, McCoy Tyner

1998 *When I Look in Your Eyes*, Diana Krall

1998 *Pure Imagination*, Eric Reed

1998 *Central Avenue*, Danilo Pérez

1998 *Standing Together*, George Benson

1998 *Sweet Georgia Peach*, Russell Malone

1999 *Why Should I Care?* Diana Krall

1999 *Jazz Has a Sense of Humor*, Horace Silver

2000 *Here's to You Charlie Brown: 50 Great Years!* David Benoit

2000 *Look Who's Here*, Russell Malone

2000 *Motherland*, Danilo Pérez

2001 *You're My Thrill*, Shirley Horn

2001 *Cruisin'*, Marc Antoine

2001 *Love Songs*, Natalie Cole

2001 *Heartstrings*, Russell Malone

2001 *Look of Love*, Diana Krall

2002 *A Song for You*, Kenny Rankin

2002 *Ask a Woman Who Knows*, Natalie Cole

2002 *Live in Paris*, Diana Krall

2003 *Salt*, Lizz Wright

2004 *Tri-C Jazz Festival 2004*, Various Artists

2004 *Girl in the Other Room*, Diana Krall

2004 *Accentuate the Positive*, Al Jarreau

2005 *It's Time*, Michael Bublé (Warner Music)

2005 *Christmas Songs*, Diana Krall

2006 *Feeling Good*, Joe Sample / Randy Crawford (PRA)

2006 *From This Moment On*, Diana Krall
2006 *Before Me*, Gladys Knight
2007 *Trav'lin' Light*, Queen Latifah
2008 *Across the Crystal Sea*, Danilo Pérez
2008 *No Regrets*, Joe Sample / Randy Crawford (PRA)
2009 *Quiet Nights*, Diana Krall
2017 *Turn Up the Quiet*, Diana Krall

VARIOUS

2009 *Love Is the Answer*, Barbra Streisand (Columbia)
2009 *American Classic*, Willie Nelson (Blue Note)
2012 *Kisses on the Bottom*, Paul McCartney (Concord)
2013 *Life Journey*, Leon Russell (Universal)
2015 *Short Stories*, Dominick Farinacci (Mack Avenue)

Index

Page numbers that appear in italics refer to illustrations.

Lightning Source UK Ltd.
Milton Keynes UK
UKHW041626271222
414474UK00001B/12